© Talib M. Aziz

PREFACE

When I began my studies in political science at the University of Akron, Ohio, I was impressed by the way political philosophy and theories dealt with the intriguing issues of politics, the depth of their analysis and their logical and systematic way of dealing with political problems. Initially, I was interested in international politics both intellectually and as a future career goal. Later however, I got into and found self-satisfaction with the field of political science namely "political thought." This interest was in part due to Professor Richard Franklin with whom I took two survey courses in Western political thought. For me that was a start in the right direction. I learned from Professor Franklin the history of political philosophy, the major issues that concerned different philosophers, and the way they approached them to find a rational solution. His objectivity and comparative analysis of various philosophical views led to me to ask whether there is a contemporary Arab or Muslim thinker with such an outlook to the political problems facing our part of the world.

There are, of course, many Muslim thinkers and intellectual leaders who are popular among the masses and whose books and writings fill the shelves of bookstores in the Middle East. For example, Ayatollah Khomeini, Sayyid Qutb, ᶜAlama Tabataba'iy, ᶜAli Shariᶜaty, Murdha Muttahiri, Muhammad H. Fadlallah and Muhammad Baqir al Sadr. I had read most of their works, and started to question the objectivity, but definitely not the sincerity, of their political views and political programs. Do they really understand or pinpoint the major sociopolitical issues facing our society? What is the scope and depth of their analysis? How about their political programs and goals? What are the objective differences between their proposals and the status quo aside from the subjective differences of ideology and beliefs between the two? These questions would never have occurred to me before I exposed myself to discourses of various political philosophers. I became intellectually and politically mature and started to question the basic assumptions of my guru, so to speak, Muhammad Baqir al-Sadr.

© Talib M. Aziz

It is then that I made my decision to write about his political thought. Why him and not somebody else? Works of other thinkers mentioned above have either been exposed by scholars in the West, or they present no major intellectual treatises of value to analyze. Most of the writings of Ayatollah Khomeini are either in mysticism or jurisprudence and the rest are political speeches. I value that he was a political leader, and not a theorist. Sayyid Qutb and ᶜAli Shariᶜati are highly exposed in the academic literature. Most of the works of ᶜAllama Tabataba'iy are about philosophy, especially about epistemology and metaphysics, while Muttahiri took the role of expounding on the thoughts of his mentor, Tabataba'iy. Fadlallah and Sadr were close friends and colleagues and were at the beginning my candidates for study. However, Fadlallah's writings are mostly about the means of Islamic political activism. This left me with only one person who I thought would be qualified to be presented as a modern Islamic political thinker and who made a sincere effort to formulate a well defined political theory.

Muhammad Baqir al-Sadr's writings cover a wide range of topics and fields. Such a broad range of intellectual work is what has made Sadr famous among Islamists in the Middle East. I had read or been exposed to most of his writings. However, I placed them under critical and thorough investigation only after my training in the discipline of political science. Here it seemed as if I was rediscovering Sadr and really understanding the political objectives of his writing. I believe that when he was exposed to Western intellectual thought such as that of Marx, Hegel, Rousseau, Locke, and others, he realized the shortcoming of Islamic scholars in dealing with political issues and thus he was determined to fill the gap. He introduced to Muslim intellectuals, who were influenced by Western political thoughts, an Islamic political theory well-elaborated and rationalized to be able to triumph over Western political theories.

This work would not have come to realization without the help and the guidance of Professor Bernard Weiss of the Middle East Center, University of Utah. I benefited from him first through the different courses I took with him in Islamic law, jurisprudence, and political thought, a discipline in which he enjoys authority. Additionally, I am greatly indebted to his thorough analysis, insightful comments, and elaborate editing to bring the study to such a standard. And my thanks to other members of my research committee, namely Professor Ibrahim Karawan, Professor Kimbell, Professor Giffen, and Professor Mossarie for their advice.

I am grateful to those who helped me with information about the life and political activism of the late Sadr, namely: Talib al-Refaᶜi, and A.H.F. (his name kept anonymous for security reasons). Both were among the founders of the Islamic Daᶜwah Party and both helped me with their historical account of the early days of Sadr's political activism. Kazim al-Ha'iri and Muhammad B. al-Hakim, both students and disciples of Sadr, provided me with information and literature they sent me about their mentor. Ahmad Kubba offered recollections about his activity and participation in organizing one of the first

© Talib M. Aziz

demonstrations that sparked popular support for Sadr in the late seventies.

Many friends and close relative helped me in the process. I would like to thank gratefully Abbas Zaini for his aid in contacting several of Sadr's associates, Jamal Barakat for realizing certain aspects of this study during our regular yet heated debates about Islamic and political issues, and Mukhtar Hashimi and Abdul A. Qatam and Abtihal Raji for their help and encouragement. My parents get the most credit for their continuous support and motivation. Unfortunately life ended so quickly for my mother that she did not realize what she had hoped to see of her son.

And finally, I am overwhelmingly indebted to my wife, Juman, for her comments, support and encouragement, without which this work could not have been achieved. After all, in front of every great woman, there is a man who takes up the credit.

T.M.A.
Los Angeles, CA
November 30, 1990

© Talib M. Aziz

INTRODUCTION

Few modern Muslim jurists have concerned themselves with social issues in their writings, been directly involved in the political process of the existing Muslim states, reshaped the existing methods of the academic teaching of the <u>hawzah</u> (religious school), or made a serious effort to stand up to the challenges the religion of Islam faces from Western philosophical doctrines. Muhammad Baqir Sadr stands tall as a pioneering figure in all the above-mentioned aspects of activist political thought. Nevertheless, up until now, no serious effort has been made by the West to study the contributions of the late Sadr. Such lack of interest or concern has perhaps been the result of relating Shi^cism to Iran only. The Iran-Iraq war reinforced this misunderstanding by depicting the conflict as part of a long history of hostilities between the Arab-Sunnis and the Persian-Shi^cas. The achievements of the great jurist from Iraq, Sadr, have been overlooked by scholars working on Islam, as if his voice had been lost in the turbulence of the Gulf War.

However, Sadr is well known for his influential intellectual writings and political activities that inspired others to follow him. He had written rather extensively on matters ranging from modern philosophy and economics to Islamic jurisprudence. His intellectual achievement was admired throughout the Muslim world. His political vision and activism were not limited to the boundaries of Iraq, but transcended most of the Middle Eastern countries. The Islamic fundamentalist movement in Lebanon and the Gulf states cannot be fully understood without relating it to Sadr's political and ideological motivation. His students and close associates constitute the top leadership of the Islamic political organizations in those countries. However, a man of such importance has received only minor attention because most of his major writings are not translated from Arabic into other languages.

© Talib M. Aziz

<u>State of the Literature</u>
The previous studies about the thoughts and political activism of Sadr can be classified into three categories.

Dogmatic Studies
Such studies are mainly written by Sadr's political followers and published by Shi`i fundamentalist political organizations that aim at proving the truthfulness of Sadr's thoughts and ideas. Although these studies are filled with biases while lacking critical analysis, they may serve as sources for understanding the influence Sadr exerted on his followers as well as different interpretations of his thought. As a case in point, the publication of the Da^cwa Islamic Party presents Sadr as an advocate of the formation of political parties; on the other hand, Khomeini's followers present Sadr as advocating a political movement led by jurists rather than a political party. Mention will be made of the following studies:

Qubanchi, Sadr al-Dyyn al-. <u>al-Fikr al-Siyasi lil Sayyid al-Shahid al-Sadr</u>. n.d.

This work is short and flashy in its presentation of Sadr thoughts. The author aims at presenting Sadr's ideas about the state, society and the scope of power of the Islamic ruler. The aim in general is to prove the compatibility of Sadr's views with the idea of "Rulership of the Jurist" (<u>Wilayat al-Faqih</u>) advocated by Ayatollah Khomeini and declared in the constitution of the Islamic Republic of Iran. Recently Qubanchi published a new work, <u>al-Madhhab al-Siyasi fi al-Islam</u> (the first edition published under a different author's name) to elaborate on these ideas and develop more analytical arguments. He followed Sadr's critique of the Western doctrines, capitalism and communism, about the state and society. He also detailed arguments supporting <u>wilayat al-faqih</u> that combine Sadr's and Khomeini's views. Qubanchi argues that Islam is a doctrine and not a theory, although the first chapter of the book is titled, "The Theoretical Basis of Islam." His definition of <u>theory</u> is similar to that of <u>science</u>. Sadr believes that the Islamic economic system cannot be studied scientifically or empirically because is not implemented in real life, i.e., the Islamic system needs to operate and perform within the society to apply scientific methods to the study of its merits and achievements. However, no critical analysis is presented in both of these works, and no major contribution is made to the study of Sadr's thought. For this purpose, it is best to refer to the original writings of Sadr.

Ha'iri, Kazim al-. <u>Tarjamat Hayat al-Marja^c al-Shahid al-Sadr</u>. Qum, Iran: 1988.

Qubanch, Sadr al-Dyyn al-. <u>al-Jihad al-Siyasi lil Sayyid al-Shahid al-Sadr</u>. 1984.

Najaf, A. <u>al-Shahid wa al-Shahid</u>. n.d.

All of these works can be considered a biography of the life of the late Sadr. Since

© Talib M. Aziz

the authors are former students or political advocates of Sadr, he is pictured as the dominating figure and genius of his time. The works convey great admiration of his personality in every aspect of his life. However, these works serve as valuable sources of information about the life and political activism of Sadr, disregarding the author's political allegiance to Sadr.

Juristic Studies

Two of Sadr's former students, Kazim al-Ha'iri and Mahmoud al-Hashimi, expounded on Sadr juristic thoughts. However, most of their works are of little value to my dissertation because they deal with principles of jurisprudence. I will only make reference to the following studies because they deal with the concepts of history.

Ha'iri, Kazim al-. "Sunan al-Tarikh, part one." <u>al-Hiwar al-Fikri wa al-Siyasi</u>. Summer 1985.

Ha'iri, Kazim al-. "Sunan al-Tarikh, part two." <u>al-Hiwar al-Fikri wa la-Siasi</u>. Fall 1985.

Ha'iri, Kazim al-. "Sunan al-Tarikh, Adwar al-Tarikh fi al-Hayat al-Ukhra." <u>al-Hiwar al-Fikri</u>. Winter 1986.

These studies were conducted by a former student of Sadr who presented his views on the historical development process. Ha'iri not only is familiar with Sadr's views and ideas, but also makes some critical analyses of Sadr's arguments. However, these studies are not concerned with making critical analyses of the general theme Sadr introduced, but rather reinforcing its rationale. Ha'iri's main arguments are about some of the juristic interpretations of Sadr to Quranic verses or other <u>shari^ca</u> sources. In this regard, Ha'iri seems to reach a different explanation of the development process of history. However, since my research concerns the thoughts of Sadr, the usefulness of Ha'iri's works rests on his extended review of Sadr's ideas and views. He in fact fills the gaps that are left out by Sadr in his writings, but narrated in lectures or private talks to his former students and colleagues. For this purpose, I will assume the views that Ha'iri attributes to Sadr are authentic.

There are two other studies that elaborate on some unique ideas introduced by Sadr in history and sociology:

© Talib M. Aziz

Adib, ᶜAdil. <u>al-A'imma al-Ithna ᶜAshar: Dirasa Tahliliya</u> (The Twelve Imams: an Analytical Study). 1979.

Amin, Muhammad Ali. <u>al-Mujtamaᶜ al-Firᶜawni</u> (Pheroahic Society). n.d.

These studies provide neither critical nor analytical studies of Sadr's view, but rather the former elaborates on his original conception and understanding of the role of the Imam in history while the latter deals with the social classes of an authoritarian regime.

Academic Studies

Aside from an article by Chibli Mellat about Sadr, Western scholarship has totally ignored Sadr, making no attempt to analyze his thought, activities, or his political impact. He, of course, was mentioned in several articles that deal with the Islamic political movements in Iraq, mainly because these articles refer to its founders or religious symbols. An example of this is:

Batatu, Hanna. Shi'i organization in Iraq: Daᶜwa al-Islamiyah and al-Mujahidin. 1986.

The same can be said about studies dealing with Islamic economics (where Sadr's works considered a pioneering in that field) where Sadr's contribution are mentioned.

Kotauzian, Homa. "Islamic Economics: Sadr and Bani-Sadr." 1983.

The emphasis on Sadr on these type of articles is marginal, and only covered as part of the total subject being studied.

Probably the first initiative taken to study Muhammad Baqir Sadr's literature and political role in the Muslim world is represented by C. Mellat in part of his doctoral dissertation. Although my efforts to gain access to the dissertation itself were to no avail, his published article represents a summary of his work.

Mellat, Chibli. "Religious militancy in contemporary Iraq: Muhammad Baqer as-Sadr and the Sunni-Shia paradigm." April 1988.

The major objective of the study was to show that Sadr's political activism was a reaction to the political events in Iraq, i.e., the Shiᶜis resistance to the Sunni domination of the political process in the country. Even Sadr's intellectual writings were correlated to the Sunni-Shiᶜi conflict. For instance, the economic and philosophical writings come as a reaction to the period of communist movement evident in the political process and control of the state apparatus. On the other hand, Sadr's writings on Islamic history and Shiᶜi jurisprudence were a natural reaction of the sectarian politics of the Ba'th regime in Baghdad.

Purpose of This Study

© Talib M. Aziz

Although there is some validity to the argument that the events of the post-1958 revolution instigated the political activism of Shi^{c}i jurists in Iraq against communism, Sadr's approach to the problem went beyond this limited political objective. He engineered a political program of long-term planning that aims at establishing an Islamic State in Iraq and the rest of the Muslim world. His writings since that turbulent political period centered around formulating a grand Islamic political theory that would function as the basis of an Islamic political system. With this in mind, the purpose of this dissertation is to show the long-term motivation of Sadr's political life and intellectual writings. Thus, the general theme of this study is to prove that Sadr's entire body of writings have one tone, aimed at one political objective.

Methodology

For that reason, my study will look at Sadr's writings from a unique angle. I will consider the whole body of Sadr's political writings as interrelated treatises that expound the Islamic theory of politics. Thus, the approach in the dissertation will be to formulate a political theory of Sadr, since I have the conviction that his later writings on history were designed to support the major theme he presented in his earlier writings on philosophy and on economics. I will examine all aspects of this political theory. He has indeed covered, in his twenty years of intellectual writings, a whole range of topics that range from religious doctrine to modern social issues. The major task then is to weave together his political ideas to bring about a systemized presentation of his political theory. For instance, I shall present Sadr's concepts on the Islamic theory of epistemology, reality, and human nature; and examine his views on human role in the society, toward nature, and human relationship to God. Sadr's late writings dealt with stages of human history and the rise and fall of political entities. He also constructed a new classification of social groups within an authoritarian rule.

Islamic political thought can be classified into three distinct types: First, the philosophical treaties that deal mainly with epistemological issues and constructing a theory of prophethood, where the emphasis in the philosophers argument is on who is the best to lead the community. In other words, these treaties, such as al-Farabi's <u>Ara' Ahl al-Madina al-Fadhila</u>, search for an ideal state and the creation of the utopian Islamic political order on earth.

The second types is juristic treaties, which were concerned not with an ideal situation, but rather with about the survival of the Islamic polity. The <u>ummah</u> (Muslim community), therefore, could be realized, according to jurists like al-Mawardi in his <u>al-Ahkam al-Sultaniyah</u>, through its unity within a political structure. Thus, the juristic objective is to defend the status quo through formulating religious doctrine that protects the existing ruler. The doctrine of course is an endeavor of interpretation of Quranic verses and quotations of similar practices of an earlier Islamic community. In this case, the juristic

© Talib M. Aziz

theory of <u>khilafa</u> (rulership) is a realistic, yet passive political doctrine that legitimizes the existing regimes, emphasizes the unity of the leadership, and advocates the unity of the <u>ummah</u> through the people's submission to their rulers.

Ibn-Khaldon's <u>al-Muqaddima</u> is the only work known to represent the third type of Islamic political thought. His theory of history gives an interpretation of the cause behind the historical dynamism. He made a serious effort to formulate an understanding of the logic of history through a careful study of the rise and fall of historical regimes of his time in northwestern Africa. No other Islamic political writer looks at history from this angle, i.e, setting aside the divine plan of history and interpreting history according to socioeconomical factors.

Sadr's political writings seem to blend all the three types of treaties in one single grand political theory. He, for example, relates the Islamic views on epistemology, reality and human nature to his interpretation of historical process. He also correlates Islamic jurisprudence to the needs of the modern political state. In this regard, he formulated an Islamic theory of economics based on the differing views of Islamic jurisprudence to show that Islam has the solution to economic problems. As a devoted Islamic jurist, he believes that Islam has provided the answers to all problems facing humanity. Islam, according to Sadr, is a package that regulates the human life and the society, and its solution can be realized only if rules and regulation are applied to all aspects of social life.

It is sufficient to mention that Sadr's diverse political writings only make sense when studied in an endeavor to discern a grand political theory according to Islamic principles. Additionally, Sadr takes the opportunity of rising historical circumstances to present and advocate some aspects of his political theory, through writings or lectures. His role was to influence history and help change it according to Islamic principles rather than to be influenced by its events, as Mellet suggests.

However, my study will not be concerned with presenting Sadr's argument for his own juristic interpretation of the Islamic sources. The scope of this research work will emphasize discovering the major theme of Sadr's political theory and not to expound on the endeavor of his juristic thought; and second, a juristic study definitely needs a well-qualified jurist well-versed with Islamic jurisprudence, which I do not claim to be. Rather, the study will take over all ideas that relate to the diverse topics covered in Sadr's literature, extrapolate their underlying theme, and present them in the form of a systematically organized political theory. For this case, I will cover <u>most</u> of Sadr's body of literature in order to come up with his grand theory. The emphasis on "most" is to exclude Sadr's mainly juristic works, which were part of his religious obligation to the religious school of grand jurist. Following are Sadr's major political writings and the date of its first publication:

<u>Falsafatuna</u> (Our Philosophy). 1959

<u>Iqtisaduna</u> (Our Economics). 1961

© Talib M. Aziz

al-Insan wa-al-Mushkila al-Ijtima^{c}iyah (Man and the Social Problem). 1961

Madha Ta^{c}ruf ^{c}an al-Iqtisad al-Islami (What do you know about Islamic Economics). 1962

Risalatuna (Our Message). 1959-1961

Ahl al-Bayt: Tanawu^c Adwar wa-Wihdat Hadaf (The House Hold of the Prophet: Diversity of roles but unified goal). 1974

Bahth Hawla al-Wilayah (Thesis on Rulership). 1974

Bahth Hawla al-Mahdi (Thesis on Messiah). 1977

al-Tafsir al-Mawdu^{c}i lil Quran (Thematic Interpretation of the Quran). 1978

Khalafat al-Insan wa-Shahadat al-Anbia' (Vicory role of man, and Witness role of Prophets) 1979

Manabi^c al-Qudra fi al-Dawlah al-Islamiyah (The Sources of Power in an Islamic State). 1979

Lamha Fiqhia fi Distur al-Jumhurial al-Islamiyah (A preliminary jurisprudence basis of the Constitution of the Islamic Republic). 1979

Khutut Tafsiliyah ^{c}An Iqtisad al-Mujtama^c al-Islami (The General Basis of the Economy of Islamic Society). 1979

Surah ^{c}An Iqtisad al-Mujtama^c al-Islami (A Perspective on the Economy of Muslim Society). 1979

Ekhtarna Lak [Collection of articles by Sadr].

There are other works by Sadr that I will make minor reference to due to their concentration on highly specialized juristic, banking and philosophical studies:

al-Usus al-Mantaqiyah lil Isriqra' (The logical Basis of Inductive). 1974

Mihaj al-Salihyyn (The Righteous Path). 1975

© Talib M. Aziz

al-Fatawi al-Wadihah (Clear Islamic Rules). 1977

al-Bank al-la-Rubawi fi al-Islam (Non-usury Bank in Islam). 1977

al-Usus al-ᶜAmah li-al-Bank fi al-Mujtamᶜ al-Islami (The General Basis of Bank in Islamic Society). 1979

Other Sadr's works are mainly for religious studies about jurisprudence and its principles.
Durus fi ᶜIlm al-Usul (Lessons on the Principle of Jurisprudence). 1974

Buhuth fi Sharih al-ᶜIrwah al-Wothqa (Thesis on Explanation of "al-ᶜIrwah al-Wothqa"). 1978

These are most of the intellectual and ideological works of Sadr. However, there are several articles, letters and lectures of his that are not compiled in books. I will refer to some of them when necessary.

Structure of the Research

The dissertation will consist of three major parts:

1. The first chapter will concentrate on the life of Sadr. I will start from 1958 (the beginning of his political activism) until his violent execution by the Ba'th government in 1980. These twenty-two years of his life constitute the period of his political activism as well as the period that he accomplished most of his intellectual writings. (Sadr had published only one work prior to 1958: Fadak fi al-Tarikh, an analytical view of the historical period right after the death of the Prophet.) Therefore, I will not be concerned with or refer to any of his activities, publications or his biography prior to the 1958 revolution in Iraq. The main objective of this chapter is to show the extent of Sadr's involvement in politics, his influence in the Islamic fundamentalist movement in Iraq, and his guidance to the religious opposition of the Iraqi regimes.

2. The second chapter will aim at formulating a definition of political theory. Setting the limit for the question "What is political theory?" will definitely help in setting the paradigm of this research since there are many different definitions to the concept of political theory. I believe that every definition is considered valid and the researcher should be consistant to scope of his or her definition. Once the definition is outlined, then it set to examin any political doctrine. In this case, there is no different approaches to the study of Islamic political theory, or for that matter, non-Islamic ones.

3. The third chapter will be the core of the study itself, because it will deal with the scope of Sadr's Islamic political theory. I shall present the theory along the line of the definition set in

© Talib M. Aziz

the previous chapter. In this case, the chapter will be divided into five sections:

a. The Meaning of History:

This covers Sadr's interpretation of history. In other words, it presents Sadr's views of the fate of humanity as a whole, not the individual human being. He views history as a progressive process that guides man into the ultimate and the absoluteness of God. History for him is an unending process and the life of man goes beyond his temporal existence.

b. The Nature of Man and Reality:

This section reviews Sadr's conceptual framework of human nature and his views of reality. He considers these views the general concepts of Islamic thought. However, I shall refer to his late work on philosophy where he develops his unique view on epistemology. The objective of this section is to answer the following questions: 1) What is reality? 2) How it is known to humans? and 3) What is his objective in life?

c. Social Process:

Here I present the realistic views of Sadr to the political environment that governs humans in general, and Muslims in particular. He defines the social class in authoritarian regimes, like the one dominating life in Iraq, in order to pinpoint the classes that have the potential for revolutionary action. The objective of revolutionary movement, according to Sadr, is to establish an Islamic political system.

d. Political Movement:

This section covers Sadr's political design for the Islamic movement, defines its goal, and their political means. He then outlines his political reforms for the office of marja^ciyah (the highest religious authority for the Shies) since he views it as the cornerstone of the Islamic movement and state. Finally, I cover his views on an Islamic state, i.e., the division of power between its main branches and centers of power.

e. The Economic Structure:

Since Sadr thinks that the Islamic economic system can perform properly only with an Islamic political system, I believed it best to leave his views on economics until last. Here I will review his views on the distribution of wealth and property rights in an Islamic society, as well as his solution to the lack of economic development in the Muslim countries.

© Talib M. Aziz

THE POLITICAL LIFE OF SADR

> Because you are a power
> Because you are a revolution
> Because you are the spark of a nation's upheaval
> You will remain for us
> You will live for us
> And your life will last
> in our way [as a source of] strength.
> Muhammad H. Fadlullah,
> in commemorating Sadr's martyrdom.

April 8, 1980 marks the day when the West started to hear and to know about Muhammad Baqir al-Sadr. Ironically, it is the day when the late Sadr was executed by the Iraqi regime. However, Sadr was not known because of his intellectual writings but only as the leader of an Islamic political movement in Iraq. His violent death did not arouse any Western criticism against the Iraqi regime because the late Sadr had publicly supported the Ayatullah Khomeini's Iran, a regime so much disliked in the West.

The Western indifference to the execution of Sadr was reinforced by the political turbulence of the aftermath of the Iranian revolution. The success of the Muslim fundamentalist movement in toppling a Western-oriented regime in Iran was the biggest political blow yet to Western interests in the Persian Gulf, an area which is vital to the West because of its huge oil reserves. The new leadership in Iran, which replaced the Shah, was determined to eradicate all Western interests in the area and politically dedicated to spreading its brand of Islamic fundamentalism to the whole region. The West and the regional political regimes in the Middle East feel threatened by what is called the "exporting of the Iranian revolution." The counter policy was then to hold the threat of Islamic revolution in Iran at bay, i.e., within Iran national borders. Ayatullah Khomeini's call for Muslims in Iraq to follow the example of the Iranian people and rise up to eliminate the corrupt secular Baᶜthist socialist regime in Iraq was seen by the regional and international powers as the first step to spread Islamic radicalism in the area, which would eventually lead to the destablization of the whole political establishment of the regional regimes.

Sadr's support of the Ayatullah Khomeini's call for political activism against the Baᶜthist regime in Iraq was considered a national security threat to the regime, and was therefore dealt with swiftly. Thousands of people were arrested, and hundreds were executed without the regular procedure of a court trial. Sadr was then regarded by the regime as the head and spiritual leader of an Islamic movement that had gained popular support due to the success of the Iranian revolution. He was seen as the figurehead of the antigovernmental forces and as the catalyst behind the mass appeal that Islamic political activism was coming to have in the countryside. To many he was the "future Khomeini" of Iraq. The Ba'thist regime accurately perceived that such a destabilizing threat to the political establishment had to be eliminated if the regime was to survive. Sadr's execution thus came as a natural response of a political regime fighting for its survival.

The Ba'thist regime in Iraq, like most regimes in the Middle East, was subject to a variety of factors contributing to political instability such that it considered the threat posed by Sadr's political activity as a grave danger to its survival. First of all, the regime was ideologically committed to Arab nationalism, which had been losing popular appeal in the 1970s due to the severe military and political defeat of nationalist regimes in the Arab world, preeminently that of Nasser in Egypt, in consequence of the failure to fulfill their promise of liberating Palestine.[28] Additionally, Arab nationalism discriminated against the largest non-Arab minority of Iraq, the Kurds.[29] Such resentment to the regime's ideology was the main factor in Iraqi civil war between the Kurds and the Ba'thist regime in early 1970s.

Second, the regime's top political leadership belonged to a small number of families of the Sunni Arab minority of the country.[30] This furthered the isolation of the political leadership from the masses. The regime was not able to appeal to the whole Arab majority. Furthermore, the internecine struggle within the political leadership created a resentment on the part of a large portion of the Arab Sunni minority and of the rest of the nationalist and secular political forces in Iraq.

Lastly, to secure its survival against increasing political foes, the regime resorted to a heavy-handed policy of political coercion and police control of the population. The tight control of the political life of the people made the regime dependent for its survival on the brutal practices of intelligence and security agencies. "One-fifth of the economically active Iraqi labor force (about 3.4 million people) were institutionally charged during peacetime (1980) with one form or another of violence."[31] The severe political oppression

---

[28]On the state of Arab nationalism after the death of Naser of Egypt, see Fouad Ajami, _The Arab Predicament_ (Cambridge: Cambridge University Press, 1981), 37.

[29]The Kurdish minority constitutes about 20% of the Iraqi population; Turkuman 2%, other non-Arab minority, 0.5%.

[30]On the composition of the Ba'thist leadership of Iraq see Hassan al-Alawi, _Shi'ism and the National State in Iraq_ (Paris: CEDI, 1989), 226-227.

overshadowed the ambitious economic policies that the regime started to implement after the rise of revenue from oil in the mid 1970s that resulted in the increase of people's income and standards of living.

Islam, after the success of the Iranian revolution in 1979, represented the main political alternative to the Ba'thist regime. Its ideology promised to unify people from different nationalities. Unlike the foreign elements of the Ba'thist ideology, such as nationalism and socialism, toward which the people could feel estrangement, Islamic principles were deep rooted in the hearts and practices of the Muslims for centuries. The Iranian revolution emerged with verbal affirmation and political dedication on the part of its leadership to the liberation of Palestine, not as the occupied land of the Arab people, but rather as the sacrad land of Islam whose sanctuaries must not come under the power of non-Muslims. Arab nationalism was, in contrast, lacking in deeply based popular political slogans. Finally, the Islamic leadership of the Iranian revolution was on the march toward ridding itself of all foreign influence, East and West alike. The slogan of "Neither East, nor West" found its roots among the masses in the region who had lived under Western colonization for decades and who still witnessed the influences of foreign powers in its affairs. Its huge oil reserves, its strategic geopolitical location and the Israeli-Palestinians conflict made the East-West rivalries more visible and intense in the area. National sovereignty and independence from the influence of either West or East have been a popular goal for nations in the region.

What made political Islam pose a grave danger to the existing regimes in the area was not simply its popular appeal, but rather the grass roots organizations that embraced its principles and political slogans. In almost all Middle East countries Islamic political groups had since the turn of the twentieth century formed political institutions and developed political programs to achieve their principal goal, that of establishing a state based on the principles and teachings of Islam. It was organizations of this sort that paved the ground for the victory of the revolution in Iran.[32] They acted as an arm and an organ of political Islam. Thus, the Iranian revolution and the program of Ayatullah Khomeini found in these organizations the means and political muscle to make the vision of exporting Islamic

[31]Samir al-Khalil, The Republic of Fear: The Politics of Modern Iraq (Berkeley, CA: University of Berkeley Press, 1989), 37-38.

[32]Such as Feda'ian Islam founded by Nawab Safawi in the late 1940s and later headed by Sadiq Khilkhali, the head of the revolutionary courts in 1979-1980; Mujahidiyn Khalq, a Socialist-Islamic organization supported by the late Ayatollah Talaqani; and Nahzat Azadi, a liberal-Islamic, founded by Mahdi Bazargan, the first Prime Minister of the revolution appointed by Ayatollah Khomeini.

revolutionary ideas come true. Some of these organizations existed in Iraq prior to the rise of both the Islamic revolution in Iran and the Baʿthist regime in Iraq. Muhammad Baqir Sadr was the one of founding fathers of an Islamic political party, the Islamic Daʿwah Party, and the political engineer of political activism through an organized political institution with defined political programs to achieve the formation of an Islamic state not only in Iraq, but throughout Islamic world. This is why it is necessary to shed light on the political life of Sadr right up to the time of his execution.

The Rise of Sadr

The Iraqi military coup d'etat of 1958 created great turmoil in the political life of the country for years afterward. It changed the structure of the political system and the social fabric of the people. The kingdom that was engineered by the British occupation forces in 1921 was replaced by a republic under the rule of a military junta. The royal family and the political establishment of the past regime were executed. The new political situation permitted a variety of political groups to participate in what amounted to an anarchical state of affairs. The military officers who led the revolt against the monarchy allowed the participation of several known political personalities from different political groups and parties in the formation of the new government. The officers led by their charismatic leader, General Qasim, in the few months preceding the coup undertook several radical policies that gained popular support, such as land reforms, withdrawal from the Baghdad Pact, and the closing of British military bases in the country.[33] Due to the deep resentment of the people toward the monarchy and its link to British imperialism the new military regime gained the support of most people, and General Qasim thus became a national hero overnight.

The Communist Party was then the most organized political party in the county. Qasim, wishing to manipulate the situation and increase his political power base within the country, was eager to use the Communists to eliminate his colleagues within the ruling junta who were loyal to the Arab nationalist political movements. In the process of the bloody street fighting that swept the entire country, especially in the northern cities of Mosul and Kirkuk where the nationalist officers attempted a military coup against Qasim, the communists became the major political force in the country masking themselves behind the charismatic appeal of Qasim and mobilizing the masses.[34]

The Shiʿi religious establishment, which was known for its political acquiescence since its last revolt against the British invasions and rule in 1920, found itself amid somber

---

[33]For a full account of Qasim's regime see Uriel Dann, _Iraq under Qassem_ (New York: Praeger, 1969).

[34]On the influence and the atrocities of the Iraqi Communist Party (ICP) see U. Zaher, "The Oppression" in CARDRI, _Saddam's Iraq, Revolution or Reaction?_, 148-150.

political challenges coming from atheist political forces of the society.[35] If left unchecked by the religious leadership, the antireligious forces might set about, so it seemed, to wipe out religion from the lives of the people. Many indicators apparent to the religious leadership showed that the whole nation was welcoming the wave of secularism and appeasing the antireligious sentiment of the new regime. The first of these indicators was the new law on civil liberties implemented by the military government, violating the Islamic laws of inheritance with regards to women's rights. Not even the public condemnation of the civil liberties law by the religious leadership could restrain the Qasim government from enforcing it. Second, the Communist propaganda, which labeled the religious establishment as reactionary and religion as a whole as an obstacle to modernization and progress of the people, began to gain momentum through the masses. The religious establishment found itself on the losing side when the mobilization of the Communist forces began to penetrate the religious establishment itself in the holy cities of Najaf, Karbala' and Kazimiyah. The Communist Party was successful in recruiting members and children of religious families. The religious leadership (<u>marja^ciyah</u>), represented by the late Grand Mujtahid Muhsin al-Hakim, took several steps to overcome this unprecedented political challenge that undermined the survival of Islam itself in Iraq, the home of supreme spiritual leadership of the Shi^ca and the place of major religious schools for the past two centuries. The Iraqi cities of Najaf, Karbala, Kazimiyah, and Samarra' house the shrines of six of the twelve imams of the Shi^cas. To undermine the religious sentiment in Iraq meant weakening Shi^cism everywhere.

During that turbulent time, there were two distinct groups within the Shi^ca's religious establishment: the traditional scholars who advocated the continuation of the apolitical stance of the religious school (<u>al-hawzah</u> al-^cilmiyah); and the political activists who advocated the involvement of the religious scholars in the political life of the people. The latter group organized themselves into a semiassociational task force known as "Jama^cat al-^cUlama'" in Najaf.[36] Their political program was designed to counter the secular and

---

[35]Hassan Shubar, "Dawr Hizb al-Da^cwah al-Islamiyah fi al-Taghyir wa-Halat al-Istirkha' al-Sabiqa" [The role of Islamic Da^cwah Party in previous period of change and relaxation], <u>al-Jihad</u>, no. 363, Oct 24, 1988.

[36]According to Talib al-Rifa`i, a colleague of Sadr and well known jurist activist in the 50s and 60s, Jama^ct al-^cUlama' consisted of ten <u>mujtahids</u>: 1) Murtada Aal Yasyyn, 2) ^cAbbas al-Rumaythi, 3) Isma^cil al-Sadr, 4) Muhammad Tahir Shaykh Radi,   5) Muhammad Jawad Shaykh Radhi, 6) Muhammad Taqi Bahr al-^cUlum,   7) Musa Bahr al-^cUlum, 8) Muhammad Reda al-Muzaffar, 9) Hussain al-Hamadani, and 10) Muhammad Baqir al-Shakhs.

antireligious trend within the society. Muhammad Baqir al-Sadr was then a young scholar and was not considered an official member within Jama^cat al-^cUlama', which was made up mainly of seniors and well-known mujtahids.[37] However his influence transcends his age and scholarly status. He was an intelligent <u>c</u>alim who earned the title of Mujtahid in his mid-twenties (a rare occurrence in the history of religious schools). Furthermore, he could exert special influence on the group through his father-in-law, Shaykh Murtada Al Yasiyn, the acting president of the group; and through his older brother, Isma^cil Sadr, a mujtahid, who held a senior position within the group.[38]

According to Talib al-Rifa^ci, Jama^cat al-^cUlama' was founded to achieve an immediate objective, which was to counter the communists' political challenge to Islam. In their political maneuvering, they were realists enough not to counter Qasim when he became the popular leader of the coup. Therefore, in their public leaflets and announcements, Jama^cat al-^cUlama' supported Qasim while attacking the communists. In response, the Qasim regime gave them access to the government controlled radio. The weekly public statements of the Jama^cat al-^cUlama' were written by Sadr and delivered by Hadi al-Hakim.[39] However, the appeasement of Qasim did not last long. Conflict between the religious leadership and the General erupted when Ayatullah Muhsin al-Hakim issued a religious decree (<u>fatwa</u>) that branded communism as atheism and forbade devoted Muslims from joining the Communist Party or helping its cause. The <u>fatwa</u> embarrassed the Qasim government's alliance with communism which forced General Qasim to abandoned the Iraqi Communist Party (ICP) once and for all. Qasim, later on, made several appeals for permission to pay a visit to the Ayatullah, but the latter refused to meet with him prior to the abrogation of the civil liberties law by the former.[40]

Jama^ct al-^cUlama' got the Qasim government's permission to publish their monthly journal <u>al-Adwa'</u> for two years. <u>al-Adwa</u>'s objective was to be the organ of Islam to counter the intensified secular and antireligious propaganda that followed the 1958 revolution. According to Talib al-Rifa^ci, this role for <u>al-Adwa'</u> was suggested by the <u>marja</u>^c of Muhsin al-Hakim. Since it was not popularly acceptable for a <u>marja</u>^c to sponsor a mass political

---

[37]Interview with Mohammad Baqir al-Hakim (once Sadr called him dearly beloved aide), <u>al-Jihad</u>, no. 5

[38]Muhammad Hussein Fadlullah, "Taqdim", a preface to Sadr, <u>Resalatuna</u> (Beirut: al-Dar al-Islamiyah, 1981) 16.

[39]An interview with one of the leading figures in the Jama^cat al-^cUlama' and the <u>Da^cwah</u> party, in January 1, 1990, who wished his identity not be revealed for security reason. Hence, I will refer to him henceforth as A.H.F.

[40]Interview with Talib al-Rifa^ci.

publication, it resorted to <u>Jama^cat al-^cUlam'</u> to take the task.[41] Sadr was given the task to write its editorial.[42] Sadr took the opportunity in his editorials to outline the basic political program of the Islamic movement, which was developing slowly. It was in the <u>Adwa'</u> that Sadr discovered his strength and the influence of his political writings.

At the same period, Sadr published his first extensive study, namely <u>Falsafatuna</u> (1959). This book offered an epistemological critique of communism and the materialist school of thought.[43] Its purpose was to show the flaws in the basic philosophical foundations of dialectic materialism. He reviewed the major philosophical schools since Plato, and attempted to prove that the materialist school of philosophy is lacking in coherence and accuracy in its explanation of the development of man's knowledge, or of the true nature of reality surrounding him. Sadr argued that dialectic materialism, the new trend in the materialist school, has too many major shortcomings to be considered the final truth of humankind. Thus, communism cannot be the answer to society's problems when its basic assumptions are false. His second work, <u>Iqtisaduna</u> (1961), was a critique of the economic theory of communism and capitalism and exposition of an Islamic theory of economics. It seeks to prove that Islam does possess ideas on the basis of which solutions to the economic problems of the day may be worked out. One of the major points the modernists, the secularists, and the communists held in common was that Islam has no answers to the rising problems of man in modern time, that Islam is only a body of beliefs concerning the salvation of man in the hereafter and has nothing to say about salvation of society in the here and now. Sadr's major task in this volume was to show that Islam is concerned about the welfare of man in this world. In fact Sadr's major intellectual achievement was his formulation of an Islamic economic doctrine on the basis of the literature of Islamic jurisprudence. None had preceded him in such an accomplishment. His final conclusion was that Islam was an economic system, which through the instrumentality of an Islamic political authority or state, provided man with an arrangement of his economic affairs that best served his needs.

In publishing Sadr's works and <u>Adwa'</u>, Sadr and the active members and

---

[41] However, <u>al-Adwa'</u>, according to Talib al-Rifa^ci, was later to become the voice of the Islamic Da^cwah party, where the official doctrine of the party was published in editorials and articles.

[42] Muhammad Hussein Fadlullah, "Taq'dim," 17.

[43] Talib al-Rifa^ci narrated to me how Sadr did not have the financial means to buy books necessary on Western philosophy. So the former resorted to a friend, an Arab nationalist and an owner of a bookstore, who was generously let him borrow the sources on materialism.

collaborators of Jama^c^t hoped to encourage a confrontation with the secular forces in the country from the level of slogan and propaganda to the level of intellectual and philosophical discussion. Sadr not only called attention to the fallacies of non-Islamic ideologies and schools of thought; he also set about to prove that Islam has an answer to the challenges facing society in the modern era. The political goal behind Sadr's publications was to direct the attention of people to Islam as the force that could guide the society through the period of modernization and progress and lift it from its present backwardness. Islam was not, according to Sadr, to be blamed for the bleak situation of the people; rather it was the abandonment of Islam by the political leadership that should be blamed as well as the impact of long years of Western colonialism.

Sadr and his colleagues confronted the secular forces on a third front through the establishment of the highly organized political party, Islamic Da^c^wah Party.[44] Steps toward founding this party first undertaken in 1957 by a group of Muslim intellectuals who felt it necessary for Muslims to group themselves in an organization and have some say in the political process and the future political outcome of the country.[45] However the actual formation of the party began in 1959, after Qasim's military coup and the establishment of <u>the republic of Iraq. The events</u> that followed the coup made it essential for concerned

[44]According to Talib al-Rifa^c^i, Da^c^wah was founded by three individuals: Mahdi al-Hakim, al-Rifa^c^i and another person whose identity should not be reviled. Sadr was later introduce to the party leadership by him and elevated to be the head of the party. However, A.H.F. gives a different account of the formation of the Da^c^wah party. The Al-Siwaki brothers (Hadi and Mahdi), who were members of the Tahrir party, proposed the idea of forming a political party to Murtada al-^c^Askari. It was the latter who contacted Sadr to set up the party's structure, and write its doctrine. According to A.H.F, Mahdi al-Hakim and Talib al-Rifa^c^i were among the first to be contacted and join the party.

[45]There are two conflicting accounts about the formation of the Da^c^wa Party. According to Salih al-Adib, one of the earlier members of the party, the first cell of the party was formed in 1957. See his article, "Rijal al-Harakah al-Islamiyah fi al-^c^Iraq yatathkarwun: Sanauat al-Muawajaha ma^c^a al-Mad al-'Ahmar" [Men of the Islamic movement in Iraq remember: the years of conflict with the red expansion], <u>al-Jihad</u>, no. 326, Feb 1, 1988; and also his new book; <u>al-^c^Amal al-Hizbi fi al-^c^Iraq</u> (Activities of Parties in Iraq), (Beirut: Dar al-Turath al-^c^Arabi, 1989), 255-256. However, Talib al-Refa^c^i trace the deliberation and the actual formation of the party to a few months after 1958 coup.

Muslim jurists and lay intellectuals to find a medium through which to face up to the challenges affecting the political future of the society. Since secularist forces in the society had acquired muscle through the formation of political parties, the conclusion of the Muslim activists was that if they were to stand up to their foes, it must be through exercising the same means. This way of thinking was inspired by the claim of the late mujtahid, Muhammad Hussein Kashif al-Ghita', that "belief could only be spread through means similar to that of unbelief." The first meeting of the Da^cwah party was held in Karbala with Sadr as one of its participants. Since then Sadr, according to the Da^cwah party, played an important role in setting its structure, writing its doctrine,[46] and later becoming its supreme jurisconsult (<u>faqih al-hizb</u>). Even the name of the party, Da^cwah ("Call"), was said to be Sadr's choice.[47] The aim of Da^cwah was to mobilize dedicated Muslim believers into the party, with the final goal of seizing power and establishing an Islamic state. The political plan to achieve such goals embraced four stages: 1) ideological indoctrination of revolutionaries; 2) political struggle against the existing corrupt regime; 3) establishment of an Islamic state; 4) the implementation of Islamic laws and the exportation of the Islamic revolution to the rest of the world.[48] This grand plan was said to be the idea of Sadr. The first stage was to take place as an underground activity with the purpose of securing the party against eventual government crackdown. Thus, the party was organized to have a hierarchical bread-cell structure. The uncovering of one cell would not affect the secrecy of the others. Furthermore, the activities of the party were not to be limited to Iraq only, but were to transcend her borders. Several branches of the party, therefore, were formed secretly in the Gulf states and in Lebanon, with unsuccessful attempts to do the same in Iran.

By the late 1960s, Muhammad Baqir Sadr was the paragon of Islamic political activism and Islamic revivalism in the Arab-Shi^ci world. All leading muslim activists such as Muhammad Hussein Fadlullah, and Muhammad Mahdi Shamsaldin in Lebanon; ^cArif al-Basri, Mahdi al-Hakim in Iraq; Ali al-Kurani and Muhammad Mahdi al-Asifi in Kuwait; and Murtada al-^cAskari in Iran are heirs of Sadr's political thinking. His books and programs

---

[46]al-Asadi, "Hizb al-Da^cwah al-Islamiyah" (Islamic Da^cwah Party), <u>Tariq al-Haq</u> (August, 1980), 46.

[47]Sadr, according to Da^cwah party, wrote four articles in the official journal of the party, <u>Sawt al-Da^cwah</u>, outlining the name, the structure, the goal, and the nature of the contemporary stage of the political struggle which is specified to be underground grass-root build up of the party and its members. The articles published in Da^cwah party publications no. 13, <u>Min Fikr al-Da^cwah al-Islamiyah: al-Shahid al Rabi^c, al-Imam al-Sadr</u>, n.d, n.p.

[48]al-Asadi, "Hizb al-Da^cwah al-Islamiyah" 48.

of political action thus became a major source of doctrine for Islamic fundamentalist groups all over the Middle East.

Back to Hawzah

Since Sadr was one of the leading mujtahids in the religious school of Najaf with a commanding edge in the field of jurisprudence (fiqh and Usul al-fiqh), his seniors in hawzah advised him to give up his political role in the Da^cwah party and in the Adwa' journal and prepare himself for becoming the future Grand Marja^c of the Shi^ci.[49] Pressure seemed to be coming from the late marja^c, Muhsin al-Hakim. Many social factions within the hawzah mounted criticism of Sadr's role in the political organization. Several individuals, led by Hussein al-Safi,[50] started a public campaign against Sadr's activities, depicting them as harmful to the survival of the hawzah, and they made their views known to al-Hakim.[51] A group within Jama^ct was influenced by the propaganda against Sadr and started showing their dissatisfaction with him.[52] Sadr's editorial in al-Adwa' raised a most disturbing question. Since the editorial articles, subtitled Risalatuna (Our Message), were political in nature, the enemies of Sadr questioned whether these views represented the views of Jama^ct at all. Muhsin al-Hakim, through his son Mahdi, exerted pressure on Sadr to give up his post

[49]According to al-Rifa^ci, Sadr took the decision on his resignation from the party at Samara' (city north of Baghdad holds the shrines of Imams al-^cAskarian) after taking khira (making one's choice through random selection of a verse from the Quran.)

[50]Hussein al-Safi was the head of the Ba^cth party branch in Najaf. He cooperated with the Islamic forces to counter the communist surge in Najaf. In fact, Jama^ct al-^cUlama' used Muhammad Reda Sheikh Radi to be the link between them and the al-Safi's nationalist and Ba^cthist forces. Hence, he was well aware of Sadr's activities. When the Ba^cthist came to power in 1963, al-Safi was appointed governor of Diwaniyah, a principality near Najaf. He later retired from political activities, and migrated to Morocco in 1970s to become a businessmen. Saddam invited him in 1985 to Iraq, and latter executed him.

[51]For a full account of the situation see Muhammad Baqir al-Hakim interview in al-Jihad no. 14 (Gambit al-Thai 1401 AH). al-Hakim also was referring to a letter received by him from Sadr, when the latter was in Lebanon, explaining the whole episode.

[52]Ibid.

as faqih of the Da^cwah party and as editor of <u>Adwa'</u> in 1961.[53] Another factor that seemed to have made Sadr yield to the pressure of al-Hakim was his future leadership in <u>hawzah</u>, i.e., the marja^ciya of the shi^cis. The religious environment in <u>hawzah</u> would not accept a highly activist mujtahid for the position of grand marja, at least not a member of a political party. The marja is usually selected from among the leading mujtahid in the fiqh and usul al-fiqh. One has to prove his capacity in these areas through the socratic method of teaching in <u>hawzah</u> for a number of years (or decades), and through publication of his juristic opinions and ideas. Since the selection of the position is highly dependent on the approval of the teachers and mujtahids in the <u>hawzah</u>, then the prospect of Sadr's becoming the grand marja of all Shi^cis was in jeopardy at stake if he continued his visible political activities.

From then on, Sadr was confined to the traditional way-of-life of <u>hawzah</u>, with less involvement in the overt political activities that might harm his marja^c status in the future. He even delayed the publication of his long awaited book, <u>Mujtama^cuna</u> (Our Society), because according to some sources, the time was not ripe for such a work.[54] However, according to the sources of the Da^cwah party, Sadr kept in touch with the party through a back channel, namely one of his pupils.[55] Fadlullah also notes that Sadr was advising some of his close associates and colleagues in the affairs and the editorials of <u>Adwa'</u>.[56]

Sadr's energetic passion for reform, therefore, was directed toward the <u>hawzah</u> itself. He realized that it was necessary to modernize the curriculum of the <u>hawzah</u>. Najaf's <u>hawzah</u>, for the past one and a half centuries, had emphasized only fiqh (jurisprudence) and <u>usul al-fiqh</u> (principles of jurisprudence) due to the rise of intellectual giants in those areas in Najaf such as Murtada al-Ansari, Khurasani and Na'ini. Since ijtihad consists mainly in the mastering fiqh and usul, other Islamic studies were considered minor or unimportant. Consequently, professors in <u>hawzah</u> paid little attention to the teaching of anything other than fiqh and usul. Sadr also was uneasy with the irregularity and irresponsibility of students toward their studies. He felt that students must be exhorted to successfully complete required courses before they could claim the rank of religious scholar (^calim).[57] He

---

[53]Mohammad H. Fadlullah, Preface to <u>Risalatuna</u> by Sadr (Beirut: al-Dar al-Islamyiah, 1981), 17.

[54]A famous saying of Sadr: "Mujtama^cuna la-yatahaml <u>Mujtama^cuna</u>" [Our society can not bear <u>Our Society</u>].

[55]Interview with A.H.F. in Jan 1, 1990.

[56]Mohammad. H. Fadlullah, Preface to <u>Risalatuna</u>, 17.

[57]Fadil al-Nuri, <u>al-Shahid al-Sadr Fada'iluhu wa-Shama'iluhu</u>, (Martyr Sadr, His Virtues and Characters), (Qum: Mahmuwd al-Hashimi office, 1984), 93.

proposed a new type of required textbook for the <u>hawzah</u> on the ground that the old textbooks were not written for the student, but rather were intellectual achievements in their fields. A textbook, according to Sadr, must take into consideration the student's ability to comprehend the subject from its basics to its latest development. Sadr's planning embraced not only textbooks of the sort used in modern academic institutions, but the formation of Western-style academic universities that hold the student responsible for completion of certain courses. Students then would be judged according to their achievement in written examinations and not according to informal questioning by their teachers, which was the traditional testing procedure of the <u>hawzah</u>.

To implement his reforms, Sadr actively participated in establishing the Usul al-Din college in Baghdad in 1964 and in setting up its academic curriculum. He later wrote three textbooks in the areas of Sciences of Quran, Usul al-Fiqh and Islamic Economics to be taught in the first and the second academic years of the college.[58] However his efforts to implement his reforms in <u>hawzah</u> itself faced stiff and consistent resistance from the students and religious establishment. The late marja, Muhsin al-Hakim, was known to oppose the creation of al-Fiqh college in Najaf, founded by the late mujtahid Muhammad Rada al-Muzafr. Nonetheless, Sadr's academic reforms for the <u>hawzah</u> were not to include the advanced studies known as "bahth al-kharij" (advance studies), but rather to be limited to the lower level of the <u>hawzah</u>'s studies. Sadr himself seemed to share the view of the majority of Shi^ci's scholars that the standard technique of teaching bahth al-kharij in <u>hawzah</u> represented the best academic format for advancing knowledge at the higher levels.

The acquiescent political activities of Sadr in the mid-1960s could be attributed to the moderate stability of the political system in Iraq. The fall of Qasim in a bloody military coup d'etat occurred on February 8, 1963. The coup sparked bloody street fighting between the rival political parties which dominated the political arena, the communist and Arab nationalists (the supporters and opponents of Qasim, respectively.) The new regime headed by Salam Arif and the Bath party were heavy-handed, and able to liquidate their rivals, the communist and all Qasim supporters within the government apparatus. Arif, nine months later, was able to eliminate his collaborators, the Ba^cthists, from the leadership. Arif's regime was able to utilize the popular resentment toward the severe methods of coercion that had been used by the Ba^cthist. Arif thus endeavored not to make new social opponents to his rule. His moderation toward the Shi^cis and its leadership resulted in a conflict-free relationship between the Shi^ci's political movement and sunni dominated political leadership. The regime at its early stage sought to gain the support or the endorsement of the Shi^ci religious establishment. Arif himself paid a visit to the late Muhsin al-Hakim, the

[58]The Sadr book in Usul is <u>al-Ma`lim al-Jadidah fi Usul al-Fiqh</u> (New features in the Principles of Jurisprudence). See Fadil al-Nuri, <u>al-Shahid al-Sadr</u>, 64; and S. D. al-Qubanchi, al-Jihad al-Siyasi, 79.

supreme mujtahid of all Shiᶜis at that time. Even though al-Hakim was not willing to give public support to Arif in the aftermath of the elimination of the two staunch rivals of Islamic fundamentalism, the communist and Bath national socialists, the rapprochement between al-Hakim and Arif brothers lasted throughout the life of the regime.[59]

This period, 1964-1968, can be labeled the "Golden Era" of the modern Shiᶜi's political involvement.[60] Free from government crack-downs, the Daᶜwah party was actively increasing its membership within the universities and within the intelligentsia. According to Daᶜwah sources, more than 1500 copies of the Daᶜwah official but secret journal, Sawt al-Daᶜwahh, were distributed to members and supporters in the University of Baghdad alone. Students used to show their commitment in an annual public march, known as <u>Màwakb al-Talabah</u>, (Students Procession) in Karbala on the occasion of the commemoration of the martyrdom of the Imam Hussein. al-Hakim, on the other hand, expanded his religious influence by increasing enrollment in the <u>hawzah</u> in Najaf, and by developing plans to establish a shiᶜi academy in Kufah, through which a college eduction would become available to shiᶜi youths who would have future influence in the political affairs of the society. He also established new religious centers and libraries in several Iraqi cities, directed by religious missionaries known as wukala' (representatives). The religious scholars of Baghdad and Khazimiyah (a religious center in the suburb of Baghdad) organized an association, similar to <u>Jamaᶜt al-ᶜUlama'</u> in Najaf, known as <u>Hy'at Jamaᶜt al-ᶜUlama' fi Baghdad wa-al-Khazimiyah</u>.[61]

Sadr, during this period, was working on two fronts. On the one hand he was preparing himself for the <u>marjaᶜiyah</u> in the distant future (due to his young age),[62] while on

[59]Abdul al-Salam Arif was killed in a plane crash in 1966, and was succeeded by his brother, Abdul Rahman.

[60]This does not mean that the relation between Arifs' regime and Islamic political activism of the Shias is free of confrontations and distrust between the two. In fact President Salam Arif was sectarian in his religious views, socialist in his domestic economic policy, and Arab nationalist in his foreign policy, positions totally rejected by the Shia religious scholars and considered non-Islamic. For details of the up and downs of the relations see interviews with Murtada al-Askari in the first commemoration of the martyrdom of Mahdi al-Hakim, Liwa al-Sadr, Jamadi al-Thai 7, 1409 A.H.

[61]The association headed by Hadi al-Hakim and Murtada al-Askari. In the late 1960s, Mahdi al-Hakim, became the most well-known outspoken member of the association. See interview with al-Askari, Liwa al-Sadr, Gambit al-Thai 7, 1409 A.H. 6.

the other hand he exerted increasing influence over Muhsin al-Hakim and acquired undisputed leverage over the decision makers of the Da[c]wah Party. To build his academic credentials Sadr started conducting regular classes in fiqh and usul.[63] In due process, many of his graduate pupils from different countries begin advocating his supremacy in the field of Islamic studies, which was highly essential for making lay people follow his religious decrees (fatwas). He also become al-Hakim's leading advisor on social and political issues. On several occasions, Sadr was the speech-writer for Hakim's public announcements on political events.[64]

Confrontation with Ba[c]th Party

The return of the Ba[c]th Party to power in July 17, 1968, brought conflict between the Shi[c]i leadership and the central government in Baghdad to a new peak. The leaders of the Ba[c]th party remembered well the negative stands of Shi[c]i's muslim activists toward their leadership in their in the 1963 regime. Muhsin al-Hakim, who issued the religious decree in the early 1960s branding communism as an atheist belief system and disallowing muslims to join the Communist party, did not give the Ba[c]th party the public support they needed when they in the same year were exterminating the communists. The Da[c]wah party was the fastest spreading political movement during Abd al-Rahman Arif's regime, when the Bath's leadership was toppled. In its 1968 comeback the Ba[c]th party faced two major social leaders who had far-reaching charisma and political clout, Muhsin al-Hakim of the Shi[c]is and Mustafa Barazani of the Kurds. The stability of the new regime was highly dependent on

---

[62]Sadr became mujtahid in his early twenties, which is very rare in the history of shia's hawzah. Most pupils attain such educational levels in their forties or fifties. Sadr's edict of ijtihad was through his mentor, Ayatollah Abu al-Qasim al-Khoei, the outstanding professor of fiqh and usul in Najaf. His exceptional intelligence brought him fame, yet made his peers envious. Ijtihad at such early age gave Sadr's opinions respect within the religious authority (mujtahid) and made him speak with an authority on religious and social matters, while facing resistance from others towards some of his political activities and religious reforms.

[63]Sadr started his first session of teaching of bahth al-kharij in Usul al-Fiqh in 1968, to end three years later, according to Tariq al-Haq, no. 4 (August 1979), 10.

[64]Abu Ali, "Lamhah Khatifah [c]an al-Shahid al-Rabi[c] al-Imam Muhammad Baqir al-Sadr" [Quick glance on the fourth martyr, Imam Muhammad Baqir Sadr], Tariq al-Haq, no. 7, (May 1980), 18.

withstanding the will of these centers of power.

Since Barazani was willing to engage in a dialogue with the regime for the solution of the Kurdish problem, the Bath party was able to negotiate and establish with him and the rest of the radical political parties (the Communist party and the nationalist groups), a national political front that patronized the Iraqi masses that supported the Ba^cth party. None of the major religious leaders or followers of al-Hakim was willing to engage in dialogue with the Ba^cth regime. None was willing to show the slightest public support for the regime. At least twice the regime made an effort to approach Mahdi al-Hakim (son of Muhsin al-Hakim and his father, a representative in Baghdad since 1964) to invite him to pay a public visit to President Ahmad H. Bakr, and in both instances the invitations were rejected.[65]

The regime then commenced a campaign to undo the religious establishment, sunni and Shi^ci, once and for all. The threat to the regime consisted in the fact that its ideological appeal to Arab nationalism was at stake. Both the Shi^ci and Sunni religio-political movements were widespread among the Arab population of the country, and this would undermine the rallying of the masses behind the secular institutions of the regime. However, to make a long story short, the regime was able eventually to corner the religious movement by advocating highly publicized radical policies that gained the support of the masses, e.g., an anti-Zionist calling for the liberation of Palestine, opposition to Arab regimes that propose a peaceful end to the conflict, the public hanging of spies linked to the West, strong ties with the eastern bloc and nonallied countries, financial assistance to radical political movements in Third World countries, and the nationalization of the Western oil interests in Iraq, to name a few.[66]

The regime undertook a first step toward limiting the power of the Shi^ci religious establishment by closing the religious schools (al-Jawadiyan elementary and high schools in Baghdad and Usul al-Din college), confiscating the land and funds set aside for building Kufah University, shutting down the publication of <u>Risalt al-Islam</u> (the only religious journal permitted by government censorship of previous regimes), prohibiting <u>Mawakb al-Talabah</u> (university students' procession in the commemoration of Imam Hussein's martyrdom) in Karbala, expelling dozens of non-Iraqi students from the <u>hawzah</u> in Najaf, and issuing a law requiring Iraqis attending the <u>hawzah</u> to join the armed forces.

Such broad but defined policies were orchestrated to limit the activities of the Shi^ci Islamic movement. The reaction of the Shi^cis' leadership appeared to be unorganized, and the Ba^cth regime seemed to catch them by surprise. The entire religious establishment went

---

[65]al-Shahada, Jamadi al-Thai 2, 1409 A.H. 13.

[66]On the policies of the Ba^cth regime, see Majeed Khdouri, Socialist Iraq: <u>A Study in Iraqi Politics since 1968</u> (Washington D.C.: Middle East Institute, 1978); and S. Khalil, <u>The Republic of Fear</u>.

into consultation to figure out possible means for dealing with the aggressive mode of the government. Hy'at al-ᶜUlama' held a meeting in Baghdad and suggested that Muhsin al-Hakim should make a visit to Baghdad, the capital, and try to mobilize Shiᶜi public support against the government.[67] al-Hakim took the initiative and took up residence in Kazimiyah, to receive devotees showing their commitment to his leadership. Sadr then travelled to Lebanon to organize public protest from abroad and use the office of Supreme council of Shiᶜi, headed by his cousin and brother-in-law Musa al-Sadr, for campaigning against the Iraqi government. Telegrams were sent by Musa al-Sadr to most heads of Islamic states and Islamic organizations calling attention to the Baᶜthist government harassment of the religious leadership in Najaf. The result of these efforts was disappointing. Only Naser of Egypt, Faisal of Saudi Arabia, 'Iriyani of North Yemen and Jamaᶜat-i-Islami of Abu al-Ala al-Mawdudi in Pakistan showed some moral support but with no tangible action.[68] However, Sadr returned to Baghdad despite the mounting threat that he might be arrested by the regime for his antigovernment activities in Lebanon. The Daᶜwah party, on the other hand, suggested to Muhsin al-Hakim that its members should organize an antigovernment public demonstration and agitate for the closing of the main bazaar in Baghdad. However, the idea was totally rejected by al-Hakim on the basis that the Daᶜwah was not prepared for such action and might swiftly face the crackdown of the regime.[69]

On his return to Iraq, Sadr, with the cooperation of Jamaᶜat of Najaf and Hy'at of Baghdad and Kazimiyah, held a public gathering in the Imam Ali's shrine in Najaf to support al-Hakim and condemn the Baᶜthist government action. Muhsin al-Hakim's

---

[67]The meeting was held in al-Karadah al-Sharqiyah, suburb of Baghdad, attended by sixty religious scholars from Baghdad and Kazimiyah. See al-Shahada, Jamadi al-Thai 2, 1409.

[68]The letter of Sadr sent to one of his friends is published in S. D. Qubanchi, al-Jihad al-Siyasi, 39-41. The letter shows that Sadr was first class political activist. He was planning with Sayyid [his name is censored in the book] to carry on several actions against the Ba`thist regime in Iraq such as asking some Lebanese students studying in Najaf's hawza to hold press conference condemning the Iraqi government against al-Hakim, contacting the press in Beirut, and distributing posters. However, the letter shows Sadr's frustration with the Lebanese from refraining to help him and refusing to show up for the press conference.

[69]The meeting between al-Hakim and leaders of Daᶜwah Party was held in June 9, 1969. See al-Jihad [official journal of Da`wa party], (Rabi` al-Awal, 1404 A.H.), 43.

statement, which was delivered to the audience by Mahdi al-Hakim, had been drafted by Sadr.[70] The next step to be taken against the government according to Murtada al-Askari, was to organize a mass demonstration in the suburb of Baghdad in support of al-Hakim.[71] Prior to the implementation of the plan, the Baʿthist government overcame the situation through its announcement that Mahdi al-Hakim was accused of plotting to over-throw the government in a military coup with the help of some generals and shiʿi businessmen who had links to Iran and the West (U.S. and Israel).[72] Such an engineered character assassination of al-Hakim by the Baʿthist government put the whole shiʿi religious movement on the defensive and diffused its popular support. Mahdi al-Hakim was smuggled out of the country, al-Askari went to Lebanon, and Muhsin al-Hakim retreated to Najaf to die few months later. His successor, Ayatullah Khoei, the mentor of Sadr, refrained from any political action against the Baʿthist government.[73]

At this turbulent and difficult time for the religious establishment, Sadr started giving lectures on the role of the Shiʿi Imams and their approaches to the tyrannic regimes of their time. He argued that the Imams had one great political plan, namely, to lay the ground for the establishment of just rule and thus to save Islam and protect its purity, even though the means employed varied from Imam to Imam. What Sadr tried to bring to the minds of the students in the <u>hawzah</u> was that one must understand historical circumstances and act accordingly. There is no one means to achieve one's goal, and direct confrontation with the rulers might not always be in the best interest of Islam. Peaceful means of resisting coercion might be the best political option since it would not bring a threat to the Islamic movement. Some of the Holy Imams resorted to supplication, others turned to the teaching of fiqh and Sunna (traditions of the Prophet), while others accepted minor political roles in order to <u>overcome tyrannical oppression</u> against the Shiʿi. Sadr even went so far as to theorize that

[70]Liwa al-Sadr, Shaʿban 29, 1409.

[71]Murtada al-ʿAskari, "Juthor wa-Khalfiyat al-Taharuk al-Islami fi Muwajahat al-Baʿth al-ʿAflaqi" (The Roots and Backgrounds of Islamic Activities in Opposition to the ʿAfliq's Baʿth), Liwa al-Sadr, Muharam 22, 1409, 10.

[72]Ibid., 10.

[73]The Baʿthist government tried to influence the selection process of the Supreme Mujtahid of the Shiʿis through a campaign to Shaykh ʿAli Kashif al-Ghita' who publicly endorsed the regime. However, Sadr and Muhsin al-Hakim's eldest son, Yousif, put their weight behind Khoei. On the selection of Ayatollah Khoei, see also Fouad Ajami, The Vanished Imam, Musa al Sadr and the Shia of Lebanon (Ithaca, N.Y.: Cornell University Press, 1986), 194.

the whole prophetic mission was designed by God Almighty according to the historical circumstance of the time of each prophet. These lectures were published in one volume named Ahl al-Bayit, Tanaw' Adwar wa-Wihdat Hadaf (House of the Prophet, Different roles but Unified Goal).

Other lectures delivered in the <u>hawzah</u> at other times were to approach the political hardship from a different angle. Sadr was emphasizing the strength of the will of the faithful as the only means to continue the message and the survival of Islam. One must not break down in the face of severe affliction. Misfortunes and difficulties are the natural processes of a just historical struggle. However, successful survival depends on the commitment of the faithful to carry on despite all odds. He reminded his fellow Shiᶜis that the Kurds of Iraq were facing overwhelming odds and hardships, and one must join hands with them, help them in any way possible and see the whole ordeal of Muslims as one which must be felt by all. These lectures were published under the title, <u>al-Mihnah</u> (The Ordeal)[74]

<u>Ascendancy to Leadership</u>

Once the charismatic leader of the Shiᶜis passed away, the Bath's government intensified its efforts to reduce the influence of the <u>hawzah</u> in Najaf through expelling its non-Iraqi students from the county (since the majority of students were foreigners), and monitoring the Iraqi students there. That put the whole <u>hawzah</u> in chaos. Sadr, in order to pressure non-Iraqi students holding valid visas to stay in the country and resist the government in any way possible, convinced Khoei to issue a religious order (hukum) to students to stay in Najaf and continue their studies.[75] Unwilling to get into conflict with the new shiᶜi leadership, the Baᶜth government postponed implementation its deportation policy. In the view of the Baᶜth leadership, Khoei had not yet built up his popular support and getting into conflict with him at this early stage might make a hero out of him.

However, the Baᶜthist regime started to crack down on the Daᶜwah Party. Many of suspected members of the party were rounded up in 1972 and sentenced to one to five years in prison.[76] Sahib Dakhiyl, known as Abu ᶜIsam, died under severe torture in 1973. Dakhiyl was the initiator responsible for the organization of the student procession held in Karbala,[77]

---

[74]al-Wihda, (an Arabic magazine of the Ministry of Guidance of the Islamic Republic of Iran), no. 5,6,7.

[75]S.D. Qubanchi, al-Jihad al-Siyasi, 74.

[76]Daᶜwah Party, Lamahat min Masirat Hizb al-Daᶜwah al-Islamiyah (Glances on the Journey of Islamic Daᶜwah Party), (n.p., n.d.), 25.

[77]Salih al-Adib, "Mawakb al-Talabah", <u>al-Jihad</u>, Feb. 29, 1988, 12.

and was also believed to be the head of the Da^cwah party branch in the capital city of Baghdad.[78] A year later, about seventy-five Da^cwah party members, some of them religious scholars, were detained by the security forces, while five people were sentenced to death (all of whom were believed to be the top leadership in the Da^cwah party) by the revolutionary court.[79] Sentencing these people (three of them ^culama') brought public outcry and condemnation from the religious establishment as a whole (including Khoei, Khomeini, and Sadr).[80] Rumors by close associates of Sadr reported that he was greatly hurt to the point that he was paralyzed for a short period of time when he heard the news of their executions.[81] In order not to set the precedent of executing religious scholars of the hawzah, Sadr issued a fatwa (religious decree) disallowing students or scholars of the hawzah to join any political party, i.e., not to join the Da^cwahh party.[82] Later that year, Sadr himself was detained and

---

[78]Sahib Dakhiyl was the editor of the Da^cwah Party underground official journal, Sawt al-Da^cwah (Voice of Da^cwah). He was detained in Sep. 28, 1971, and later executed. See, al-Jihad, Jan. 3, 1983.

[79]The five sentenced to death were: 1) Shaykh ^cArif al-Basri, 2) Sayyid ^cIz al-Din al-Qubanchi, 3) Sayyid ^cImad al-Tabrizi, 4) Mr. Hussein Chalukhan, and 5) Mr. Nuri Tu^cmah. On their life and story of their detention and execution see, Islamic Da^cwah Party, Shuhada' Baghdad (Martyrs of Baghdad), (Tehran: Islamic Da^cwah Party, 1403).

[80]On the reaction of Ayatullah Khomeini to the execution of five people of Da^cwah, known as al-Shuhada' al-Khamsah (the five martyrs), see al-Jihad (journal) (Rabiy^c al-Awal 1404), 44.

[81]al-Jihad, July 20, 1987.

[82]This fatwa became the one single issue widely discussed in the literature of Shi^ca's Islamic movement in Iraq. The opponents of forming political party (which is considered a Western phenomenon) argued that Sadr reversed his opinion and disbelieved in the organization of political party as acceptable religious means for the political struggle (jihad). The Da`wah party and its advocates produced some evidence that shows that Sadr's fatwa was only a political tactic to safeguard the hawzah from further government crackdowns, see al-Jihad (journal) (3, 1404) 44-47. The former group advocates popular political movement thats do away with hierarchical cell structure (similar to Hizb Allah, party of God), and they claim that it is the only

taken from Najaf to Baghdad for interrogation, but released shortly by the security forces.[83]

In the post-Hakim era, Sadr was recognized in the hawzahh as a marja while (as mentioned above) the Supreme Marja of the Shi^{c}is went to his mentor, Ayatullah Khoei.[84] Meanwhile, Sadr was considered the heir apparent of Khoei. However, the marja^{c}iya position seemed to be a heavy burden. He had to continue his classes in the hawzah in fiqh and usul. However,the normal teaching in the hawzah together with the responsibilities of the marja^{c}iyah take up most of the daily hours of a mujtahid. This resulted in great pressure for Sadr, who devoted much of his time to politics. In addition to setting up regular classes in fiqh and usul which lasted several years, as marja^c Sadr was supposed to set aside time for public appearances in his private court to accept visitors, and answer questions about Islam and issues of personal conduct either in person or through letters. Other major tasks of the marja^c are to distribute religious funds sent by the faithful among causes which he sees as serving the interests of Islam.

Sadr, as a marja^c, also had to send representative from among the ulama to areas and masques in need of religious services. Since the number of his muqallid (followers in religious decrees) was not widespread, Sadr's responsibility was less than that of Khoei, for

---

purely Islamic means of organization, and, above all, it is in accordance with the line of the Imam (Khomeini); see Ali al-Kurani, Tariqat Hizb Allah (The mean of Party of God); and S.D. Qubanchi, Buhuth fi Khat al Marja^{c}iyah (Studies in line of Marja^{c}iyah), (n.p., 1984). The latter group claims that party organization is also Islamic since it is an effective means of jihad jurisdiction that is legitimized by approval of grand mujtahid, like Sadr and Muhsin al-Hakim. They also cite that the Party of God structural organization is no different from that of Da`wah party at all, except in name and rhetoric. See M.H. Fadlullah, "Mn Yaqud ^{c}Amaliyat al-Taghir fi al-Ummah, Hizb al-Ummah aw Ummat al-Hizb" (Who Leads the Process of Change in the Nation, the Party of the Masses or the Masses of the Party), al-Muntalaq, no. 27, 28, 29 (10, 11, 12, 1985); and Interview with Fadlullah, al-Jihad, Dec 14, 1987, 9.

[83]S.D. Qubanchi is the only one to cite that Sadr was detained by the government in 1971 but was not imprisoned because of his poor health, but rather was tied to his hospital bed. See al-Jihad al-Siyasi, 25.

[84]Another marja^{c}s in Najaf was Ayatullah Khomeini. Also, there were others in Qum, Iran, such as Shari^{c}atmadari (d. 1985), Gulbaygani, Mar^{c}ash-Najafy; and in Mashhad, Iran, ^{c}Abdullah Shirazi (d. 1986).

example. His <u>muqallids</u> mostly consisted of intellectuals, college students and upper middle class people and mainly Iraqis, especially Muslim fundamentalist activists and Da^cwahh party members.

Since a <u>muqallid</u> must follow the opinion of the <u>marja</u>^c regarding the acts of worship and Islamic regulations of daily life, a <u>marja</u>^c must produce what is called <u>al-Risalah al-^cAmaliyah</u> (Treatise on the Practice of Islamic Laws) for people to refer to. Sadr first recorded his opinions as footnotes to Muhsin al-Hakim's <u>Mihaj al-Salihyn</u>.[85] Also by then, most of Sadr's writings on jurisprudence appeared as a result of his lectures in the <u>hawzah</u>.[86] Out of his lectures in fiqh was published, <u>Buhuth fi al-^cUrwah al-Withqa</u> (Investigation into the Sure Bond) a standard jurisprudence textbook, and in usul he published <u>Buhuth in ^cIlm al-Usul</u> (Studies in The Principles of Jurisprudence).[87] In these works Sadr presented his views about the derivation of religious laws.[88]

Sadr felt that most mujtahids wrote their treatises in a style that made them impossible for the general public to understand, even though the whole purpose of these treatises was used by the people. Their language is full of the terminology of fiqh, which is

---

[85]Every shi^ci-person must follow the opinion of mujtahid with regard to his religious duties. Once the mujtahid die, one must choose the most knowledgeable among the living mujtahids. The tradition in the hawzah is that the new marja` produce their opinions in the form of footnotes to the previous marja so people can figure out the difference in opinion between the two and follow the new one.

[86]The normal procedures of publication conducted in hawzah are that some students (mostly the brightest) would write and edit the lectures of their mentor. The students then gain a written permission from his mentor for the publication of the work under the professor name with subauthor of the student.

[87]The fourth volume drafted by Sadr's student and mujtahid graduate of his hawzah, Mahmuud al-Hashimi, under the title of Ta^carud al-Adilah al-Shar^cyah (The Contradictions within the Indicators of Religious Law), (Beirut: Dar al-Kitab al-Lubnani, 1980). al-Hashimi is considered one of the brightest students of Sadr to gain <u>Ijtihad</u> in his thirties. He later was appointed by Sadr as his representative in Iran after the revolution.

[88]Since these works are out of my field of studies, I refrain from making any comments or annotated bibliography about them.

hard for laymen to grasp the meaning of, not to mention adhering to. The fatwa employed are a thousand years old, and their stipulations related to problems of earlier days, not to contemporary problems. Sadr aspired to produce a new Risalah cAmaliyah that would reflect the needs and understanding of contemporary people. His al-Fatawa al-Wadihah is unique in its class, and is praised by the youth and the intellectuals of the Sunnis and Shicis alike for its straightforward language and for its detailed expositions of the fatwa and of their bearing upon contemporary problems.[89]

Sadr even proposed a new classification for the fatwas. The traditional classification consists of two categories: cIbadat (acts of worship), and Mucamalat (acts of relationship).[90] Sadr thought that such a bipolar scheme is too broad and awkward since scholars had to ignore some laws, or place some laws in an inappropriate category just to satisfy the traditional classification.[91] Therefore, Sadr intended that his Fatawa al-Wadihah would consist of four volumes: 1) cIbadat, which includes the personal acts of worship that require niyah on the part of the worshiper but would not include such acts as al-amr bil macruf wa-al-nahi 'an munkr (enjoining good and forbidding evil) or jihad (holy war) because they involve public participation; 2) Properties (Amwal) including such matters as public wealth, the property of the state, the public economic resources such as Zakat (even though it is a form of worship); and private money, the private ownership of property; 3) Private life, including such matters as family law (marriage, divorce), and inheritance law; and finally 4) Public affairs.[92] However, Sadr was able to publish only the first volume (cIbadat), in 1976, probably because of the turbulent years that followed, which climaxed in the events of the Iranian revolution.

In the Fatawa al-Wadihah Sadr seemed to take a more conservative view with regard to the derivation of Islamic laws. According to him, the only sources for the derivation of Islamic laws are the Quran (the Holy book) and Sunna (the tradition of the Prophet). The other two sources, cAql and Ijmac (rational reasoning and consensus, respectively), were not considered valid sources by him unless they are supported by Quran or Sunna.[93]

---

[89]Sadr had invited Shaykh Muhammad Jawad Maghniyah from Lebanon to help him edit al-Fatawa al-Wadihah to make its stylistic writing easily grasped by a laymen.

[90]All the Rasa'il al-cAmaliyahs are classified according to the classification of Sharaic al-Islam of al-Muhaqqiq al-Hilli (d. 1277).

[91]Sadr, al-Fatawa al-Wadihah, (Beirut: Dar al-Tacruf li-al-Matbua't, 1981), 95.

[92]Sadr, al-Fatawa al-Wadihah, 132-134

In his spare time, Sadr, with the help of one of his students,[94] was writing a philosophical work that would compliment his earlier book, <u>Falsafatuna</u>. He had come to believe that the Aristotelian epistemology had too many shortcomings to be considered the undisputable means of proof in the scientific age. Philosophy and science had been considered compatible from the days of Aristotle until the modern age of scientific revolution. Aristotelian logic had worked perfectly to link philosophical reasoning to scientific proofs. However, nowadays empirical data and mathematical principles are the only acceptable facts for the positivists philosophers as well as for dialectical historical materialist philosophers of the nineteenth and twentieth centuries. In <u>Falsafatuna</u>, Sadr had used Aristotelian methods in trying to prove the existence of God and refute the materialist school of thought that denies the existence of a metaphysical realm. Now Sadr was trying to discover a concurrent method of proof that would relate philosophy to scientific experiments. His efforts led him to explore inductive logic as the basis for human knowledge in both philosophy and science. His book, <u>al-Usus al-Mantiqiyah li-al- Istiqra'</u> (The Logical Basis of Induction), is considered as Sadr's most outstanding philosophical achievement.[95] Sadr himself recognized its worth and was eager to publish it in Western languages.[96] When he was asked why he wrote this book, he replied in his famous statement that <u>"the age of borrowing from the west must come to an end, and we must export our</u>

---

[93]M.B. Sadr, <u>al-Fatawa al-Wadihah</u>, 98.

[94]A letter sent by Sadr to Kazim al-Ha'iri, one of his students, admiring him for his essential role in deriving and completing the theory of inductive logic. (al-Ha'iri is one of the few students known to gain their <u>ijtihad</u> from Sadr.) For a copy of the letter see, Hassan Nuri, "Ma^ca al-Shahid al-Sadr Muhaqqiqan" (With Shahid Sadr as an Inquirer), <u>al-Hiwar al-Seyasi</u>, no. 28-29, (April-May 1985), 70-71.

[95]Zaki Najib Mahmud, the contemporary Egyptian philosopher, according to Mohammad H. Fadlullah, had praised Sadr's <u>al-Usus al-Mantiqiyah</u> and wished the book to be translated to the Western languages to prove that Arabs have great philosophers.

[96]Sadr considers this work as his major intellectual achievement. He wanted to translate this work into Western languages. According Sheikh F. al-Sahlani, Sadr paid a sum of money to the head of the Philosophy Department at the University of Alexandria in Egypt to translate the work into English. Three copies of the translation were sent to Sadr in 1980, shortly before his execution, and unfortunately were not published.

achievement to them." In <u>al-Usus al-Mantiqiyah</u> Sadr critiques the basis of the Islamic philosophy (the offshoot of the Aristotle's philosophy) which he argued for in his previous book, <u>Falsafatuna</u>. He came to the conclusion that the Aristotelian logic and concepts of epistemology have their shortcomings. Thus, Sadr developed his own epistemological concepts which are based more or less on the standards of empirical philosophy. He argues that experimental-scientific techniques are valid formulas to know the physical as well as the metaphysical world.

By early 1977, Sadr completed his last major work, <u>Durus fi ᶜIlm al-Usul</u> (<u>Lessons in the Principles of Jurisprudence</u>) in three volumes, to be used as a text book for beginners in the <u>hawzah</u>.[97] The book was what Sadr had envisioned a textbook ought to be. He introduced the students to the history of the subject, explained in detail the concepts, and gradually introduced the students to the field of <u>usul</u>, its latest trends, and the major accomplishments of the great <u>usul</u> thinkers. The book's eloquence and style surpassed the traditional textbooks, which made it the standard <u>usul</u> text of Shiᶜi's <u>hawzahs</u>.

As a <u>marjaᶜ</u>, Sadr was aware that the <u>marjaᶜiyah</u>, the Shiᶜas only true source of political leadership, lacked an adequate institutional underpinning. Even though it was a thousand years old,[98] it still lacked those features that characterized effective political

---

[97]Sadr dedicated the book to one of his students (one of closest and most admired), Abd al-Ghani al-Ardabili, who faced sudden death in Iran. Sadr mentioned that Ardabili asked him to write the book on usul to be taught in the latter's new established hawzah in Iran. Sadr, therefore, in a rush, finished the work in two months. See Dedication of <u>Durus fi ᶜIlm al-Usul</u> (Cairo and Beirut: Dar al-Kitab al-Masri, or al Lubnani, 1978), 5

[98]Sadr divided the history of <u>marjaᶜiyah</u> into four different stages: First, the period of "Individual <u>marjaᶜiyah</u>", which begins with companions of the Holy Imams until the time of `Alamah al-Hili (d. 1325), where the <u>marjaᶜ</u> served only as the source of religious laws for the Shi`is masses. Second, the period of "Institutional <u>marjaᶜia</u>" which was formed by al-Shahiyd al-Awal (d. 1374), where the marja' sent representatives to various areas for religious preaching and collections of religious taxes. Third, the period of "Central <u>marjaᶜiyah</u>," characterized by consolidation of power within one <u>marjaᶜ</u>, which began with <u>mariaᶜiyah</u> of Kashif al-Ghita' (d. 1813). The grand <u>marjaᶜ</u> became a dominant authority on the affairs of the Shi`is all over the world. Fourth, the period of "Popular <u>marjaᶜiyah</u>" which began during the Western colonization of the Muslim world, where the <u>marjaᶜiyah</u> was directly involved in the political affairs of

leadership. In particular, it lacks the means of enforcement which would enable the marja[c] to make his appointed representatives all over the Shi[c]i world obey his decisions. The Marja[c]s traditionally conducted their policies and made decisions on the basis of their own individual styles, depending on an inner circle of close associates and family members to gather information, issue political statements, or make decisions. Thus, there was no fundamental pattern either for the process of making decisions, or for the content of those decisions. This inconsistency had resulted in social confusion that weakened the relationship between the marja[c]iya and the people. Furthermore, a marja[c] did not train the [c]ulama' who were second- or third-in-command and pass knowledge and expertise to them, but rather each new marja[c] would start from square one to conduct the course of their business. Therefore, each marja[c] differed from all others in his leadership capacity, crisis-management ability, or experience in political affairs.[99]

To enhance the power of the marja[c]iyah in the society and upgrade its effectiveness, Sadr wanted to transform what he called the "individualistic marja[c]iyah" into an "objective marja[c]iyah." The marja, according to Sadr, must conduct his affairs and guide his people on the basis of an organized multibranched institutional infrastructure in order to overcome all the weaknesses mentioned above. He, therefore, proposed to organize research, planning, and executive capabilities for the marja[c]iyah based on a division of labor and distribution of responsibilities. To conduct the affairs of the ummah, the marja[c], according to Sadr's plan, should set up the following committees:

1) a committee to manage educational affairs in the hawzah

2) a committee for the support of Islamic intellectual studies,   research, and writings on essential social subjects.

3) a committee responsible for the affairs of those [c]ulama' who represent the marja[c] in other cities.

4) a committee for public or external relations

5) a committee for the support of the Islamic movement

6) a committee for financial affairs

The marja[c] himself must assume the top position in the hierarchy in order to become a powerful leader in the society.[100] However, he realized that "the individualistic conduct of

---

the Muslims to protect religion and defend the right of Muslims, and in several cases, lead their struggle against imperialist powers. See, Sadr, "al-Mihna," Sawt al-Wihdah, (n.d), 56.

[99]These points are outlined in M.H. Fadlullah's speech on al-Marja[c]iyah wa-al-Tahazub (Marja[c]iyah and Political Party) giving in Fourth Conference of Muslim Group, 1982.

[100]Sadr, "Utruhat al-Marja[c]iyah al-Salihah" (Thesis on

affairs in the practice of the marja^ciya has some positive features such as the quick response [to political issues], and insurance of a high level of supervision and self-command, so as to secure the <u>marja^ciyah</u> against the penetration of unwise individuals into the stages of planning, but the features of the other process [objective <u>marja^ciyah</u>] are much greater and more important."[101] Furthermore, the prevailing selection process of the "individualist <u>marja^ciyah</u>" has emphasized the personal suitability of the marja^c himself to carry on the traditional functions of <u>marja^ciyah</u>. The two most important components of this suitability are that the <u>marja^c</u> be the most knowledgeable of scholars in the <u>shari^cah</u> (A^clamiyah) and that he not deviate from its principles and code of ethics in his life (^cAdalah). However, the selection of a personally suitable <u>marja^c</u>, according to Sadr, is not enough to achieve the goals envisioned for the "objective <u>marja^ciyah</u>." "It requires a foundation (of person), within the <u>hawzah</u> and within the nation, who believed in these goals in one way or the other."[102]

Close Encounter With Ba^{cth}

By early 1977, the Ba^cth regime took the boldest step yet to limit the popular religious activities of the Shi^cis by banning the annual ceremonies commemorating Imam Hussein's martyrdom. The regime had tried but failed to prohibit such ceremonies since 1970, especially in the religious cities of Najaf and Karbala. However, the Ba^cth leadership was determined that year to use any means necessary to stop the traditional people's walk from Najaf to Karbala, an event that generates high passion and religious sentiment. Tens of thousands of Shi^cis from all over Iraq participate in the pilgrimage, which usually takes four days to travel about fifty miles. Such acts were seen by the regime as hindering their policy of secularism, and providing the religious authorities (the reactionary forces of the society, as labeled by the Ba^cth's propaganda) with popular support.

The governmental banning of the procession of Sufr 1497 AH (1977), unlike proceedings years, provoked popular riots in the city of Najaf. People were determined to violate the authorities' prohibition against sanctions against the annual walk to Karbala'.[103] Organizers of the procession distributed leaflets that called on people to participate in defiance of the authorities for the sake of protecting their religious rights.[104] The public

---

Suitable Marja^ciyah), in al-Ha'iri, <u>Mabahith</u>, 94-95.

[101]Ibid, 96.

[102]Sadr, "Utruhat al-Marja^ciyah," 93.

[103]For detailed accounts of the uprising see, Ra^cad al-Mussawi, <u>Intifadat Sufr al-Islamiyah fi Iraq</u> (Sufr Islamic Uprising in Iraq), 2nd ed., (Qum, Iran: Amair al-Mua'minin, 1404 AH).

hearings organized by the Ba^{c}th Party and the governor of Najaf did not ease the situation, but rather ended in chaos.[105] An estimated thirty thousand people began their procession holding banners citing verses from the Quran such as "the power of God is above theirs" and "victory shall come from God."[106]

The regime's security and police forces were not able to stop the multitude in Najaf. When the procession was ten miles away from Karbala, the regime was in a dilemma whether to let them enter the city, make their ritual visit to Imam Hussein's shrine and face humiliation, or confront them with a large military force and prevent them from proceeding. First the regime resorted to face-saving dialogues with the leaders of the procession.[107] A group of distinguished personalities and ᶜulama' (amongst them Muhammad Baqir al-Hakim) informed them that the regime was willing to lift the ban on the procession if the rioters would not chant anti-government slogans.[108] However, the anti-Baᶜthist sentiment of the participants was so high that it prevented any dialogue with the al-Hakim group. The government then mobilized a military brigade (tanks, helicopters and fighter jets) to block the way to the city of Karbala'.[109] However, hundreds of the rioters were able to get into the city because many officers and soldiers were sympathetic to the procession and were unwilling to obey the government orders to fire on a peaceful demonstration chanting religious slogans.[110] The government then mobilized large numbers of Baᶜth Party cadre, security and police personnel to suppress the procession in the streets of Karbala and detained as many as they could. As a result, hundreds were imprisoned and many were injured.

The government then formed a special revolutionary "security" court (Mahkamat al-Thawrah) headed by three high ranking Baᶜth Party leaders to try the defendants.[111] After a

---

[104]Ibid., 66-68.

[105]Ibid., 71-73.

[106]Raᶜad al-Mussawi, Intifadat Safr, 68-69.

[107]Ibid., 95-99.

[108]Some of the slogans were: ya Saddam shil eidk, ja'iysh wa- shaᶜb ma yiridk (Saddam take off your hand, the military and the people don't want you), and Jassim qulla lil Bakr, Dhikr il-al- H'ssiyan ma yin dither (Jassim, governor of Najaf, tell Bakr, the President, the Memory of Hussein can not be obliterated).

[109]R. al-Mussawi, Intifadat Sufr, 101.

[110]Ibid., 102-103.

mock trial the court verdict was business-as-usual for the Ba^{c}th regime in dealing with civil disturbance: seven people were sentenced to death (all were the organizers of the procession), and fifteen to life imprisonment, including Muhammad Baqir al-Hakim. The incident also caused a split within the Ba^{c}th leadership itself. Some high-ranking members of the Party were judging the action of the regime as unduly suppressive and they seemed hesitant to take harsh actions against the rioters. The extremist group led by the Saddam-Baker factions won the round and dismissed the moderate group, including the members of Special Revolutionary Court, from their government and party positions.[112]

The imprisonment of Muhammad Baqir al-Hakim prompted a public outcry within the hawzah for his release. Khoei sent missionaries to the presidential palace asking for al-Hakim's release. al-Hakim's life imprisonment was reduced to a few years, and soon he was released. However, the regime suspected Sadr of having a link to the riots. The riots were highly organized, which suggested a relation of the underground Da^{c}wahh Party to the uprising. In fact, according to Da^{c}wahh literature, the whole plan of the procession was orchestrated by party branches in Najaf and Karbala.[113] M. B. al-Hakim, the head of the group negotiating on behalf of the regime with the rioters, also was a close disciple and personal representative of Sadr. His failure to gain concession from the rioters whose links were with Da^{c}wah, the Sadr's forefront organization, was one of the signs that made the regime think that there was a behind-the-scenes conspiracy played by Sadr. The regime's security forces detained Sadr and sent him to Baghdad for questioning, but released him shortly in order not to instigate another riot by the hawzah and the people demanding his release (since Sadr by then had established his credibility as a well known faqih, and his marja^{c}iya was slowly spreading in the Shi^{c}i world).[114] It was later revealed by M.B. al-Hakim that the plan for the uprising was engineered by Sadr to break out after his arrest by the government.[115] He had planned to lead a public revolt against the regime which might

---

[111]The tree members of the court were:1) Ezat Mustafa, Minister of Health; 2) Hassan Ali, and 3) Falih Jassim, all members of the Regional command of the Ba^{c}th party.

[112]RCC decision in March 23, 1977.

[113]Ra^{c}ad al-Mussawi, _Intifadat_, 106-112. This book is considered to represent Da`wah views since Shaykh Mahdi al-Asifi, Da^{c}wah Party's spokesman, was its editor. Also, a private conversation with Muhammad Baqir al-Nasiri, the current head of _Jama^{c}t al-Ulama_, confirmed the deep involvement of Da^{c}wah with the organization of the procession in 1977.

[114]al-Qubanchi, _al-Jihad al-Siyasi_, op. cit., p. 89.

lead to his arrest and execution. However, Mohammad B. al-Hakim did not elaborate on why Sadr refrained from his original plan for the uprising.

The Final Episode: Showdown to Bloody End

The moment the leaders of the Ba‘th regime thought that their suppression measures in 1977 had once and for all put an end to any religious opposition for years to come, revolutionary stirrings in Iran shook the world and set fire to efforts to achieve political stability in the area. By 1978 a revolution led by the religious leadership centered in Najaf was well in the making against the powerful regime of the Shah, which had the support of the internal security agencies and the help of U.S. intelligence services. The Shi‘i capital of religious studies was again in the center stage instigating political upheaval, however not directed toward the Ba‘th, though troublesome to the Iraqi regime. Ayatullah Khomeini, the leader of the Iranian uprising, had been residing in Najaf for the past fourteen years, benefiting from the Ba‘th enmity toward the Shah to launch a broad campaign against the monarchy in Iran. He was provided with easy access to Iraqi Persian broadcasting to beam his political messages to Iran, and this made it possible for him to be approached by his political collaborators. However, such favors (which in any case were severed in the aftermath of the Saddam-Shah Algiers agreement in 1975 that ended the hostility between the two regimes) did not elicit pro-Ba‘th sentiment from Khomeini, who witnessed the Ba‘th's oppressive measures toward the hawzah of Najaf and toward the Shi‘i's religious leadership. In several instances, Khomeini sent messages through his political associates condemning Ba‘th's campaign against Muslim activists in Iraq. Each time he was reminded not to interfere in the internal affairs of Iraq. Khomeini, to show his discontent with the Ba‘th regime, had halted his regular teaching classes in hawzah for several days.

The revolution in Iran awakened once again the political activism of the religious leadership in Iraq. They felt a part of the uprising in Iran. The revolution seemed to demonstrate that an oppressive regime could in fact be challenged and defeated, and that Islam ideology and movement are capable of leading masses toward establishing the dreamed of Islamic state. It showed that blood sacrificed in the process of revolution can encourage other devotees committed to the cause of Islam. Thus, the oppressive measures by the regime could be turned into the means for achieving victory.

Upon Khomeini's deportation by the Ba‘th regime (from the pressure of the Shah of Iran) to France, Sadr paid a visit to him through security forces encircling Khomeini's residence in Najaf.[116] Such a visit meant great moral support to Khomeini since the marja‘s

---

[115]A telephone conversation with Muhammad Baqir al-Hakim in 1985.

[116]M.R. al-Nu‘mani quoted in al-Ha'iri, Mabahith ‘Ilm al-Usul, 114.

themselves, in the hawzah tradition, do not visit each other. Later on Sadr would emerge at the center of the Iraqi political arena to stir and instigate antigovernment activities in Iraq for the next two years, and to emerge as the main political challenger to the Ba^cthist rule.

Sadr undertook several acts to show his deep commitment and full support to the revolution in Iran.[117] He first sent a long statement to support the revolution of the Iranian people, while Khomeini was in Paris, declaring his support and praising the uprising.[118] Secondly, right after the success of the revolution and return of Khomeini to Iran, Sadr sent one of closest disciples, Mahmood al-Hashimi, to Iran as his representative and personal contact with its leadership.[119] Both actions were considered clear violations of the government policy of "wait and see" toward the events in Iran.[120] Sadr even challenged the Ba^cth government policy of instigating and supporting the uprising of the Arab population in Iran, and their demand for more rights from the revolutionary regime of Ayatullah Khomeini. Sadr sent a telegram calling the Arabs in Iran to obey the leaders of the revolution because the Islamic republic represented the state formed by the Prophet where people from different nationalities and ethnic groups lived in tranquility.[121]

Thirdly, Sadr took the initiative to submit six different studies that concern the foundation of an Islamic state, which was later published under the title al-Islam Yaqud al-Hayat (Islam Governs [Man's] Life). One of them was a jurisprudential treatise on the religious reasons for forming an Islamic government. In this treatise Sadr also outlined the

[117]In a personal letter to his ex-pupils and disciples in Iran, Sadr expressed his personal admiration for the leadership of Khomeini, and demanded their full support to the authority of Khomeini. Sadr expressed that Khomeini's marja^ciyah mad achieved the goals of the "Objective marja^ciyah," which he has theorized years ago. For the text of the letter see, al-Ha'iri, Ibid., 145-146.

[118]The message was not publicized because Sadr's disciple living in Iran thought the announcement of such statement endangered Sadr's life in Iraq. For full text of the message see, al-Ha'iri, Mabahith ^cIlm al-Usul, 142-145.

[119]Ibid., 114.

[120]Because of the 1975 agreement between Iraq and Iran, the Ba^cth government took a positive stand to show their support to the Shah. Saddam, then the vice president of RCC, had declared in one of the party meetings in Basrah that "al-Shah baqii, baqii, baqii" (The Shah will survive, will survive, will survive).

[121]For text of the telegram see, Ibid., 147.

structure of an Islamic state, the functions of each branch of government, the responsibilities of the marjaᶜ in the state and the legitimacy of his absolute authority according to Shiᶜi Islam. Sadr's views were compatible with Khomeini's teaching concerning what is known in jurisprudence studies as <u>wilayat al-faqih</u> (reign of the jurist). The treatise seems to have major impact on the authors of the constitution of the Islamic Republic of Iran. One can find many of Sadr's ideas and views on the structure of an Islamic state in the final draft of the constitution in Iran.

Sadr's second important studies, <u>Khalafat al-Insan wa Shahadat al-Anbia'</u>, is a sociopolitical essay that deals with the question of rights and obligations of the ruler and the ruled in the Islamic state. He considers the marjaᶜ as the legitimate successor to the prophets and the holy imams; however, the marjaᶜ carries no responsibility for initiating new Islamic laws, but rather interprets Islamic laws to fit circumstances. On the other hand, man's purpose in life is to uphold the command of God to creating a better social environment on earth. Man is superior to other creatures of God because he is capable of carrying such responsibilities through the exercise of his free will. His mission in earth is to be God's vicar, and the chosen people (i.e., prophets and holy imams) are to guide man to carry on his great mission. The marjaᶜs role in the state, thus, is to be the vicar of the chosen ones by witnessing or watching over men as they seek to achieve the goal designed by God for them.

The third essay, <u>Manabi' al-Qudrah fi al-Dawlah al-Islamiyah</u> (The Sources of Strength in the Islamic State), is an attempt by Sadr to show that the Islamic polity "possesses great capabilities in leading the nation toward progress and in overcoming and eliminating backwardness" such as is true of no other form of state that governs muslims. These elements of strength are related to: 1) the nature of ideology of the Islamic state; and 2) the psychological and ideological nature of the muslim. The goal of the Islamic state is not merely a materialistic one, but is also a spiritual one that is divinely guided. Thus, the policies of the state are to conform to moral standards that protect justice in the society. Any Muslim, according to Sadr, is historically, culturally and emotionally linked to idea of an Islamic state.

The other three essays deal with the basic principles of the economy of the Islamic state and the structure of its banking system, which are very similar to the ideas Sadr presented in his works twenty years age. It is proof that Sadr had conformed to his early <u>ijtihad</u> about these issues.

Sadr, at that time, started giving politically oriented lectures in the <u>hawzah</u>. These lectures, fourteen in all, were compiled in one volume called <u>Muqadamat fi al-Tafsir al-Mawduᶜi li-al-Quran</u> (Introductions to the Thematic Interpretation of Quran). In these lectures, Sadr dealt with the process of social change in history. Referring to verses from the <u>Quran</u>, Sadr distinguished two types of laws that govern the historical process: those which have outcomes over which mankind has no control; and those that mankind is able to maneuver in order to bring about a historical change for better or worse. He then introduces a new conception of social stratification under the heading of "al-Mujtama^c al-Fir^{ca}uni" (Pharaonic Society). At the extreme top and bottom of the social hierarchy and his opponents, the mustad^cafin (oppressed). Other social classes are either beneficiaries of the oppressive system or they are political passivists. However, all social classes save the mustadh^cafin, according to Sadr, are doomed by history and destined to be punished by God. What is Sadr implying is that the saved are the politically activated mustadh^cafin, who seek to eliminate injustice and establish a form of government ordained by God. If people have the will, Sadr suggests, they could change the course of history. One must not think that historical conditions are beyond the capacity of man to change. The mustadh^cfin must not only think to overcome the unjust circumstances but also seek the guidance and the power to form a just social and political system that will best serve man's materialistic and spiritual needs. Sadr's last lecture was a dramatic speech that concentrated on the commitment and the sincerity of his pupils, the principles of Islam and its goals. At the end of the speech, he intimated that the days of his life were numbered. More specifically, he hinted to the hawzah that he was planning for direct political opposition that could very well result in his execution.[122]

However, Sadr's boldest political step in the war of nerves against the regime at that period was his fatwa (decree) prohibiting Muslims from joining the Ba^cth party or its affiliate organizations. Such a step was so brave and dangerous that even some of Sadr's representatives in different Iraqi cities were hesitant to publicize the fatwa overtly because they feared for their own safety, or for Sadr's survival. To make known the contents of his fatwa, Sadr resorted to other means such as encouraging his students to ask him questions during his regular sermons in the hawzah regarding one's participation in the Ba^cth party. This way Sadr made his position known publicly. People expected severe government action against Sadr. However, the real igniting of the situation came from Iran.

Ayatullah Khomeini, relying on his sources in Najaf, had broadcast a message to Sadr calling on him to stay in the hawzah and not to leave Iraq despite government harassment.[123] Although Sadr was indeed facing an expected detainment or possibly an

---

[122]M. B. Sadr, Muqadamat fi al-Tafsir al-Mawdu^ci li-al-Quran (Introductions to the Thematic Interpretation of Quran) (Kuwait: al-Tawhid al-Islami, 1980), 219.

[123]For texts of Khomeini's message to Sadr, see al-Ha'iri, Mabahith ^cIlm al-Usul, pp. 117-118. Khomeini had discredited Sadr by addressing him as Hujjat al-Islam wa-al-Muslimiyn, a title used for a lower ranking ^calim even though Sadr was then a marja^c of a well known reputation and usually addressed by title Ayatullah al-^cUzma [Grand Ayatollah]. However, after Sadr's death, Khomeini started addressing him as Ayatollah Sadr.

execution, he was not in any case planning, according to Fadlullah, to leave Iraq at all.[124] However, Khomeini's message and Sadr's response to him,[125] which were heard by millions in Iraq, set off a wave of public demonstrations in several major Iraqi cities in support of Sadr and in praise of Khomeini.[126] Najaf was the most turbulent one, where many delegations from different parts of Iraq held riots and were received by Sadr at his residence. Sadr had to inform his devotees and representatives to call it off. Since these delegates represented the core of his popular support, Sadr, according to al-Nuᶜmani, did not want to expose his real strength to the regime and he wanted to secure some protection for his supporters from future government crackdowns.[127] Sadr told one of the Daᶜwah's members that "the regime's quiescence for the moment reveals a great hidden danger, thus we should use precautions and prudence in our action."[128]

The government crackdown anticipated by Sadr followed a period of relative ease in Iraq. Most of Sadr's representatives as well as hundreds who participated in the declaration of bayᶜa (allegiance) to Sadr were rounded up and imprisoned. Then Sadr himself was detained and taken to Baghdad. His sister, Amina al-Sadr (known as Bint al-Huda), went to

---

[124]In private talk with Sayyid M. H. Fadlullah in 1982.

[125]For the text of Sadr's reply to Khomeini, see Ibid, p. 123. The message shows Sadr's deep respect and commitment to the leadership of the latter. He first addressed him as Ayatullah al-ᶜUzma al-Imam al-Mujahid (the Grand Ayatollah, the Worrier leader) titles never used in communiques between marjaᶜ themselves. Sadr, addressing himself as spokesman in the name of the Iraqi people, expresses his appreciation to Khomeini's paternity over the welfare of Najaf and its Hawza, and calling on Khomeini as the leader of Muslims to liberate Palestine. The reply was considered by the Baᶜth leadership the most disturbing to their authority in Iraq, and in the Arab World since the party claims to be the force that holds the banner to liberate all Arab lands.

[126]Their chanted slogans were: Bism al-Khomeini wal Sadr, il-Islam duma' mintisr (In the name of Khomeini and Sadr, Islam always victors) and ᶜAsh, ᶜAsh, ᶜAsh al-Sadr, wil Din Dawman mintisr (Long life to Sadr, and religion [Islam] always victors.)

[127]al-Nuᶜmani quoted in al-Ha'iri, Mabahith ᶜIlm al-Usul, 119.

[128]Quoted in al-Jihad, May 2, 1983, without revealing the name of the Daᶜwah Party member.

the holy shrine of Imam Ali and gave a fiery speech instigating people to demonstrate against the government and show their anger in order to protect their leader [Sadr] against rash action of the part of regime. Once the news diffused about the arrest of Sadr, riots broke out in Baghdad, Basrah, Diala, Samawah, Kut, Diwaniyah, Karbala and other cities. The bazaar in Najaf closed down and riots erupted in which angry people clashed with police; and the whole city seemed to be under siege when the government beefed up their security efforts. The spread of violence in the country forced the regime to free Sadr on the next day.

The detention of Sadr gave the Ba‘th regime a clear idea about the extent and size of social support behind him. His opposition to the regime had made him a national leader and a galvanizing core of popular opinion, and his presence had become a threat to the survival and legitimacy of the regime. Although Sadr possessed no mass media means to express his views, such a shortcoming was compensated for by the Arabic broadcasting service of Tehran radio which was beamed to Iraq. Also the regime was not willing to deport him outside the country, taking a lesson from the mistake of the late Shah when he forced Khomeini into exile, to become the national hero to all opposition groups. The policy of the regime was to deprive Sadr of his political power within the country, then proceed to remove him from the scene, once and for all.

In keeping with this plan, the regime was determined to cut off Sadr's political allies within the country, i.e., his ᶜulama' representatives in different parts of the country and the members of the Daᶜwah Party. Iraq witnessed the mass arrest of Muslim activists, who faced severe torture and summary executions. Well-known ᶜulama' in major Iraqi cities were quickly executed and the mosques they served in were shut off from public worship. Any ᶜulama' who cooperated with the regime and supported its policy were detained. Muslims activists, a majority of them Daᶜwah party members, who participated in the demonstration against the regime in support of Sadr before and after his arrest, were detained and hundreds executed were after summary trials. Available government documents show that the "Revolutionary Court" had passed at least twnety-two sentences of death against 258 people.[129]

Simultaneously, Sadr was placed under house arrest and his contacts with the outside world severed; at the same time, the regime kept channels of dialogue open through some ᶜulama' (loyal to the regime) and officials, the purpose being to get political concessions from him. The government demanded first of all total surrender of Sadr to its will. Fadhel al-Barak, the head of Security Agency, during his interrogation of Sadr in Rajab 1400 AH, wanted him to give up his support for the Iranian revolution and make a public statement in support of the regime policy toward Iran. When Sadr showed his unwillingness to yield to such demands, the regime relaxed its demands and softened its language. The Ba‘th leadership, through its new mediator, Shaykh ᶜIsa al-Khaqani, wanted Sadr to fulfill one of five conditions in order to spare his life: 1) relinquish his support of Ayatullah

---

[129]al-Jihad, May 2, 1983.

Khomeini and of the Iranian regime; 2) issue a statement in support of one of the government's nationalist policies such as the nationalization of foreign oil companies or granting national autonomy to the kurds; 3) issue a <u>fatwa</u> forbidding association with Da^cwah Party; 4) reverse the <u>fatwa</u> that prohibited joining to Ba^cth Party; or 5) be interviewed by an Iraqi or foreign newspaper on strictly religious matters. By then Sadr, according to his personal secretary al-Nu^cmani, had concluded that his days were numbered and he was prepared to reject any government demands in anticipation of his martyrdom.

The prospect of becoming a <u>shahid</u> (martyr) had underlain Sadr's thoughts and actions for years. He had reached the conclusion that the regime of the Ba^cth in Iraq possessed an overwhelming power and that it was impossible for the Islamic movement to topple the regime. However, the survival of the regime could only mean the vanishing of religious sentiment and belief among the Iraqi people. The only measure Sadr thought powerful enough to instigate people into political action against the Ba^cth was his own violent death. He wanted to emulate the political action of Imam Hussein whose violent death when faced with overwhelming odds of the Umayyad rule in the seventh century A.D. caused the Umayyad regime to lose its legitimacy and sparked a series of violent uprisings. The Abassi revolution, which finally ended Umayyad rule, was instigated by the call to avenge the blood of Imam Hussein and <u>Ahl al-Bayt</u> (Household of the Prophet). Sadr was quoted as saying that "not all people could be motivated by thought; the majority need blood to stimulate them." Further, "the Iraqi people need the sacrifice of a holy blood like that of Imam Hussein to awaken them."[130]

Sadr's martyrdom was not the outcome of the Iranian revolution but rather went back to the mid-1970s when the Ba^cth rulers consolidated their power through progressive economic programs that upgraded the standard of living of people through severe coercive measures against their political opponents, while at the same time advocating radical foreign policies that were highly popular at home and in the Arab World. Furthermore, the Iraqi people were unwilling to take any action against the regime which was restricting their political rights or freedom of expression. Sadr, in 1976, considered emulation of the Hussein revolution as a means of provoking antigovernment activities. The plan was that Sadr and some of his close associates would lead a public protest in the Shrine of Imam Ali in Najaf. Sadr would give a speech criticizing government abuses of religious and human rights, while others would try to mobilize people in the Shrine. He anticipated that the regime's security forces would retaliate in a heavy handed manner. The plan was to continue the riots until death came to Sadr himself. Other associates of Sadr and the religious establishment in Najaf would mobilize the populace in antigovernment actions, i.e., general strikes, demonstrations, riots and so on. However, the success of the plan depended on the support of the <u>culama'</u> and the religious community to achieve its goal. Sadr hoped to seek

---

[130]Interview with A. Kubba.

legitimacy of his plan from a highly vocal political advocate, Ayatullah Khomeini. Yet when Sadr met with Khomeini to get his approval of his plan, the latter answered: "I don't know." Sadr, failing to secure the consent of the hawzah behind his plan, reconsidered the idea of martyrdom. He thought that without the marja‘iyah approval his violent death would be of no political significance and people would regard it as a political suicide.

Nonetheless, during the years following the Iranian revolution Sadr came to the conclusion that an Islamic state in Iran led by a marja‘ would be interested in utilizing his martyrdom in its effort to carry on the struggle. Signs were given to Sadr by the Iranian leadership that the Islamic republic was supportive of this move. The Iranian propaganda reinforced this idea when it called for the liberation of holy places in Iraq. Messages were broadcast from the Iranian Radio network to the Iraqi people calling on them to rise up behind their leader al-Sadr and relinquish the unislamic regime of the Ba‘th. Sadr felt confident that Iran would hold up the "torch" of his martyrdom, and that the exiled Iraqi ‘ulama' would lead the revolt after him. The Islamic Republic in Iran had provided Sadr with the two vital factors that were missing from his earlier "Husseini Revolution": the legitimacy of his move; and the assurance of the continuation of the struggle. There was also a psychological reason that contributed to Sadr's revival of his martyrdom plan. He had witnessed the establishment of an Islamic state which he had striven to realize throughout his life. Once his vision had come true in Iran through the marja‘iyah of Ayatullah Khomeini (which he regarded as an "objective" marja‘iyah since it accomplished the goal of establishing an Islamic state),[131] Sadr felt his martyrdom to be essential to the continuation of the Islamic movement. He had told al-Khaqani, the Ba‘th regime's mediator, that

> whatever I had sought for in my life is to make possible the
> establishment of an Islamic government in earth. And after its formation in
> Iran under the leadership of Imam [Khomeini] it makes no difference for me
> whether I am alive or dead because the dream I wished to attain and the hope
> I wanted to achieve had come true, thank to God.[132]

Once the Islamic fundamentalist groups (e.g., the Da‘wah party and Islamic Action Organization headed by al-Shirazi and al-Mudarsi brothers[133]) had witnessed the regime's

---

[131]Sadr considers the marja‘iyah of Ayatollah Khomeini as an "objective" one not because it established the institutional structure which Sadr proposed, but rather because Khomeini merely had achieved its goals. See al-Ha`iri, Mabahith, 146.

[132]al-Nu‘mani is quoted in al-Ha'iri, Mabahith ‘Ilm al-Usul, pp. 162-163.

[133]Munazamat al-‘Amal al-Islami (Islamic Task

harassment of their leader, they resorted to armed struggle against the Ba^cth's officials. The climax of their antigovernment operations was an attack against a high ranking official and Ba^cth Party ideologue, Tariq Aziz, currently the Foreign Minister, in Mustansiriyah University. Aziz was supposed to deliver a speech to Ba^cth Party members among the university's student body regarding the regime's stand towards Iran. Muslim activists who infiltrated the ranks of Ba^cth party threw a bomb at Aziz, killing his body guards and causing Aziz some injuries. At the public funeral for those slain at al-Mustansiriyah University, a bomb was thrown at the procession, killing several people.[134] The regime was in a state of shock when thus faced for the first time with the resort to armed struggle by Shi^cis, the backbone of the rank and file of the Ba^cth party. Saddam Hussein, the new president of the republic, shouted during a visit to victims of Mustansiriyah in the hospitals, calling for revenge against perpetrators. The regime's tactic of labelling the muslim activism as the work of Iranians foreign elements in the country was not effective, because after deporting more than 132,000 Iraqis of Iranian origin to Iran Muslim activism was still showing its strength in antigovernment activities in the country. Moreover, Sadr, the symbol of the Islamic movement, was the descendant of a well-distinguished Iraqi family of known political activism in modern Iraqi history. The Ba^cth regime, striving for its legitimacy, embraced the goal of total liquidation of the Islamic movement at any cost. On the 31st of March 1980, the powerful Revolutionary Command Council (RCC) passed a law threatening all (past and present) members of Da^cwah Party or its affiliated organizations, or people working for its goals, with the death sentence. The law left no room for sparing Sadr's life.

Organization) is a splinter group from Da^cwah party. Their leader, Muhammad Mahdi al-Shirazi, was one of the first group, according to Mahdi al-Hakim, to join the Da^cwah party. In early the 1970s he and his brother, Hassan (assassinated in Lebanon in 1980), formed their own organization, al-^cAmal al-Islami as a result of disagreement with Da^cwah on issue of leadership of the party and the political tactics. When al-Shirazi announced his marja^ciyah in 1970s, Muhammad Taqi al-Mudairsi and Hadi al-Mudarsi headed al-Amal, while Shirazi assumed the title, the spiritual leader of the organization. For their political thought, see, Tawfiq al-Shaykh, ^cAn al-^cIraq wa-al-Harakah al-Islamiyah, Hiwarat ma^ca al-^cAlamah Muhammad Taqi al-Mudarisi (On Iraq and the Islamic Movement, Interviews with Muhammad Taqi al-Mudarisi, (London: al-Safa, 1988).

[134]Chibli Mallat, "Religious militancy in contemporary Iraq: Muhammas Baqer as-Sadr and the Sunni-Shia paradigm, Third World Quarterly (April, 1988), 728.

Sadr, on his part, had left no room for retreat and reconsideration of his anti-Ba^cth campaign. While he was under house arrest he smuggled three messages to his associates calling on the Iraqi people to resist the regime in any way possible.[135] In these messages, he had placed himself as their leader, speaking in their name and demanding from the government political and religious rights for all people, Shi^cis and Sunnis, Arab and Kurds. He even appealed to the members of the Ba^cth party when he accused their current leadership of violating the principles of the party itself. He challenged the Ba^cth leadership on the legitimacy of their rule calling on them to allow the people for only one week to express their feelings toward the regime. In one of these messages, Sadr gave his ultimatum to the people: they should topple the regime and establish an Islamic government instead.

> It is incumbent on every Muslim in Iraq and every Iraqi outside Iraq
> to do whatever he can, even if it cost him his life, to keep the jihad and
> struggle to remove this nightmare from the land of the beloved Iraq, to
> liberate themselves from this inhuman gang, and to establish a righteous,
> unique, and honorable rule on the basis of Islam.[136]

He was so sure of his immanent extermination by the regime that he tried to set up a committee of his associates, which was known later as <u>al-Qiyadah al-Na'ibah</u> (Substitutional Leadership), to be his successor and lead the struggle against the regime after him.[137] The committee was supposed to be composed of five people. Even though the names of the committee were not disclosed by Sadr himself, it is widely believed that it would include his most trusted pupils or trustees: 1) Muhammad Baqir al-Hakim, 2) Kazim al-Ha'iri, 3) Muhammad Mahdi al-Asifi, 4) Mahmuud al-Hashimi, and 5) Muhammad Baqir al-Nasiri.[138] Sadr intended to present the committee to Khomeini for approval in order to

---

[135]According to Da^cwah Party members, these voice-recorded messages of Sadr were supposed to be published and distributed to the people inside and outside Iraq, but were censored by his associates (fearing the regime reprisal on Sadr's life) and were not made public until after his death.

[136]For full text of Sadr's three messages to the Iraqi people, in Arabic; see al-Ha'iri, <u>Mabahith ^cIlm al-Usul</u>, pp. 147-153; and its translation in English, see Abu Ali, <u>A Glimpse of the Life of The Martyred Imam: Muhammad Baqer al-Sadr and His Last Three Massages</u>, (Date and place of publication unknown), 16-19.

[137]al-Nu^cmani quoted in al-Ha'iri, <u>Mabahith</u>, 159-160.

[138]All of them are now part of the Supreme Assembly of the Islamic Revolution in Iraq (SAIRI), founded in 1982,

assure the legitimacy of their leadership after his death.[139] However, the official formation of al-Qiyadah al-Na'ibah did not materialize, because the regime expedited action to finish him off.

The security forces rounded up Sadr along with his sister on April 5, 1980, and detained them in the Headquarters of the National Security Agency in Baghdad. Three days later, his body was brought back to his uncle, Muhammad Sadiq al-Sadr, in Najaf for secret burial. However, the whereabouts of Bint al-Huda, sister of Sadr, were not disclosed by the regime, even though it is widely believed that she was executed too.[140] Two weeks later, Ayatullah Khomeini issued a statement on the execution of Sadr and his sister and called on the Iraqi people and the armed forces to overthrow the Ba‘th regime.[141]

Some Final Remarks on Sadr

Sadr had set up a revolutionary strategy for the implementation of his plan to bring about major changes in his surroundings, the society, the political system, the religious establishment, and even the world in general. He disliked the whole environment around him. Unlike the utopian Rousseau, who had no hope of changing his social environment and in consequence lapsed into a state of despair, Sadr believed in his capacity to impose change and reform the world. He was an utopian in one sense, but an optimistic one, who believed the historical outcome would be on his side. His enthusiasm for revolt against the establishment, his inner belief that change is immanent in history, emboldened him to embark upon revolutionary course. The contemporary history of the hawzah in Najaf had

---

where al-Hakim acts as its president, al-Hashimi as its spokesman, al-Nasiri, until two years ago, as the chairman of its General Assembly.

[139]al-Ha'iri, Mabahith, 159.

[140]According to one of Sadr's cousin, the family of Sadr still hopes that the regime has spared the life of Amina al-Sadr (known as Bint al-Huda), although, the propaganda of the Islamic movement refers to her as the martyr Bint al-Huda.

[141]The reason for the two weeks' delay of the announcement by Khomeini was to gather accurate information about the event through the foreign ministry. However, one reliable source told me that when Sadr's associate tried to reach Khomeini and inform him of the execution of Sadr, Khomeini's aides would not give access to the Ayatollah, claiming that Sadr is an American agent. Such a labeling of Sadr is wide spread among some ulama, because of Sadr's strong criticism of socialism.

never seen a jurist that was so antiestablishment as Sadr. All the previous religious reformers wanted to change the society, in a manner which enabled the <u>hawzah</u> to function as an agent of change. All the previous secular reformers wanted to do away with the <u>hawzah</u>, which they regarded as an agent of stagnation. Sadr emerged as a unique figure in history, wanting to change society along religious lines while finding the <u>hawzah</u> with its current structure inadequate as the means of change. Therefore, he was the target of criticism from both secular and religious enemies. However, his involvement in politics in his early life as well as his early death were fortuitous and were not, in my view, the result of long-term planning on his part, stretching over many years. Here I differ with the conventional wisdom of the revolutionary Islamists who believe otherwise. My view is supported by the following considerations:

First, Muhammad Baqir al-Sadr, as a young student and scholar of jurisprudence, was dedicated entirely to his religious studies and was not active in the political affairs of the turbulent years of the post-1958 coup in Iraq. He was considered the "genius and exceptional" student of the <u>hawzah</u>. His involvement in political activism came via encouragement from his colleague and friend, Talib al-Rifa^ci. The latter introduced Sadr to the founders of the Da^cwah Party,[142] who saw in him the charismatic jurist who could legitimize their political activities within the <u>hawzah</u>, because of his high credentials there. However, once he was engaged in the activities of the party, he assumed the highest rank among his peers, and came to be regarded as the <u>faqih</u> of the party, a position entailing supervision of the whole gamut of activities of the party. His intellectual capacity, which came to be socially noticed and admired by the insecure religious establishment of that time, especially after the publication of his work, <u>Falsafatuna</u>, made him the ideologue of the party and of the political movement at large. Later on, Sadr became the religious leader of the Islamic movement that spread out of Najaf to a large part of the Muslim world. Not even his sudden resignation a few years later from his leading position in the Da^cwah party reduced his influence and charismatic appeal. In fact his exit from the party was in part a political move intended to open the way to the highest symbolic leadership of the Shi^ci communities, the <u>marja^ciyah</u>. Activist Muslim jurists and the Islamic movement were hoping for Sadr's elevation to the Supreme <u>Marja^c</u> of the Shi^cis everywhere. It seemed to be only a matter of time, since Sadr was undisputably a resourceful jurist of the <u>hawzah</u>. "He is," Khomeini exclaimed, "the jewel of the religious schools." It was possible, many thought, that the era of political acquiescence of the <u>marja^ciyah</u> could be put to an end.

Second, Sadr's <u>fatwa</u> restraining students of the religious schools from joining an Islamic political party, coupled with his resignation from the Da^cwah party, was seen by

---

[142]See an interview with Mahdi al-Hakim on the history of the Islamic movement in Iraq in <u>Liwa al-Sadr</u>, (Jan 12, 1990), 12.

some as an indication that Sadr had changed his views about the legitimacy of the formation of the political party. They claim that Sadr later in his life was in fact in the line of Ayatullah Khomeini, who championed a political struggle of the masses organized by the jurists from the mosques as opposed to a party-dominated struggle. Even al-Ha'iri, who until 1985 was the jurist of the Da^cwah party, suggested that the later Sadr <u>may</u> have changed his view when he advocated the idea of the <u>marja^ciyah al-mawdu^ciyah</u>.[143] However, I believe that Sadr, as acquainted with his political theory suggests, believed that there was a role for both the party and the jurists. He adhered to the idea that an Islamic state can come through the struggle of the organized, committed few of the <u>ummah</u> to lead the political offensive against the tyrants. The role of the jurist is to guide the political party and give legitimacy to their actions. His political program centers around the idea that a successful political struggle can be achieved only through gradual pedagogy and a long process of education of the people, since not all Muslims can be considered zealous advocates of Islamic political goals but live more or less passively within an inherited Islamic environment. In order to establish a healthy and strong political state, the strategy then must be to concentrate on organizing the few who are committed to the political goals of Islam, who will create the revolutionary conditions, and lead the political struggle. What I conclude is that Sadr believed that the party should function as the political arm of the <u>marja^ciyah al-mawdu^ciyah</u> for the purpose of mobilizing the people behind the political program advocated by the Supreme Jurist.

Third, Sadr's firm commitment to the principle of leadership of the supreme <u>marja^ciyah</u> stopped him from challenging the existing <u>marja^c</u> of his time, Hakim and then his mentor, Khoei. The publication of his interpretation of the religious laws in the mid-70s cannot be interpreted as confrontation with or distaste for the political quiescence of Ayatullah Khoei. He in fact justified his early indirect announcement of interest in the <u>marja^ciyah</u> as a means of protection of his life from government crackdowns. He thought that the government would spare his life due to the customary practice of the regimes in Iraq and Iran, which was not to execute any leading jurist. A case in point was the expulsion of the Ayatullah Khomeini from Iran by the Shah's regime. Clearly, Sadr misjudged the extent of the Ba^cth regime's commitment to such prudence. Rather, the regime considered any political dissent as a threat to its survival. Accordingly, the Ba^cthists dealt heavy-handedly with political opponents without heeding foreign pressure or world public opinion. At the publication of Sadr's <u>al-Fatawa al-Wadihah</u>, members of Da^cwah party and Sadr's admirers started making references to him, thus considering him as their <u>marja^c</u> and guiding leader.

Finally, in his final two years, Sadr did not champion direct political opposition to the Ba^cth government because he felt the conditions were not ripe to make such opposition successful. However, he was dragged into public opposition against the regime by the

---

[143]al-Ha'iri, <u>Mabahith fi ^cIlim al-Usul</u>, 161.

Iranian leadership and those in Iraq who were influenced by the events of the Iranian revolution, especially with the Da^cwah party and among Sadr's close associates. According to al-Nu^cmani, Sadr was not pleased with the public procession, which was organized by the Da^cwah to pay allegiance to his leadership, because he felt that the Islamic movement would then expose its members and supporters to government attention and crackdowns. If Sadr had felt that the political conditions were in a truly revolutionary stage, he would not then have feared the regime's eventual oppression. However, the Iranian leaders went ahead with their public campaign in their Arabic broadcasts to the Iraqi people, asking them to take the lead behind Sadr and topple the Ba^cth's regime.[144] They encouraged Islamic political organizations in Iraq to organize demonstrations and protests (similar to the tactics of the Iranian revolutions) in which people shouted slogans claiming the spiritual leadership of Sadr. This may have put Sadr in an awkward position. He felt pressured to counter his political beliefs and go along in supporting the masses who were calling for his leadership. As a religious jurist, he was constrained to side with those people who needed his guidance. I believe he was not actually consulted by the leaders of Iran nor by the leadership of the Islamic movement in Iraq. Evidently, he would listen to the messages of Ayatullah Khomeini and other Iranian leaders on the radio urging him to revolt against the government. On the other side, some of the first public protests and demonstrations in support of him and of the Iranian revolution were spontaneous and unplanned for by the Islamic organizations. These were certain started by some enthusiastic individuals who were influenced by the spectacular success of the revolution in Iran.[145] It was only then that the Da^cwah party welcomed these political moves, and decided to put pressure on the marja^cs in Najaf (Khoei and Sadr) to initiate a movement like that which had emerged in Iran under the leadership of Ayatullah Khomeini.[146] The leadership of the party reached a conclusion that

[144]One of the examples of how Sadr was pushed into unplanned direct confrontation against the government was when he was hospitalized in 1979, and one of the Iranian ulama asked Talib al-Rifa^ci to write a get-well telegram (in Arabic) to Sadr. However, the draft was rejected on the basis that its language was mild and did not include harsh statement against Saddam and the Ba^cth party. Al-Rifa^ci refused to write such statements because they would endanger Sadr's life.

[145]An interview with Ahmad Kubba, one of the Da^cwah members who initiated the first demonstration after the Friday sermon of Ayatollah Khoei in Masjid al-Khadrah in Najaf, in 1978. He said that he had no order from the party to start the demonstration. Rather the party officials discouraged such a move. He then had supported public protests only after the success of the revolution in Iran.

historical conditions were ripe to start the political struggle against the Baᶜthist regime. The Iranian experience showed them that huge public demonstrations restrain the regime from crushing the multitude of protestors. Their blunder rested on their overestimation of the revolutionary frame of mind of the masses in Iraq, whose general admiration for the revolution in Iran was undeniable. Additionally, the assumption that the behavior of the Baᶜth regime toward public protest would be similar to that of the Shah was utterly wrong. Such miscalculation by the Islamic leaders in Iran and by revolutionaries in Iraq made Sadr and the rest of the political activists in Iraq pay a deadly price.

---

[146]Ayatollah Khoei advised Sadr, via the latter's representative in Kuwait, that he should not involve himself in a political struggle then because the Baᶜthist government would certainly kill him at a time, when the hawzah needed his services.

DEFINING POLITICAL THEORY

Without a revolutionary theory, there cannot be a revolutionary movement.

Lenin

Sadr did not systematically set forth a political theory. We do not have any work by Sadr himself that bears a title such as "On political theory according to Islam." What we find, rather, are intimations here and there of a political theory. His voluminous writings incessantly betray a central theme, a grand theory that he developed but never formally presented, mainly because he was not given sufficient time to do so. Like many great thinkers, his writings dealt with scattered topics without assembling major ideas into a unified and coherent schema. Although he had the desire to write extensive works in sociology and politics, he was occupied with duties tied to his religious status as a <u>marja^c</u>. Death came so suddenly he could not bring to realization his long envisioned work, <u>Mujtama^cuna</u>. Fate did not give him the time he needed. The task here is to discover his political dream, ponder the different fields Sadr covered in his books, and to read between the lines in order to extract his political theory.

<u>What is Political Theory?</u>

There has been heated debate in the discipline of political science over the past century, starting with the rise of empiricism after the industrial revolution in the West, over the definition and the utility of political theory. A first group, the behaviorists, place the study of politics under the strictures of scientific methods; that is they subject every hypothesis to empirical verification. For them, a thesis in any social science discipline is valid only by virtue of the weight of observed data. The second group, the traditionalists, consider personal observations and judgments of great political thinkers as having a validity equal to that of empirical data. A philosopher or thinker may refer to his or her individual account of nature of the political environment and give his or her own views with regards to the pattern of political life, referring to the system of values to which he or she subscribes.

It is the political philosopher's derivation of his ideas from his *system of values* that causes behaviorists to reject the whole body of political literature of the past two thousand years since Plato. The validity of values cannot be determined through scientific experimentation, and their frame of reference includes such things as God's will, social beliefs, or cultural myths. On this basis, the traditional political theories are rejected because they can not be substantiated by acceptable scientific methods or supported by scientific data.

The positivist school of thought and Karl Marx waged the first major attack on the entire body of literature of traditional political theory. Marx, for example, considered the traditional political theory as mere ideology, an expression of the values of a certain historical period of economic development.[120] Ideology aims to support the dominant class of a particular historical epoch. Once the means of production develop, the ideology will be replaced by a new ruling class and a new historical period. The entire superstructure of the socioeconomic system, such as values, norms, political institutions and social relations is in a continuous progressive process of change.[121] Ideology, therefore, is a false consciousness that aims to legitimize the authority of the dominant class. It is only under the communist system, where the means of production is publicly owned, that the ideology will endure forever. It legitimizes the authority of all, not one class over the other. Therefore, Plato's and Aristotle's political theory are not applicable to day and can be considered backward and reactionary theories.

The positivists, on the other hand, reject the idea of standard values and adhere to the view that values are relative and changing from time to time and place to place. Reality, for them, is limited to the phenomenal world, and we can depend only on science to furnish us with physically observable facts to know and discover reality. Accordingly, "science could give us no information about the relative validity of the different goals men might espouse for their opinions about the good referred to subjective emotions rather than to objective facts."[122] The political theorist, thus, should not take the liberty of advocating values he preferes and proposing a political system and ideas that other people should institute. Such value judgments are subjective and do not represent the facts about reality.

[120]Karl Marx, <u>On Society and Social Change</u>, edited by Neil J. Smalser (Chicago: The University of Chicago Press, 1973), 10.

[121]Ibid., 5.

[122]Dante Germino, "The Revival of Political Theory," in the Richard H. Cox, ed. <u>Ideology, Politics and Political Theory</u> (Belmont, CA: Wadsworth Publishing Co., Inc., 1969), 107.

From a different point of view, both Marxists and positivist disregard any political thought that advocates a universal truth regardless of their practicalities or their philosophical accuracy. For the former, even philosophical treaties represent some forms of ideologies, and ideology is described as "bodies of thought held by the social classes,"[123] an illusory knowledge and does not represent the real truth of the social reality. For the latter, any political thought that prescribes universal truth and social values that cannot substantiated by empirical data is not worth considering. For that matter, ideologies and political treaties of well-known philosophers in history are treated equally, both represent a reflection on what is the good life of the community and of man, and set a program for the structuring of the political environment. These reflections in the traditional political theory are rejected on the basis as nonverifiable; thus they are considered worthless to the understanding of politics.

However, there are those who distinguish between political theory and ideology and counter the Marxist-Positivist schools by what is known as the normative political school. There is a great difference, they argue, between the philosophical discourses of Plato and Hegel and what was advocated by Hitler and Napoleon. The formers's works aim to study objectively the nature of the political environment, and, in the process of their investigations, prescribe a political program for achieving social harmony. Consequently, they refer to philosophical arguments to understand the true nature of reality and human nature. "The political theorist is or strives to be a philosopher, and a philosopher, as Plato saw so clearly, is a lover of wisdom and truth."[124] The objectivity of their thought is judged by the validity of the critical assessment of the nature of the political reality they are examining. In fact, the idea advocated by the behavioralist school is that a scientific argument free of value judgments is untrue. The postbehavioralist movement in political science, which a rose as a result of the rapid political change in the Third World and the social instability of the First World in the sixties, renounced the behaviorist stand that political science inquiries be limited to the realm of empirical investigation. Post behaviorism champions the introduction of values in the political science because political thinkers have a "major task in society" and their "responsibility is to protect the human values of civilization."[125] Moreover, values had played an important role in scientific research in terms of formulating a hypothesis,

---

[123]Kenneth Minogue, "Nietzsche and the Ideological Project," in Noel O'Sullivan, ed. "The Structure of Modern Ideology (London: Edward Elgar, 1989), 30.

[124]Dante Germino, Beyond Ideology: The revival of Political Theory (New York: Harper & Row, 1967), 11.

[125]S. P. Varma, Modern Political Theory (New Delhi, India: Vani Educational Books, 1985), 36.

deriving generalizations, deciding the topics of investigation, and giving preference to the type of scientific method to be conducted.

On the other hand, ideologists are political adventurists, or as Germino liked to call them *publicists*, who seek political goals in their advocated thoughts and ideas. Their aim is not to enrich human understanding of the political environment, but rather to gain immediate political goals. Their arguments are simplistic, although they may use philosophical arguments to arouse popular enthusiasm. Publicists such as statesmen, politicians, and political propagandists usually have opinions and some understanding about politics, while philosophers go beyond giving opinions and try to discover the real essence of politics, keeping in mind the controversy between the two groups concerning the term *politics*, for politics means different things to different people. In Aristotelian terms, politics is defined as the whole set of social operations within the *polis*, includes the family structure, the control of slaves, revolutionary movements, and political process; i.e., it is the master science. To Max Weber, it is the struggle to gain power or to influence those in power, including the struggle between groups and states; i.e., it is the control of and the exercise of influence over others. For those who advocate the system theory, or are concerned with the structure of the state rather than the dynamics of politics, politics comprises the activities of the political institutions, or the authorative allocations of powers and values.[126] Definitions of politics have the important function of establishing the scope and agenda of political thought and research. Even if it is assumed that the term *politics* is part of the vocabularies of both the philosopher and the publicist, their approaches to the study of politics may differ greatly. In general, when a philosopher is in the process of examining of any subject matter, he treats it with a careful analysis that penetrates its roots.[127] He may, during the course of analysis and study to discover the truth about the nature of things, allow particular values to play a role but not to the extent of giving his investigation of true nature of political reality its ultimate shape. What makes philosophers different from publicists is that while both work from a self-endorsed set of values, the latter seeks certain goals to achieve while the former seeks to discover the political reality; however he or she may or may not be involved in political affairs of his society. In fact, it is hard to imagine a political thinker writing about the heated issues of his society without some direct participation in politics. It is such deep concern for and involvement in political issues that makes him aware of the demanding issues of his time.

On the other hand, political philosophy in general is a conviction of philosophers about the civil society.[128] Philosophy, in the Platonic definition, is the quest for wisdom.

---

[126]George E. G. Catlin, "Political Theory: What is it?", <u>Political Science Quarterly</u> (March, 1957), 1-6.

[127]Leo Strauss, "What is Political Philosophy?," <u>Journal of Politics</u> (August, 1957), 3.

Wisdom is to know and understand the essence of reality, i.e., the knowledge of the whole that goes beyond the phenomenal world to include the metaphysical. Political philosophy is defined as belonging within the scope of holistic wisdom, and entails a value judgment on the ability of human being to attain that wisdome. Political philosophy, according to Leo Strauss, who is in the tradition of the classical political philosophy of Plato and Aristotle, is the thought of a philosopher who seeks "to replace opinion about the nature of political things by knowledge of the nature of political things."[129] Further, he adds that "political philosophy is the attempt truly to know both the nature of and the right, or the goods, political order."[130] However, the distinction between ideology and political philosophy must be clear before one can proceed to the task of defining political theory.

The main difference between political philosophy and ideology is that while the latter seeks the mobilization of people in support of a specific idea to achieve certain political goals, the former has no genuinely practical goal. In fact, political philosophy is considered the intellectual discourse of the few, understood by some, and beyond the reach of the majority. A political philosopher has no desire to attract the multitude to his ideology, even though he has the desire to change their political environment or personal beliefs. Philosophers are supposedly searching for the truth rather than to inspire others or shape the course of political events. Therefore, they are not writing for their own time, but for generations to come. They appeal not to the emotion of the masses, but to the reason of the intellects. Accordingly, philosophers attempt to be logical, while publicists incite emotions in order to incite action. The latter has the purpose not to enhance the understanding of others as much as to make them enthusiastic, to mobilize them, and to have control over their lives and thoughts. They seek to persuade others to follow their guidelines. Ideology establishes the boundaries of political actions, defines the enemy, uses simple language to make ideas cross over easily into people's minds, and tries to maintain people's aspirations through a utopian vision of an ideal and immanent civil society. Ideology is a means for changing a society. However, political philosophy wants to enhance the knowledge of man and not necessarily to promote immediate personal or societal interests. This is why political philosophy is prosaic and monotonous for many, while political ideology is exciting and appealing. Accordingly, one finds that political philosophy tends to incorporate a measure of ideology in order to acquire appeal vis-**Error!**a-vis nonphilosophers, but rarely does ideology utilize philosophical explanations of its main ideas. Ideological writers borrow their ideas

---

[128]Sabine, "What is Political Theory?," _Journal of Politics_ (Feb, 1939), 7.

[129]Leo Strauss, "What is Political Theory?" _Journal of Politics_ (August, 1957), 344.

[130]Ibid.

from one philosophy or another. For this reason, ideology is considered a simplification of philosophy.

One of the main characteristics of ideology is a utopian outlook that challenges the political environment by "advocating a conception of the good life, and describing the forms of social action and organization necessary for their achievement."[131] Political theorists too have such ideological interests and not merely the interest of writing philosophical treaties. They have always been "concerned with prescribing the goals which citizens, states, and societies ought to pursue. His (i.e., political theorist's) aim is to generalize about right conduct in the political life and about the legitimate use of power."[132] However, his concerns are not historical situations, rather he wants to provide a solution to an intriguing political question facing man in his social environment. Consequently, political theory is a political philosophy and ideology. In other words, political theory is political philosophy applied to concrete social circumstances. It is the logical and systematic character of its construction of civil society which makes it more a philosophical study than an ideological one. "[T]he great political theorists of the past saw themselves as going beyond opinions to arrive at a critical <u>understanding</u> of man's role in society."[133] On the other hand, political theory can fill the role of giving advise regarding ways and means of achieving the objectives that it propounds. Theories, for example, are interested in causation and are systematic in the way they form their major concepts, assumptions and solutions; they are also objective in their treatment of values. They can serve as a scale by which to judge critical issues in politics. Political theories at large are not only the philosophical means for explaining political phenomena, but also function as an ideology. Political theories set standards with which people are able to construct beliefs. For this reason, a political theory presents universal settings in a way that can affect the outcome of policy-making process. Political theory is thus (as stated above) applied political philosophy. Hegel regarded political theory as "not subjective ideology but experiential science."[134] The ideological side of political theories is that "they are influential not because they are right but because they are believed."[135]

---

[131]P. H. Partridge, "Politics, Philosophy, Ideology," in Richard Cox, <u>Ideology, Politics and Political Theory</u>, 116.

[132]Andrew Haker, <u>Political Theory: Philosophy, Ideology, and Science</u> (New York: MacMillan Co., 1961), 2.

[133]Dante L. Germino, <u>Beyond Ideology: the Revival of political Theory</u> (New York: Harper & Row, 1967), 5.

[134]Dante Germino, "The revival of Political Theory," 105.

[135]Ibid., 10.

Generally, political theory deals with all the concepts that political philosophy is concerned with. Each political theory introduces its own visions and assumptions about the nature of reality, of human beings, the historical process, society and the state, and of the relationships of the individual to history and civil society. Most political theories comprise four components: epistemology, psychology, ethics, political doctrine. Epistemology entails the definition by a theorist of his assumptions about reality and the nature of the world. Theorists are divided along the three main schools of philosophical thought, rationalism, empiricism and theological voluntarism. The first school emphasizes the rule of reason as the primary source of knowledge.[136] Reality, for them, can only be discovered through reasoned discourses. Accordingly, reality is the invisible and metaphysical in essence. The ideal "forms" can be discovered only through rational reasoning and are the basis behind the visible world. Reality is what the mind beholds, not what appears to the eye. The temporal world is only the reflection of the ideal and everlasting reality.

Empiricists on the other hand tend to be causality-minded (etiological) in their philosophical approach. They completely reject the ideal forms of reality. The starting point for them is the physical world, the realm of visible things. Nothing goes beyond what we see and feel through our senses. The realm of ideal Platonic *forms*, the metaphysical world, has no reality in itself since it cannot be perceived by our sensual perceptions. There is nothing to be discovered beyond the world of immediate experience, whether forms or ideals or even God. Human beings can discover only general laws that govern the physical world and the logic behind the phenomena which occur in it. Scientific experimentations are the means of knowing the world around us, not philosophical reasoning.

The third school of thought is theological voluntarism. The central theme of this school of thought is that the divine will determines the whole of reality and that ultimate truth must be derived exclusively from a revelation from God. Every thing in this universe is a reflection of God himself. Neither reason nor experience are sufficient means to knowledge. Faith is the main source of understanding the true nature of the world.[137] In contrast to theological rationalism, which emphasizes the harmony between revelation and human reason, theological voluntarism affirms a radical discontinuity between revelation and reason, invalidating the latter as a source of truth about ultimate things. The implication of this kind of thought is that a good society and good government implement the laws and standards communicated by God to mankind through prophets, as opposed to laws and standards inherent in nature which the human reason is able to discern on its own.

The second component of a political theory, its psychology, embraces its views

---

[136]Encyclopedia of Philosophy v. 7, "Rationalism," by Bernard Williams.

[137]Encyclopedia of Philosophy, v. 8, "Voluntarism," by Richard Taylor.

about human nature. Here too political theorists are divided between the two schools of thought: the developmental and the behavioral. The question asked here is whether human nature by essence is good. The developmentalists take an optimistic view about the nature of man. Man is, after all, a rational being. Through reasoning, man is in a state of growing and developing his capacity to control and change his environment for the better. Through reasoning, he has the capacity to discover the ultimate, and to make it his destiny to achieve the ideal world. On the contrary, behaviorists think that man is the product of his environment. His thought and perception are shaped by his surroundings. Man cannot transcend his nature because his attitudes and beliefs are the reflection of his environment. Man is conditioned to have a certain state of mind, and does not have the ability to change the world around him.

Rationalists and empiricists are divided between these two views of human nature, whereas theological voluntarists tend to embrace a more synthetic way of thinking. For them, man is born subject to environmental conditioning but has the capacity to develop and transcend beyond his environment. Crucial to his development is his capacity to know God and to understand his commands and laws. Furthermore, he has the will to obey or rebel against his Creator. Man is not limited to a single set of behaviors. He can change the world in conformity to the will of God, or he can take the opposite route and suffer, confining himself to (to borrow from Hobbes' language concerning the state of nature) the "nasty, brutish, and short" world around him.

The third component is ethics. Political theorists give some attention to ethical questions. Absolutists consider there is only one standard of moral values that applies to every man in all circumstances. What is good for Americans is good for Iranians too; and what is good for the prophets of Israel is good for modern man. The values of good and evil, right and wrong are unconditional. Unlike the variability of human desires, moral laws apply to all people, all the time, in all places, with respect to all moral instances. Relativists, on the other hand, consider there is no one rule of truth. Moral standards change when circumstances change. Ethical values are the byproducts of social beliefs. The absolutists belong to the rationalist school of thought. Rationalism is historically inclined toward normative thinking about civil society. If one is to know what is a good society, one must also know what is meant by good. The concern of rationalists, thus, is with concepts of good, justice and beauty. If society aims to achieve such standards, then society is considered good. Rationalists believe the purpose of the state is to facilitate the attainment of these ethical values. The idea of Aristotle's teleology is to look for the end product of things in general, and the civil society in particular. For the normative thinkers like Plato, Kant, and Hegel politics and ethics are interrelated. Their concern is with what should be done about the shortcomings of the civil society. They do not like what they see in the world, but are still optimistic and believe in the capacity of man to transform the existing world into an ideal one. For the relativists, ethics is seen as intimately bound up with culture. A set of values that is considered good in one culture might be viewed as evil in an other culture because the environmental and social conditions in the two culture are different. Empiricists are relativists. They do not believe, for example, in the natural law of the traditional philosophers. Ethics and politics are two separate concerns. Because they accept experience as the only source of knowledge,[138] ethical values possess no universal validity at all. On the other hand, religious voluntarists are more like absolutists.

Finally, political theory must offer a political doctrin that prescribes ways of dealing with political reality. Each theorist views the world from a different angle, and looks at the political situation through a different lens. It is this component that gives the theory political relevance. What empiricists see as important in politics is not the *telos* of the society (justice and beauty) that the state should promote. Empiricists are realists in their approach to the analysis and the study of civil society. This is why the Humes of the world are always Machiavellian. They try to look at past descriptions to solve present situations. Their approach to the study of civil society is within the scientific mode, not with the ethical mode. Rationalists, on the other hand, regard the *ideal* form of the society as the higher reality and every thing else as imperfection, oppression, and injustice. This ideal political reality might be found in the "state of nature" or in the futuristic utopia. Politically speaking, the rationalists tend to be utopians bent on creating an ideal society as envisioned in the mind and sharply critical of the existing political environment, which they regard as having divided human beings, turned one against the other, and driven them into constant conflicts. The rationalists envision a world free of conflicts and oppression, and the human beings in harmony. Rationalists, thus, are universalists who see the whole of humanity as governed by the natural laws. In contrast, Aristotle as well as Marx bridged between the two extremes, by being both political realists and utopian. On the other hand, religious voluntarists tend to be utopian in their view of political reality.

Such diverse views about political reality make a difference in how political theorists perceive the right political action and approach to social change. There are major differences between violent revolutionary action aimed at change in existing regimes and peaceful means of developing the political reality. Theories, therefore, can be classified into two categories according to their ideas about social change. The first comprises radical theories that propose rampant change of the society as part of a natural process of development. These theories see the history of mankind as a series of stagnation and growth cycles separated by periods of rapid social change, called revolutions. These revolutions are not based on some preexisting set of rules, practices, and social structures of its predecessor. Marxism stands at the summit of this body of political thought. The second category comprises conservative theories, which consider incremental change of the society as the

---

[138]<u>Encyclopedia of Philosophy</u>, v. 2, "Empiricism" by D. W. Hamlyn.

soundest way of assuring survival. Conservatives view revolutions and radical changes in history as bringing only destruction and illness to the society. Gradual development of the society is not only the natural way for man to progress in history, but the preferred course of political action; thus, revolutions must be contained from jeapordizing man's survival. However, there is no clear cut distinction as to where each philosophical school of thought stands on the issue of social change. While Marx, an empiricist, favors revolution, Locke, also an empiricist, on the other hand, advocates a gradual process of change within the society. In contrast, religious theorists, in general, believe that political tyrants on earth are God's punishment to man. Believers must obey their rulers, and in the process try to change the society gradually through appealing to the authority in charge.

Moreover, political theory serves the purpose not only of studing the problems facing the civil society but also, given its ideological bent, of providing prescriptions for maladies within given political situations. It is, therefore, not a value free intellectual exercise such as is found in pure philosophy. Political theorists have a vested interest in changing the world around them. Their prescriptions for social illnesses are designed to assure the survival of humanity. Political theorists grow out of political crises that beset civil society. This is why historicists like Dunning, Sabine, and McIlwain assumed that all political theories are historically conditioned. People of ideas, philosophers and the like, reflect their understanding of the world surrounding them, and express their anger in it. Sabine, one of the renown historicists of this century, defined political theory as "an intellectual tradition and its history consists of the evolution of man's thought about political problems."[139] He explains that a political theorist "is thinking about something that has actually occurred and that has been the stimulus of his thought."[140] In other words, historicists suggest that there can be no universal truth, except that all ideas are a product of a historical period and can not transcend it.[141] To understand one particular political theory is to locate it within particular historical circumstances to which theorists are reacting. Such relativism does not give answers to the perennial problems of politics or postulate timeless values. To the contrary, the values and ideas of the past emerge out a particular age and people. Our modern belief system is in fact the production of the past. There is nothing in the minds of today's thinkers that is not the outcome of the intellectual discourses of ancient history. According to Hegel, everything in the body of ideas has been worked out, nothing

---

[139]George H. Sabine and Thomas L. Thorson, <u>A History of Political Theory</u>, 4th ed. (Hinsdale, IL: Dryden Press, 1973), 3.

[140]Sabine, "What is Political Theory," 4.

[141]David Easton, "The Decline of Modern Political Theory," <u>Journal of Politics</u> (February, 1951), 40-43.

else is left to be discovered. For the West, the history of ideas reaches back to Greek antiquities while for the East it is rooted in ancient religion. The existing moral values are the *telos* of the past, and the past's ideas are the embryo of today's beliefs.

In sum, a political theory entails three kinds of factors: a factual statement about the circumstances that occasioned the theory; a causal statement about what would be the likely outcome of the current state of affairs; and the valuational statement suggesting what ought to happen or what should be the human action to change the course of events.[142] While the first statement represents the political philosophy component, the second and the third represent the ideological components. Because of the ideological aspect, political theorists tend to be optimistic in their view of man's future. Political theories, in general, define the good political order and take the view that people have the capacity to achieve and build such an ideal order. Regardless of how political theorists view human nature (wicked or saintly), they view man as having the capacity to contribute to the realization and survival of utopia.[143] A political theory has two sides, the empiricist side, where the theorist uses his analytical skills to give a descriptive account of the prevailing political conditions; and the normative side, where he gives his prescription for the reorganization of the political life of the society.[144] The importance of political theory lies in its practical application. It serves as the blue-print for practice. Its insights into the political environment and its affirmations about the true nature of political actions serve as a guide for the restructuring of civil society, the establishing of new social institutions, the reorganizing of social behavior, and the reallocation of resources.

The building blocks in the construction of a theory are the independent variables that represent the basic facts. However, are not laws made up of similar elements? Does that mean that theories and laws are similar. The answer is no. Laws, although built of such variables, are themselves considered as facts. They constitute associations between the factual variables. Laws do not "say why a particular association holds, they cannot tell us whether we can exercise control and how might we go about doing so. For the latter purpose we need a theory."[145] Theories, in contrast to laws, are not to be considered as facts

---

[142]Sabine, "What is Political Theory?," 6.

[143]Glen Tinder, "What Should be Political Theory Now," in John S. Nelson, ed., *What Should Political Theory Be Now?* (Albany, NY: State University of New York Press, 1983), 153.

[144]Om Bakshi, *The Crisis of Political Theory: An Inquiry into Contemporary Thought* (Delhi: Oxford University Press, 1987), 6.

[145]Kenneth N. Waltz, *Theory of International Politics* (NY: Random House, 1979), 6.

of life, but rather are the body of statements that explain the relations and associations between variables. These explanatory statements are the nonfactual elements of the theory.[146] They are made up of assumptions, which "are not assertions of fact. They, [thus], are neither true nor false."[147] Therefore, a theory can be refuted only by another theory, while the validity of laws must be confirmed directly by carrying out experiments. Theories, hence, are judged on the basis of the structural coherence, the plausibility of their assumptions, and the accuracy of their generalizations.

Because laws belong to the realm of the factual, they are used as the building blocks of theories. Theories are systems of statements that entail laws. One of their functions is to give a new understanding to the relations between observable facts or variables around us. These facts must have a role to play, otherwise they represent only useless data. "The real problem [then], to return to Rousseau, is what role is to be assigned to facts when writing a theory."[148] Theories make possible the ordering of data, and become a useful tool in selecting facts that are most relevant to the problem being analyzed.[149] Without theories, the real facts of life would have no order or meaning. Theories act as the spirit that is breathed into the body of data and make the data meaningful. They "indicate what is connected with what and how the connection is made. They convey a sense of how things work, how they hang together, of what the structure of realm of inquiry may be."[150] Thus, political theories enable us to better understand the political life that surrounds us. Policies can not be carried on without having some sort of theory about the political environment. A theory makes us understand not only the world around us, but also the outcome of its process, so our actions could be directed toward achieving a certain goal. It is the striving attain of goals that makes political theories essential for people in politics, the principal goal being to influence the political process and direct of the outcome. As Arnold Brecht plainly put it:

> It is the function of the political theorist to see, sooner than others, and to analyze, more profoundly than others, the immediate and the potential problems of the political life of the society; to supply the practical politician, well in advance, with alternative courses of action, the foreseeable consequences of which have been fully thought through; and to supply him not only with brilliant asides, but with a solid block of knowledge on which

[146]Ibid., 10.

[147]Ibid., 6.

[148]Haker, _Political Theory_, 7.

[149]Kenneth W. Thompson, "Toward a Theory of International Relations", _American Political Science Review_, 735.

[150]Kenneth Waltz, _Theory of International Politics_, 12.

to build.[151]

Generally, the structure of the theory consists of four elements.[152] <u>Paradigms</u>, the foundation of any theory, are the particular conceptualizations of the phenomenon being explained by the theorist. A paradigm, therefore, must underscore and fully explain the relationships between the variables of the phenomenon under consideration and the manner in which they operate. The behaviorist may choose the scientific approach to deal with the phenomenon he is investigating, while others may choose a more philosophical approach. <u>Concepts</u> are ideas or thoughts that are used as labels assigned to a class of phenomena. Theorists may attach different meanings and definitions to the same concept. Therefore, these concepts must be carefully defined and their relations to the paradigm must be demonstrated. Additionally, a theory must define the <u>logical relationship</u> between concepts and state clearly if they are positive, negative, or independent of one another. Those relationships must be linked theoretically. In fact, the structure of a theory "depends on the kind of relationship statements it contains and their relationship to one another."[153] Finally, these abstract aspects of the theory must be validated on the basis of empirical data, i.e., <u>variables</u>.

Islamic Political Theory

We should highlight some of the distinct features of an Islamic political theory. Islam is a revealed religion and the revelations from God are considered real facts. The major body of facts in Islam is found in the <u>Qur'an</u>. The Qur'an's authenticity, for a Muslim, is unquestionable. For a theorist who is a devoted Muslim, the verses of the <u>Qur'an</u> are the factual variables with which to build a theory. These verses may contain historical data, social regulations, moral values, or sets of beliefs, all of which are taken as revealed truth which is beyond questioning. Revelation in Islam, as in the Judaism and Christianity, is not the only source of truth, but is the most important one since it embraces the words of God. The religious mind considers that a human may not have the capacity to grasp the ultimate truth of God, being finite and of limited capacity. It is the mercy of God that has made available to man facts that are beyond his ability to know, particularly those facts that are essential to human salvation.

However, this does not mean that religious theorists totally deny the ability of the

---

[151]Arnold Brecht, <u>Political Theory</u>, 20.

[152]Graham C. Kinloch, <u>Sociological Theory: Its Development and Major Paradigms</u> (New York: McGraw-Hill Book Co., 1977), 12.

[153]Ibid.

human intellect to discover and know the truth. It is the function of the human mind not only to understand the revelations of God, but also to know the physical world and observable facts around him. These kinds of truths must be searched for by man himself in order to facilitate his survival on earth. The Shi‘i jurists (faqihs) assign an even greater role to man's intellect. The basic tenets one holds must be believed through one's intellect and reasoning powers. A Shi‘i (mainly of the usuli school of thought)[154], for example, should be led by his reason to believe in God. The five tenets of belief in Islam-- tawhid, (the unity of God), ‘adalah (the justice of God), nubuwah, (prophethood, both that of Muhammad and of all previous prophets), imamah, (the role of the perfect guided leadership of humanity), ma‘ad, (the resurrection of man and the day of judgment) --all must be believed in as a result of intellectual reasoning. To accept these tenets of belief as part of a cultural tradition or simply because they are mentioned in the holy books is not acceptable to Shi‘i jurists. If someone does not use his intellect to believe in the tenets of Islam he is considered as blindly following his ancestors' religion, which is highly condemned by God in the Qur'an. That is why it is customery among the shi‘i jurists to write rational treaties to prove the existence of God and the five tenets of Islam. Sadr himself had supplemented his book of Islamic regulations, al-Fatawi al-Wadiha, with a preface devoted to rational proofs for the basic beliefs about God, the prophethood of Muhammad and the massage of Islam. Sadr in this essay used the philosophical argument he developed in his book, al-Usus al-Mantiqiyah lil Istiqra'. His method of proof was inductive, one which sought to derive conclusions about God, Muhammad, and Islam from observable facts. The preface was later published independently and subtitled, al-Mursil wa-al-Rasul wal Risalah (The Revealer, the Messenger, and the Message). Man is given an active role in proving the existence of God, not to mention his being accorded an ability to understand his responsibility in this life, and his accountability in the hereafter. This standpoint led Sadr to produce a rational argument to convince Muslims to adhere to the principles of Islam. He believed that once Muslims are presented with rational arguments about their religion, they would not deviate from their beliefs because, according to Sadr, Islamic beliefs are compatible with man's fundamental needs.

---

[154]Shi‘a, from a jurisprudence point of view, are divided into two main schools of thought: the akhbaris, which consider the Quran and Sunna as the only sources for deriving Islamic laws; and the usuli, which regards the principles of jurisprudence (which is considered as the logic of fiqh) as a valid source of deriving laws. On the foundations of the two schools and the historical intellectual conflict between them which ended in the defeat of the akhbaris in the late eighteenth century, see Sadr, al-Ma‘alim al-Jadidah lil Usul (Tehran: Maktabat al-Najah, 1975), 5-89.

Nonetheless, Sadr never embraced the idea that human rationality could make man capable of discovering or implementing the political system that is best for his needs and survival. Human reasoning is able to give an accurate judgement when it comes to analysis of physical experiments, but this is not the case when it comes to analysis of social problems. Knowledge gained from physical experiments is pure knowledge, but the results of social experiments are always tainted with bias.[155] Such lack of objectivity in the study of social phenomena is due to several factors, according to Sadr: 1) The duration of a physical experiment is relatively short. Therefore scientists can cover virtually all aspects of the phenomenon and come to their conclusions. In contrast, a social phenomenon might transcend the life span of the scientist, and what he observes in his study are but some of the effects and features of the phenomenon; thus, conclusions are related to part of the reality. 2) Man has a vested interest when it comes to making conclusions about social phenomena, while scientists, in general, have no personal interests in manipulating the data and results gained from experiments on physical matters. Sadr cites that a capitalist economist, when analyzing the social benefit of the banking system, would be predisposed to defend the social benefits of usury. 3) Even if an unbiased social analyst were available to discover the best social system, he should be committed to the ideal he is proposing for the society. For example, Marx's descriptive work as a social scientist was not enough to pinpoint the ills of capitalism; his commitment to utopian communism was also a factor. 4) Man is the product of his environment, and is not expected to transcend what he knows. "A man who is convinced of the soundness of the prevailing system cannot be expected to look for a better system."[156] Sadr gave an example of how the United States of America was not able to enforce the law banning alcohol because drinking is part of the social norms of the society even though science shows the negative impact of drinking upon the society.

Sadr therefore concluded that man is in need of an immortal being, i.e. God, to show him the right and ideal social settings and a political system that is best for his survival. Only God, through his revelation to prophets, could provide humanity with the best social system. All other man-made social systems have their shortcomings. They cannot serve the full range of human interests throughout history. The best political order, according to Sadr, is the one ordained by God, the creator of man himself, who is attentive to man's development and needs and is the best protector of his interests. Islam is the final revelation of God to

---

[155]M.B. Sadr, "al-Insan al-Muᶜasir wa-al-Mushkilah al-Ijtimaᶜyah" (The Contemporary Man and the Social Problem), in al-Madrasah al-Islamiyah, 3rd ed. (Beirut: Dar al-Zahra', 1980), 24.

[156]Sadr, Islam and School of Economics (a translation text of Sadr's al-Madrasah al-Islamiyah), translator name unknown (Albany, CA: Muslim Students Association, n.d.), 42.

man; thus, an Islamic political system is the best system, one which serves the salvation of man both in this life and in the hereafter.

Sadr's Grand Poltical Theory

One of the indications that led me to believe that Sadr had a political theory in mind is his systematic way of dealing with the political crises of his time. Unlike other jurists, he did not resort to mere political propaganda to defend Islam in the face of great political challenges, but rather studied alternative and even antireligious political ideologies that were overwhelming the political arena in an attempt to develop a more intelligent and scientific response that took into account the elements of political theory mentioned above. In his research, he wanted to look at other ideas objectively, notwithstanding the Islamic character of his own beliefs. This is noticeable, for example, in Sadr's admiration for Marx's thought and political philosophy. Other Islamic political activists and jurists attack Marxism from the stand point of the failure of Marxist regimes in the world. Some have gone so far as to consider Marxism as part of the an international Jewish conspiracy to weaken religious devotion among Muslims and Christians and to achieve a worldwide Jewish hegemony. Sadr, on the other hand, called Marx "the genius" but regarded his exceptional intellectual prowess as limited by European social experience in the nineteenth century.[157] Thus,"the Marxist solution to the social problem is diluted."[158] Sadr's approach was to counterattack Marxism not with rhetoric but with a grand political theory. Marxism has applied dialectical materialism "to history, society, and economics; and thus, it became a philosophical doctrine concerning the world, a method of studying history and society, a school of economics and a plan in politics."[159] Sadr wanted an Islamic response that would cover all aspects of political theory and would not resort to name calling and emotional attacks. Sadr clearly outlined his program of inquiry:

> It is necessary, therefore, to inquire about Islamic philosophical convictions concerning life, the universe, society and the economy. We must also inquire about its legislation and procedures, in order to obtain a complete overview of Islamic ... thought, comparing these Islamic convictions to other forms of conviction regarding the procedures they pursue and the doctrines the adopt.[160]

[157]Sadr, _Muqaddimat fi al-Tafsir al-Mawdu^ci lil Quran_, (Kuwait: Dar al-Tawjih al-Islami, 1980), 79.

[158]Sadr, _Falsafatuna_ (Beirut: Dar al-Ta^caruf, 1980), 31.

[159]Sadr, _Our Philosophy_, translation of _Falsafatuna_ by Shams C. Inati (London: Muhammadi Trust, 1987), 14.

[160]Sadr, _Our Philosophy_, 32.

Consequently, Sadr classified the subjects of his theoretical investigation under three headings, each of which became the title of a book. First, <u>Falsafatuna</u> (Our Philosophy) covers epistemological questions aiming at refuting empiricism and most especially dialectical materialism; Second, <u>Mujtamaᶜuna</u> (Our Society) covers sociopolitical questions, that is to say, questions relating to the role of man within social settings and to the ideal social order and the attainment of man happiness through it; and, third, <u>Iqtisaduna</u> (Our Economics) deals with the structuring of economic activities within the proposed Islamic social order. However, Sadr, after publishing his first volume, was under pressure from readers to write about Islamic economics and to delay the proposed volume <u>Mujtamaᶜuna</u>.[161] It was due to the impact of Marxism that the readers were eager to know if Islam has any socioeconomic perspective. Otherwise, Sadr would have proceeded with goal of constructing an Islamic political theory in a systematic way from A to Z.

Sadr went on to openly denounce the existing political movements in the Muslim World which adopted nationalism as a basis of their political theory.[162] Nationalism, according to him, is nothing but

> an historical and linguistic tie and not a philosophical principle or an ideological doctrine, and it occupies neutral position *vis-a-vis* different philosophical, ideological, social or religious system of beliefs. The (nationalist) movements are in need of specific views towards the universe and life as well as a specific philosophy to mold the foundations of civilization, the process of its [historical] progress and the structure of its society.[163]

It is this lack of doctrinal beliefs that leads these movements to link their nationalist creed to one school of thought or another. People in the East carry a resentment towards the West because of the long history of colonization. For this reason nationalist movements in the Arab World, for example, adopted a naturalized form of socialism called "Arab Socialism."[164] Both nationalism and socialism are part of the European experience and are totally foreign to Muslims' traditional system of belief. Sadr traced back the basis of the nationalist socialist movement to the historical development of West.

The philosophical foundation of the West is empiricist in its epistemological

---

[161]Sadr, Preface to 1st edition of <u>Iqtisaduna</u> (Beirut: Dar al-Taᶜaruf, 1981), 27.

[162]Sadr, Preface to 2nd edition of <u>Iqtisaduna</u>, 14.

[163]Ibid.

[164]Sadr, <u>Iqtisaduna</u>, 15.

principles. Western man is always linked to the physical world around him. This led him to disbelieve in the metaphysical world. Such disbelief led him, after he was Christianized, to the point of bringing the God of Christianity down from heaven to earth through the doctrine of incarnation. Such strong attachment to the physical environment was also noticeable in scientific research, which tried to relate man's existence to the natural developmental process of life on earth. Western man is brought up to believe that he is in a constant struggle with his environment. Physically, he must satisfy his desires and passions like other creatures around him, which consequently has led him to the belief that he must exploit the environment in order to amass wealth and satisfy his materialistic needs. Economically the West was able to develop quickly in modern history because every member of the society was part of a whole system that maximized his or her personal interests. Western economic development, according to Sadr, was due to the fact that the European social system was a reflection of the system of beliefs of Europeans. Even the personal freedom advocated strongly in the West was a result of the European's belief that he alone was responsible for his survival. He must have full authority over himself. In fact, such an individualistic view led to the development of one of the great philosophical schools in the modern European history, namely positivism. Socialism, however, is a natural response to overcome the shortcomings of the individualist foundation of the capitalist system in the West.[165]

On the other hand, man in the East,[166] being shaped by heavenly messages, is more attached to the hereafter than to this world. A Muslim is not obsessed with materialistic needs, but rather is subject to constraints over his desires and passions. It is this preoccupation with the metaphysical that led Muslims to have negative stands toward the exploitation of the environment and made them resentful of the materialistic life. In the long run, unproductive and lazy attitudes toward work resulted. The attachment to the metaphysical also led them to see their actions as being continually under the surveillance of a supernatural authority. This belief led them to be less inclined to have a sense of personal freedom of choice. Moral value is consequently centered around the welfare of the community. Along with this communalism is a global outlook which makes it obligatory for believers to carry the message of heaven to all people, contrary to the European emphasis on national survival. A political theory, for Muslims, must take into consideration their system of beliefs and must find roots in their ideological commitments. It must overcome the

---

[165]Sadr, _Iqtisaduna_, 18-21.

[166]Sadr uses the concept "East" to refer to non-Western civilizations, generally, the civilizations influenced by divine religious teachings. These include the home lands of Judaism, Christianity, Islam, Zoroastrian, Buddhism, and Hinduism. The Afro-Asian civilizations are centered on God, while the European civilization is centered on man.

Muslims's negative attitude toward exploitation of nature and elicit from them a powerful dynamic energy to develop the economy and eliminate backwardness. The theory must take into account the belief of Muslims in the supernatural stock-taking of their behavior and not impose on them alien notions of individual freedom of the sort central to Western moral values.[167]

It was within these guidelines that Sadr wanted to construct his Islamic political theory. He saw Islam as a complete system of beliefs that does not need to borrow from other ideological doctrines. The paradigms and basic concepts and principles of his theory are derived from Islamic teachings. He wanted all trained muslim jurists, the 'ulama', to join the endeuvor to prove that Islam is the final salvation of humanity. All other doctrines and creeds fall short of the perfection found only in Islam.

Sadr's universalist outlook on social problems made him repudiate the traditional approach of Islamic jurisprudence. As Islam had lost control over political life, jurists (faqihs) had come to look at Islamic laws entirely from the stand point of individual problems. In their juristic deliberations, they typically responded to the daily problems faced by faithful Muslims in what in reality amounted to un-Islamic social environments. Their effort was thus confined to regulating individual behavior in accordance with Islamic teachings. Such an outlook caused jurists to undermine the social import of Islamic laws. Sadr gave two examples to prove his point. The jurists generally agreed that since the obligations that make up the Shari^cah cannot be determined with certainty, doubt concerning these obligations necessarily accompanies all effort to fulfill them. If so, one must exercise a cautious hesitation with regard to one's daily actions. One cannot be entirely sure whether one's behavior is according to the will of God or not. Such thinking is not, however, feasible with regard to the formation of laws guiding the community. Social laws must be decidedly either lawful or prohibited in order to be enforceable by the political authority. A society as a whole, Sadr argues, cannot function on the basis of cautious hesitation. The natural social relations and the economic and political welfare of the society would come to a halt.[168]

The second example that Sadr cites to show the failure of the traditional jurisprudence to develop a social vision is the application of the jurisprudential principle of "la Darar wala Dirar" (no damage and no mutual infliction of damage). He argues this principle was applied in such a way that Islamic laws were rejected by jurists only because these laws, when executed, might have harmful effects on an individual. For example, since the confiscation of property for the purpose of achieving a public good violates the individual right of property ownership, the jurists decreed that action was unjust, and should

---

[167]Sadr, Iqtisaduna, 21-23.

[168]Sadr, "al-Itijahat al-Mustaqbaliyah li-Harakat al-Ijtihad" (The Future Trends of the Process of Ijtihad), in Ikhtarna Lak, 2nd ed. (Beirut: Dar al-Zahra', 1980), 79-80.

be considered illegal. Had the jurists approached the problem from a socially-oriented viewpoint, and become aware of the positive effects such actions had on the welfare of the society, then there would be no reason to adhere to these principles. Any damages, harms and disadvantage that might be inflected on the individual would be compensated by the well-being of the community as a whole.[169]

As a result of the <u>al-janib al-fardi</u> (individualistic tendency) of fiqh, jurists resorted to finding escape routes for Muslims when facing circumstances not favored by Islam. For example, when a Muslim deals in financial relations based on usury, which is prohibited by Islam, the jurists would try to find some arrangement to overcome such problems. This basic financial relationship is essential or unavoidable in the life of an individual. Meanwhile, the jurists in their sanction of the western-styled banking transaction would not try to ignore the negative effects of usuary on the community. Their main concern is to purify the individual behavior, not the social relations of the whole community. Such an attitude of jurists has affected their understanding of the sources of Islamic laws (<u>Qur'an</u> and <u>Sunnah</u>). An order by the Prophet not to use a well, for example, might be interpreted by jurists as either forbidding, or warning. However, the prohibition might be interpreted as only a temporary order by the Prophet while acting as a leader.[170]

Sadr wanted to give a social meaning or perspective to the <u>Shari^cah</u>. In his book review of Maghnia's <u>Fiqh al-Imam al-Sadiq</u>, he concurs with the author's view that in respect to acts of worship one must be restricted to the literal meaning of the indicators and passages of <u>Shari^cah</u>. On other matters, one can give a broad social interpretation to these sources of law.[171] Sadr's socially oriented outlook on Islamic jurisprudence would make it possible for him to develop the grand political theory he had in mind. In contrast, the traditional individualistic view of jurists would hinder this effort and make it difficult to instigate the creation of an Islamic state. The socially oriented outlook is not only new to the study of Islamic jurisprudence, but is revolutionary in its nature.[172] It is a sincere effort to

---

[169]Sadr, "al-Itijahat," 80-81.

[170]Sadr, "al-Itijahat" 81-82.

[171]Sadr, "al-Fahm al-Ijtima^ci lil-Nas fi Fiqh al-Imam Ja^cfar al-Sadiq" (The Social Understanding of Indicators in Jurisprudence of Imam Ja^cfar as-Sadiq), <u>Ikhtrna lak</u>, 97-99.

[172]M.H. Fadlullah, "^cAlamat Istifham ^cAla Tariq Harakat al Quwah fi al-Dawlah al-Islamiyah" (Question Marks on the Route of Movement of Power in the Islamic State), <u>al-Tawhid</u> (Tehran) n. 21 (March 12, 1986) 90., referring to Sadr's new topology of <u>fiqh</u> subjects; and Ha'iri, <u>Mabahith</u>, 57-61, referring to Sadr's new school in <u>jurisprudence</u>.

modernize Islamic jurisprudence in order to bring it into line with the trends developed in the West by allowing Islamic jurists to place the social well-being of the community alongside individual salvation. Sadr, well before the establishment of the Islamic Republic of Iran, set the standards for the possibilities of applying Islamic law to the social settings. Like Marx, who saw Hegel as walking on his head and tried to make him stand on his feet, Sadr was determined to turn Islamic jurisprudence (fiqh) right side up.

Moreover, Sadr also wanted jurists to turn from the traditional methodology of Qur'anic studies, which explicates Qur'anic verses one by one from the first surah (chapter) to the last, to a more "objective" style of finding the general themes covered by the Holy Book.[173] An incremental study of the Qur'an might take several years and would result in an encyclopedic compendium of Islamic studies, but it would not give an understanding to the basic concepts and themes that, according to Sadr, God wanted man to grasp and believe. The Qur'an is a book of guidance, but if Muslims do not understand all aspects of its message, it will be difficult for them to see the guidance in it. For Sadr, theoretical studies of the major themes of the Qur'an are the only way to make the Holy Book an influential guide for the people.[174] The social function of the interpreter in the tajz'i (incremental) methodology is negligible because he focus his attention on literal meanings and the historical circumstance behind particular verse(s). However, an interpreter of mawduᶜi (objective) methodology tries to find a Qur'anic solution to currently prevailing issues.[175] While the former's field of inquiry is history, that of the latter is the existing social norms and system. The objective interpreter is a full participant in the affairs of the people, and his inquiry aims to mold social life according to divine will.

When Sadr compared the studies in jurisprudence with those in the Qur'anic commentaries, he found the former to be more socially advanced than the latter.[176] Jurists had classified the issues of jurisprudence according to social needs in order to come up with a general understanding of the basic themes of Islamic law. Hadiths are classified into topics such as family issues, acts of worships, financial transactions, and so on. This objective type of inquiry had given jurists the ability to discover the general guidelines within each area. Once these guidelines are known, jurists can make judgements on new circumstances. However, inquiry of this sort was not extended to the Qur'an.[177] While the jurists show a comprehensive understanding of the basic principles of jurisprudence, the concepts

[173]Sadr, Muqaddimat, 9-14.

[174]Sadr, Muqaddimat, 34-37.

[175]Ibid., 18-22.

[176]Ibid., 15-16.

[177]Sadr, Muqaddimat, 17-18.

developed by the Qur'anic commentators are fragmented.[178] Students of the Qur'an must instead be able to discover theories from the Holy Book that concern the prevailing human conditions of the time. Only in this way can the Qur'an serve its main purpose as a source of guidance to human.

Jurisprudence itself must have a broader view of its subject matters and not be limited to themes and details relating to the various jurisprudential topics. It must carry on a deeper investigation to derive the basic theory behind each compartment of Islamic law. As Sadr had phrased it:

> We know that behind each set of laws for the various issues of life there are basic theories, which are related to certain aspects of the Islamic canons such as the Islamic economic doctrine. The Islamic canons that related to marriage and divorce and the relations of woman with man, [for example], entail a general theory about woman and man and the role of woman and man. These general theories should form the basic foundations of the general outlook of jurisprudence[179]

Sadr wanted to extend his mawdu^ci (objective) research methodology, as he likes to call it, to other Islamic fields of study. Likewise, when he studied the life of the twelfth Holy Imams of the Shi^cahs, he was trying to find the general role of the Imams' mission.[180] He expressed his dissatisfaction with the previous historical studies of the lives of Imams. Each one of them had adopted different political functions in order to deal with the existing oppressive regimes. This would imply a contradiction between the actions of each Imam, and mean that the Imams had conflicting views. The Imams' actions and practices are divinely ordained, implying that their contradictory actions all have divine approval; therefore, Sadr wanted the historical studies to concentrate on finding the ultimate goal that all Imams tried to achieve. All Imams, during their mission, wanted to achieve that goal and adopted a different course of action. These actions by the Imams were to complement each other in order to reach the final goal of their mission.[181] In this way, Sadr wanted to solve

---

[178]Ibid., 18.

[179]Ibid., 24-25.

[180]Sadr, "Dawr al-A^cimah fi al-Hayat al-Islamiyah" (The Role of Imams in Muslims' Life), in Ikhtarna Lak, 60-61; originally the articles were a speech delivered for the "Linguistic Society" in Najaf in 1966. The same idea also was expressed in his Dawr al-A^cimah, 57-149, where he fully detailed the role of the Imams' missions in period that extended two and half centuries.

the contradictory nature of the Imams' actions.

Generally, throughout his Islamic inquiry, Sadr tried to discover the social concepts of Islam and relate them to the prevailing political conditions, an emphasis rarely adopted by other jurists before him. He wanted Islamic teaching to be part of the dynamics of social life. His emphasis on the <u>mawdu^ci</u> approach to all field of Islamic studies is related to his need to formulate an Islamic political theory. Consequently, one finds that his epistemology drew upon Islamic philosophy and his interpretation of history upon <u>Qur'anic</u> interpretation, while in writing on the means of political struggle he employed a historical analysis of the early period of Islam, and in his prescription of the Islamic political state, he employed Islamic jurisprudence. Having witnessed the ignorance of the people about the basic principles of Islam, which made them susceptible to the influence of Western thought, he was determined to revise all standards of traditional Islamic teachings and make it possible to derive a grand political theory based on Islam. He thought that such a mission was necessary in order to attach people more deeply to Islam again. The reason that the general teachings of Islam are foreign to Muslims is that they live in an environment unattached to the meanings of these principles. This situation is similar to one who knows how to speak his own language but has only a vague idea about the basics of its grammar.[182] For Sadr, Muslims must know the theoretical basis of Islam to be immune to the influence of the sociopolitical theories of the West.[183]

However, Sadr does not consider himself to be constructing an Islamic political theory, but rather thinks of himself as *discovering*, or deriving it from the Islamic sources.[184] His belief is that Islam clearly has a grand political theory, on which underpins the entire body of its teachings. The fundamental principles of belief, the ritual acts of worship, the set of rules regulating individual behavior, standards of ethics and social values, as well as Islamic laws and legislation, are mere reflections of the "Grand Islamic Theory." He considers the Islamic theory as the foundation upon which rests the superstructure of Islamic knowledge, including such things as laws and regulations. He developed an Islamic theory of economics and in so doing made an intensive effort to *discover* what is underneath the different laws of the various Islamic schools. His assumption is that these laws were derived by Muslim jurists from a basic and commonly held theory. The differences between the schools arise from the efforts of jurists to use their reasoning powers in applying fundamentals to circumstances as they rise, or to make them compatible with cultural

---

[181]Sadr, "Dawr al-A^cimah," 70.

[182]Sadr, <u>Muqaddimat</u>, 27-28.

[183]Ibid., 29.

[184]Sadr, <u>Iqtisaduna</u>, 388-389.

standards. They are comparable to the differences between the British, German, Italian and American laws. Although capitalism represents the underpinnings and the ideological basis of these countries, their laws represent a reflection of their different historical and social heritages. The Anglo-Saxon culture is different from the Germanic, from the Roman and so on, which results in different legislation and sets of social-juristic rules. Since the grand theory underlying the Islamic sciences is not clear-cut as are those of capitalism or Marxism concerning which one can directly go to writings of Adam Smith or Marx, Sadr suggests that one can extrapolate the theory, the substructure in this case, from the superstructure.[185] One, in this case, must disengage all effects of historical circumstance, individual juristic reasoning, and limited interpretation of the general principles in order to truly get a clear embodiment of the theory.[186] The jurists sometimes unknowingly tried to justify current historical situations, or misread the reasons behind the Islamic traditions, which led to a misunderstanding of the principles of Islamic political theory. He concludes that the theory he is *discovering* goes beyond his mere ijtihad, but rather represents the foundations common to the various Islamic schools of thought. His efforts are aimed at revealing the blueprint behind all Islamic teachings and knowledge down through the centuries.

---

[185]Sadr, Iqtisaduna, 391.

[186]Ibid., 404-429.

The Meaning of History

The continuous logic of history is not a random process, but rather an objective in nature.

Sadr

The interpretation of the historical process is the corner- stone of Sadr's political theory. Even though his views on history emerged in his later discourse, he clearly defined the paradigm of his theory in them, and outlined the basic concepts of his grand design for society. Without a clear understanding of his vision of history, his other political concepts seem to lack a focus. The historical process seems to act, in Sadr's political theory, as the thread that links all the beads and clarifies other social elements.

The Nature of History

Sadr views history as a causal process and as working according to a well-defined pattern.[187] This understanding of history grows out of his general Islamic beliefs. Man and his environment exist by virtue of divine creativity and thus must have meaning. History unfolds according to a specific set of rules and its natural processes are not random, for God's actions are not without meaning. God has implanted within his creation a well-defined system that links the effects of all elements in the historical process to each other. However, the historical process itself is not a self-contained mechanism, but rather has two sides: the materialistic side, where man and nature have great impact on the process; and the metaphysical side, where the Deity's will has full control over its <u>telos</u>.[188] Therefore, the materialist side does not comprise the totality of the historical process. It is the will of the Almighty that prevails in the end.

---

[187]Sadr, <u>Muqaddimat fi al-Tafsir al-Mawdu^ci Lil-Quran</u> (Kuwait: Dar al-Tawjih al-Islami, 1980), 23.

[188]Sadr, <u>Muqaddimat</u>, 44-59.

Consequently, Sadr defined the historical process as causal in respect to its mechanical workings, divine in respect to its goal, and social in respect to its impact on human life.[189] While the physical forces may act independently, their impact extends into a wider arena, because the process encompasses the whole human realm. This is why the effect of small social forces or influential personalities within the society is felt throughout the social system. Accordingly, Sadr is able to take account of the Marxist notion that the change in the means of production may reshape the social structure of the society, while at the same time finding room in his theory of history for the Hegelian notion that ideas are the prime factors shaping history. On the other hand, the historical process, considered as a totality, is shaped according to the will of God. It is true that history follows a dialectical course of development, but it operates according to a divine pattern. Materialistic conditions as well as idealistic conditions have effects on the final outcome of the historical development. Nonetheless, the Deity has its own way of directing the development of history according to its own will. The story of history has a built-in divine logic. To understand history one must be aware of the telos of history as ordained by the Deity.

The sunan (laws) of history are general conditions that govern the historical process, conditions that determine outcomes of historical development. If one is to understand history, one must understand the laws. Sadr classified three types of historical laws of development: First are the *voluntaristic* laws, those which involve human agency as a determiner of outcomes.[190] Through these laws man can have control over the destiny of his life. They function as if they are physical laws of nature. Once man has acted, he will because of these laws witness certain consequences without fail. Sadr finds a reference to these laws in the Qur'anic statement that God would not change the environment of people unless people change within themselves. He also notes that the Quran mentions that the collapse of society would be the natural outcome of the control of corrupt-wealthy

---

[189]Ibid., 76-78.

[190]Sadr does not assign any label to his conceptual definition about historical laws, but rather he explains their functions. For example, he defines the first type of these laws as historical laws "similar to causative principle." See, Ibid., 84. Since the outcome of such laws can be conditions according to the will of man, I took the liberty to call them *voluntaristic* laws. He expounds that these laws function like the natural process of boiling water, when at certain pressure and heat the water starts to boil and transfer from liquid to gas. Man is in control of providing the conditions, but once conditions are met, then the result will follow. Historically speaking, man's free will has a direct influence on the historical process.

individuals over the affairs of the society.[191]

Second are the *naturalistic* laws. These consist of inexorable patterns that are evident in the historical process and that cannot be changed by man's action.[192] Man, at some stages of history, may deviate from these patterns, but eventually he will be subdued by them. Thus, man must realize that he is part of a divine historical design. If one society tries to challenge or change the social roles of males and females, for example forcing women to work outside the home and men to be homemakers, these actions would lead to the destruction of society because women are naturally created to nurse children and men naturally have the physical ability to confront the physical demands of the outside world.[193] For Sadr, such a social violation is limited in duration, and the divine design for history will eventually prevail. Sadr also mentioned that if a society should legalize the homosexual relationship, such a society would eventually be doomed to annihilation. He believes that the espousal of religious beliefs and norms is also part of the divine design. If people choose not to espouse such beliefs and norms, they would also suffer disintegration in the end.[194] The Quran specifically mentions this,

> So set thy purpose for religion as a man by nature upright--the nature
> (framed) of Allah, in which He hath created man. There is no altering (the
> laws of) Allah's creation. That is the right religion, but most men know not.
> (30:30).

Third are the *deterministic* laws. These govern history's movement toward its final goal or outcome (telos).[195] God has full control over the direction of the historical process and enforces it on man. While man through the voluntaristic laws of history has an impact on the outcome of specific historical development, the deterministic laws govern the entire

---

[191]Sadr, Muqaddimat, 88-89.

[192]Defined by Sadr as "the historical laws formulated in away as the natural course of historical process." See, Sadr, Muqaddimat, 93.

[193]Ibid., 95-96.

[194]Sadr, Muqaddimat, 97-99.

[195]Sadr defines these laws as "similar to definitely-assured-to-happened principle." He gives the example of the eclipse of the sun or the moon where neither human knowledge nor will could change the natural course of the event. Here the will of God has direct impact on the historical process. See, Sadr, Muqaddimat, 89. Therefore, I refer to these laws as *deterministic* laws.

historical process from creation to eternity. God, according to Sadr, has a grand design for history. The whole historical process is a divine drama unfolding since the creation of Adam and operating according to God's will. The entire process will culminate in the coming of the Savior (Mahdi, the twelfth Imam) and the establishment of a justice and social system on earth that will prevail over all the injustices of man.

Stages of Historical Process

Sadr recognized three stages in the history of man: 1) the stage of rearing (Hadanah), which started with the creation of Adam and Eve and ended with their becoming dependent upon the earth; 2) the stage of unity or solidarity (Wihdah), which preceded the rise of social differences between men (as a social group, not as individuals); 3) and, the stage of dispersion or discord (Tashatut), which will last until the coming of the Mahdi.[196] Sadr, however, did not specify the historical stage that immediately proceeds the coming of Mahdi. One may gain an understanding of his views about the first stage from the book Mawsuat al-Imam al-Mahdi written by his cousin, Muhammad al-Sadr which he reviewed and prefaced.[197] Sadr did not give details on each of the periods, but his pupil and disciple, Kazim al-Ha'iri, has presented a critical analysis of Sadr's opinions in three articles published under the title al-Tafsir al-Mawdu'i lil-Quran al-Karim (Thematic Interpretation of the Quran) which I will refer to extensively.[198]

The first stage refers to the rearing of humanity as a whole not just to the creation of Adam and Eve, because their creation represents the creation of all mankind. It is considered a rearing stage because Adam and Eve were protected from facing any physical needs or environmental difficulties. They were provided with abundant resources in a 'heaven-like' environment. Man also during this period must grow into maturity and be provided with

---

[196]Sadr, Muqaddimat, 203.

[197]Three volumes reviewed by Sadr are: Tarikh al-Ghybah al-Sughra (History of Minor Occultation [of Mahdi]), Tarikh al-Ghybah al-Kubra (History of Greater Occultation), and Tarikh ma b`ada al-Zuhur (History of the Post-Coming of Mahdi). Sadr preface was published separately under the title, Bahth Hawla al-Mahdi (On Mahdi). However, Muhammad al-Sadr published additional volume title, al-Yawm al-Maw^cud (The Promised Day).

[198]See Kadim al-Ha'iri, "al-Tafsir al-Mawdu^ci lil Quran al-Karim," al-Hiwar al-Fikri wa al-Siyasi (Published by the Islamic Center for Political Studies, Tehran) v. 30-31 (Aug 1985), 51-90; v. 32 (Nov., 1985), 40-65; v. 33 (Summer 1986), 47-76.

faculties to help him in his earthly mission.[199] The <u>Quran</u> refers to the creation of Adam by Allah as the creation of all men on earth, not in heaven.

> And when thy Lord said to the angels, 'I am setting in the earth a viceroy.' They said, 'What, wilt Thou set therein one who will do corruption there, and shed blood, while We proclaim Thy praise and call Thee Holy?' He said, 'Assuredly I know that you know not.' And He Taught Adam the names, all of them; then He presented them onto the angles and said,'Now tell Me the names of these, if you speak truly.' That said, 'Glory be to Thee We know not save what Thou hast taught us. Surly Thou art the All-knowing, the All-wise.' He said , 'Adam, tell them their names.' And then when he had told them their names He said, 'Did I not tell you I know the unseen things of the heavens and earth? And I know what things you reveal, and what you were hiding.' And when We said to the angles, 'Bow yourselves to Adam'; and they bowed themselves, save Iblis; he refused, and waxed proud, and so he become one of the unbelievers. And We said, 'Adam, dwell thou, and thy wife, in the Garden, and eat thereof easefully where you desire; but draw not nigh this tree, lest you be evildoers.'Then the Satan caused them to slip therefrom and brought them out of that they were in; and We said, 'Get you all down, each of you an enemy of each; and in the earth a sojourn shall be yours, and enjoyment for a time.'(2:30-36)[200]

The purpose behind this long quotation of the verses is that it summarizes all the events and features of the first stage. First, the superior nature of man to angels is his ability to learn and acquire knowledge. This characteristic of man had made the angels bow to him. Second, Allah made man responsible for his actions through sanctions on his behavior. Man was created with free will and with the ability to violate the sanctions and commands of his Lord. Third, there is a system of reward and punishment for the purpose of restraining man from committing sins and encouraging him to do good deeds (in this life in the form of enjoyment and burden of guilt and in the hereafter, heaven and hell).[201] Three features, knowledge, free-will, and reward and punishment, are to enhance the progress of man in his life on earth. The lack of any one of these features would make man's existence on earth undesirable.[202] Such analysis was envisioned by the angels when Allah presented them with

---

[199]al-Ha'iri, "al-Tafsir al Mawdu^ci lil-Quran," <u>al-Hiwar al-Fikri wa-al-Siyasi</u>, (Aug., 1985), 63.

[200]<u>The Koran Interpreted</u>, translated by A. J. Arberry (NY: MacMillan Publishing Co., 1955), 33.

[201]al-Ha'iri, "al-Tafsir," 62-63.

his vicar, i.e., a creature having free agency. Their response was that man would eventually commit sins and bloodshed, unless some control measures were imposed on him to limit his behavior.[203] Being vicar of God implies that man has the freedom to choose, and without the ability to distinguish between good and bad, he would wander aimlessly and ultimately go astray. However, God's remedy was that man would acquire the knowledge (the names), as the first control mechanism of his action. The new creature (mankind), who was chosen as the vicar of God on earth, would have the capacity to learn and progress according to the guidance of God, which would be sent to him. Messengers of God would act as witnesses and lead man to the proper course of action to fulfill his role on earth.[204]

Man was faced thereafter with a dilemma to test his action and force him to go through a decision-making process to test the use of his knowledge to control his behavior. His creator had warned him of his enemy (Satan) and against eating the fruit from a specific tree. The prohibition was to give the father of humanity the experience of controlling his sensual urge and to prepare him for the responsibility of living on earth. Resources on earth are limited and man is supposed to acquire a reasonable amount of them to satisfy his needs.[205] Through a rational dialogue full of lies, Satan won Adam's confidence and seduced him to eat from the tree and violate God's prohibition. God therefore warned Adam again of his enemy and made him take full responsibility for his action. Man thus was presented with his second behavioral control mechanism, punishment and reward. He was left to face the difficulties and enjoyment of life on earth and to receive God's warnings from time to time.[206] Furthermore, man was allowed to repent of his action and was able to gain his Lord's forgiveness. He was able to reconsider his action and behave according to Allah's will. From this point of view, man's experience with Satan was for his benefit in order to prepare him to repent whenever he deviates from his purpose in life. The sinful action allowed man to experience spiritual feelings and made him live up to the responsibilities given him by God through repentance and praying for God's mercy. By then, man's mental faculty (rational reasoning, spiritual feelings) had developed to the capacity of his role as vicar of God on earth.[207]

---

[202]Ibid., 65.

[203]Sadr, <u>Kalafat al-Insan wa Shahadat al-Inbia'</u> published in <u>al-Islam Yaqwod al-Hayat</u> (Iran: Islamic Ministry of Guidance, n.d), 138.

[204]Ibid., 138-139.

[205]Sadr, <u>Khalafat al-Insan</u>, 152.

[206]Sadr, <u>Khalafat</u>, 71.

The second historical period is parallel, but not identical, to the <u>state of nature</u> of the social contract theorists (Hobbes, Locke, and Rousseau). Men at one time maintained a harmonious social life. Unlike the state of nature, there has always been some sort of social setting and man cannot be portrayed without society for man is a social animal, to use the Aristotelian proverb. The social relationship was the outcome of man's physical needs for such items as food and shelter. His search for survival forced him to cooperate with others.[208] Eventually he found himself using the help of other men and cooperating with them for his survival. Man possesses the natural instinct of self-love. This instinct makes him more dependent on others to secure his needs and interests. The more he gets the less satisfied he becomes and the more eager the demand for more. This ultimately results in an increased complexity of his social relationships. Generally, man's social relations are driven by his self-love: the more he gains physical satisfaction, the greater his desire for additional commodities.

Sadr has recognized two aspects of man's physical livelihood: First, every man has specific on-going 'primary' needs connected with his physiological being--nutritional, sexual, rational, and sensual needs; and second, there are no limitations to the quantity of these needs and commodities, because they are dependent on the complexity of life and social relations and the demands of the changing environment. The extent of man's experience in life, the widening of his knowledge, and the complexity of his social relations make his 'secondary' needs grow and expand.[209] These latter needs are different from one person to another, one society to another, and from one historical period to another. For example, modern technology has made electricity one of the basic needs of man. This need, however, was not a fact of life in the past century, and is not a basic for the Amish people, living within the most technologically advanced society, the United States. The function of a social system, therefore, is to recognize, and organize, the social relationships between men according to these needs. Similarly, the best social system for humanity should satisfy man's *primary* needs and should have a progressive nature so as to keep in touch with the development of society in attempting to satisfy the *secondary* needs.[210]

At the unity stage, humanity was considered in the <u>Quran</u> as one nation, as men lived together in harmony:

The people were one nation; then God sent forth the Prophets, good

---

[207]Sadr, <u>Khalafat,</u> 152-153.

[208]Sadr, <u>Iqtisaduna</u> (Our Economics), 14th ed. (Beirut: al-Taᶜaruf, 1981), 338.

[209]Ibid., 338.

[210]Sadr, <u>Iqtisaduna,</u> 339.

tidings to bear and warning, and He sent down with them the Book with the truth, that He might decide between the people touching their differences; and only those [people] had been given it were at variance upon it, after the clear signs had come to them, being insolent one to another; then God guided those who believed to the truth, touching which they were at variance, by His leave; and God guides whomsoever He will to a straight path.(2:213)[211]

Mankind were only one nation, then they fell into variance. But for a ward that preceded from thy Lord, it had been decided between them already touching their differences.(10:19)[212]

Man at this stage had not yet formed a state, and the social units that he formed were free of any form of social exploitations.[213] He was guided by the Divine knowledge, distinguishing between good and evil and refraining from the latter. The simplicity of life made his livelihood needs and expectations simple. The faculties that God implanted in man's nature (fitra) enabled him to form a monotheistic society that adhered to the worship of God alone, which meant, in practical terms, the rejection of nondivine standards of behavior and of deviation from the role of vicar of God on earth. The social responsibilities in these social units were performed by all members, and even messengers of God did not have special hierarchical privileges. They functioned only as guides and advisors.[214] The commitment to the guidance of God was the only security that kept these social units, in that historical stage, in tranquility. There was no need for political leadership or any form of social enforcement agencies in order for man to conform to a certain course of behavior. It was only deviation from God's way-of-life that would endanger the survival of a peaceful and just society:

So set thy face to the religion, a man of pure faith--God's original (fitra) upon which He originated mankind. There is no changing God's creation. That is the right religion; but most men know it not--turning to Him. And fear you Him, and preform the prayer, and be not of the idolaters, even of those who have divided up their religion, and become sects, each several party rejoicing in what is theirs.(30:30-31)[215]

[211]The Koran, trans. Arberry, 56-57.

[212]The Koran, trans. Arberry, 226.

[213]Sadr, Lamha fiqhiyah Hawla Dustur al-Jumhuriyah al-Islamiyah, published in al-Islam Yaqwod al-Hayat 4-5.

[214]Sadr, Khalafat, 152.

[215]The Koran, trans. Arberry, 108.

The third stage started with the rise of differences between people. Men, by nature, possess different capabilities and talents. The complexity of the social life gave growth to livelihood needs, which resulted in the uneven distribution of goods and possessions between people. Men with extra talents and more physical powers gained the upper hand in social relations, and began to exploit others who were weak or had fewer talents to acquire the material goods.[216] A contradiction in social life, which took the form of oppression by the powerful few of the weak, became the major phenomenon of this historical stage. The oppression took different forms with various degrees of intensity, but the social contradiction lasted through all ages and generations and permeated various types of social systems.

Sadr differs from Marx on the origin of the social contradiction. Marx relates the contradiction to the growth of means of production. The development of each new means of production gives rise to new social relations and thus to a new type of exploitation, one class of the society exploiting another class. So, "the handmill gives you society with the feudal lord; the steam-mill, society with the industrial capitalist."[217] In other words, the contradiction originates in the economic environment in which man lives. The people who possess, or have access to, the means of production have full control over social relations and social arrangements. In order to change the social arrangement and end the exploitation of the many, one must take from the few their access to the means of production and allot it to the society as a whole. In sum, the historical development of societies is tantamount to the development of its economic conditions; the social revolution is the abolition of ownership of capital by the elite class of a society.

Although Sadr pictured the rise of contradictions in the social relations as due to the changing economic conditions of the society, he regarded the real cause behind it not as consisting of external-environmental conditions, but rather as resting within man himself. Man is not always the product of his environment, but the environment is shaped by his activities. The development of economic conditions is his doing, and social relationships are developed and organized to meet his needs. It was his intellectual and physical capabilities that made it possible for man to advance his living conditions. Without these faculties, the external conditions would have stayed the same since the dawn of history. The reason behind the rise of the social contradiction is that man deviated from the way-of-God.

The changes in the conditions surrounding man would only serve as instigators of man's mental capabilities. They act as 'raw materials' for the human brain to work on. Change of environmental conditions gives man the ability to develop new tools or means of production to counteract the effects of the changing conditions. Consequently,

[216]Sadr, _Lamha_, 4.

[217]Karl Marx, _The Poverty of Philosophy_, 109.

...the natural forces of production do not, by themselves, reach their [state of] perfection and growth, or quicken their development and maturation, but rather they only instigate the senses and the thinking of man. Their natural development, thus, is not [the result of a] dialectical process, and the positive effect [i.e., the emancipation of life] does not emerge out of this development. Rather, the forces of production are governed by an historical factor that is superior to them.[218]

The superior factor, according to Sadr, is the human mental faculty. If production itself, in the Marxist definition, "is natural activity against the environment, performed by many people to satisfy their materialist needs, and where the social relations become its natural outcome"[219] then the whole process of production must have been preceded by two factors: thought and language. Thought (fikr) allows the human being to change the nature of his environment to meet his needs, e.g., from wheat to flour to bread. Unless there is such a faculty, we cannot suppose man would respond to the new changes in the environment. Animals, for instance, are not able to effect radical change in the environment.[220] Language, as the physical (phonic) side of thinking (fikr), allowed the participant in the production activity to communicate, and thus facilitated the development of production. Language itself is not the natural outcome of economic conditions as are social relationships, but is rather the outcome of needs to exchange views and thoughts. "We don't find one Marxist --not even Stalin-- who would dare to say that the Russian language for example had changed [or developed] after the socialist revolution to a new one."[221] Hence, the primary factor behind the contradictions that exist in society is, according to Sadr, not the changing economical conditions (forces of productions) but rather the contradictions within man himself.

At this historical stage, man had deviated from his fitra and started abusing his talents and power to oppress and alienate others. His deviation led him to adopt a new kind of worship and turn away from his creator. Once there was no control over his behavior, he fell deeply into sin, and social corruption grew. The society, once a coherent and harmonious entity, became divided and conflict-ridden. Classes and groups opposed each other. The social dilemma was that the powerful would get even more powerful, and thus more corrupt and abusive, while the weak became more weak and subject to more oppression. In general, the history of mankind during this period was a struggle between these two groups. The historical process can be defined between two poles of political

[218]Sadr, Iqtisaduna, 108.

[219]Ibid.

[220]Sadr, Iqtisaduna, 109.

[221]Ibid., 109.

thinking, those who would like to protect their interests and keep the existing system of alienation indefinitely and those who would like to revolt and change the existing oppressive system of social relations with a just one.

The natural course of action for the deprived and weak was to lead a revolution against the corrupt and oppressive political regimes. The history of revolutions, according to Sadr, has taken two different routes to confront the unjust social structure.[222] The first type are revolutions that advocate the elimination of materialistic forms of oppression in the society. They are considered forms of alienation which the oppressed encounter every day. These feelings of the masses (that they are underprivileged) lead them first to a silent opposition. When oppression continues, they organize their effort in vocal political movements that give force to their demands upon the system. These groups eventually resort to violent actions when all other means are exhausted. Revolutions of this type of movement mobilize masses on the basis that a new system would transfer the wealth and resources to all members of society and eliminate special privileges for the upper and dominate classes. However, such revolutions, while concerned about certain kinds of social needs, are short-sighted. The masses would continue to face other forms of alienation in the post-revolutionary system. The oppressed of yesterday would become the master, and thus, the oppressor of today. The whole historical process would repeat itself. Thus, "the revolution would only change the position of exploitation, but would not accomplish the elimination of it."[223] That is why Marx probably thought there is a dialectic process in history where each rising class resorts to oppressive measures and means to protect its interests against other groups, i.e., every thesis gives rise to an antithesis.

The second type of revolutionary process is one that tries to eliminate the source of alienation and does not merely emphasize elimination of its materialistic contradictions.[224] It is a revolution that would resort to the creation of new social values that would put an end to all sources of exploitation. The revolution would advocate the values of justice, righteousness and equality that stem from belief in God is the only revolution that would secure man from the domination and the exploitation of other powers. It is the total surrender of man to God that would free him from surrendering to others. When the revolution advocates the equality of all people, it must be on the basis that all are equal before God and no one group has special rights with respect to others. When revolutionaries try to eliminate the means of control of the dominate group it is not because of a belief that they do not have the right to reign, but because all people have an equal right to govern before God and act as His vicar on earth. Sadr called the latter type of revolution the 'real

---

[222]Sadr, _Khalafat_, 156.

[223]Sadr, _Khalafat_, 157.

[224]Ibid., 157.

revolution' (<u>thawrah haqiqiyah</u>) and the former the 'relative revolution' (<u>thawrah nisbiyah</u>).[225]

Prophets and messengers of God were the pioneers to lead the struggle for the latter type of social revolution. The divine missions of prophethood had the complete answer to the social problems facing man. Unlike other social movements in history, the purpose of prophethood was not to wither away social contradiction (the facade of the problem) but to solve the inner contradiction of man. The revolutions and the messages of prophets were concerned with eliminating the alienation of man, and also helping him to overcome the psychological tendency of oppression of his human nature.

On the social level, God sent his messengers with codes of law that would put an end to the alienation, and eliminate the oppression of man. For this reason, prophets led social revolutions of the oppressed against the oppressors. Throughout history, the followers of all prophets were from the deprived classes.

And We sent not unto any township a warner, but its pampered ones declared: Lo! we are disbelievers in that which ye bring unto us.(34:34)[226]

Even so We sent never before thee (Muhammad) any warner into any city, except that its men who lived at ease said, 'We indeed found our fathers [follow upon certain trend], and we are following upon their traces.(43:32)[227]

Said the Council of the unbelievers of his [Noah] people, 'We see thee not other than a mortal like ourselves, and we see not any following thee but the vilest of us, inconsiderately. We don't see you have over us any superiority; no, rather we think you are liars.'(11:27)[228]

The message of the prophets (and religions) became the cry of the oppressed for generations that followed them. The great religions of the world, e.g., Christianity and Islam, were embraced by the deprived and the poor and were opposed from the start by the elite.[229] The prophets' concern was the liberation of man from his sins and from his unjust social environment. The goal of the prophets was to create a just social system that protects the rights of every individual within the social structure. Hence, "the idea of the state originated

---

[225]Sadr, <u>Khalafat</u>, 158.

[226]<u>The Glorious Quran</u>, trans. M. M. Pickthall, 456.

[227]<u>The Koran</u>, trans. Arberry, 200.

[228]<u>The Koran</u>, 242.

[229]Sadr, <u>Iqtisaduna</u>, 116.

[first] with the prophets, whose main role was to establish a flawless state whose structure and principles were founded by God, the most High."[230] The reason behind the revelation of religion that contains shari^ca, or cannon laws, was to lay the ground for the formation of a political system that would end all forms of human oppression and alienation. That is why Sadr considers the Prophet Nuh (Biblical name, Noah) as the first advocate and the founder of a political state. His message was the first universal religion that had elaborated a shari^ca (codes of laws) to govern people. In every epoch of history, God reveals his commands and message to prophets as a basis for social conduct. The great universal Divine messages to Ibrahim (Abraham), Musa (Moses), ^cIsa (Jesus) and Muhammad were to be the higher (constitutional) laws of political states.

On the personal level, prophets were to refine human behavior according to man's fitra (inner knowledge). Man was driven by his passions and self-love into sinful action and social corruption. Unless man could be liberated from his tendency toward evil behavior, then all efforts at eliminating social injustice would be impotent. Without freeing man from his sins, social injustice would soon be replaced by new forms of social injustice. The prophetic message carried the spiritual guidelines that would purify human nature. Man would be in constant struggle against his sins. He would be trained to lead the fight against his corrupt desires and excessive passions. The prophetic mission would make man responsible for his actions before divine authority. Such divine guidance is the only control mechanism that would prevent man from exploiting his fellow man.

The prophets have led the struggle against injustice on two levels: the greater (or more precisely, fundamental) struggle (jihad al-Akbar) to confront man's inner passions and corrupt tendency, and the lesser (or minor) struggle (jihad al-asghar) to eliminate the manifestation of personal corruption in the society.[231] Prophets directed their followers to rotate the battle fields of struggle from self to society, and from society to self. This is the only way, according to Sadr, for humanity to eliminate all forms of exploitations and oppression. The prophets throughout history were the source of *real* social revolution when they led the struggle against corruption in society, and the corruption in the human self. Hence, he plainly affirms that,

> ..we believe that it is not possible for the *real* revolution (emphasis added) to be disassociated from revelation and prophethood, and their extension in history of mankind; similarly, that it is not possible for prophethood and Divine message in any way to be detached from the social revolution against exploitation, opulence, and oppression.[232]

---

[230]Sadr, Lamha, 5.

[231]Sadr, Khalafat, 159-160.

[232]Sadr, Khalafat, 160.

Development of Historical Process

The historical process is a social affair where the main participants (or elements) are man, nature, and God.[233] They correspond to the three types of historical laws (sunan) mentioned above: voluntaristic, naturalistic, and deterministic, respectively. Though other social theories had recognized only the first two elements, Sadr thought that their shortcoming stems from the fact that history itself is kalimah (literally, word; meaning creation) of God. Without including the role of God in history, our understanding of the process of historical development is meaningless. Sadr, hence, recognizes three type of relations man would be bound to: 1) social relations between man; 2) economic relations between man and nature; 3) vicarage (estikhlaf)/religious relations between man and God. It is the last type of relation that makes his Islamic theory superior to non-Islamic theories. Historical process is the byproduct of this relationship. While the positivist theory of man would only recognize the effect of economic relationship on the social one, or vice versa, Sadr discloses the effects of the third relationship on the other two. He claims that the failure of man-made theories to solve the social problems facing man throughout history is due to their discounting of the prime dynamism of the historical process, which has a direct effect on man's life. To illustrate Sadr's point of view, I will explain two interpretations of historical development from social and economic aspects.

Ibn Khaldun is considered the first to give a theory of the historical development of man from the standpoint of his social relationship. The major concern of his Muqaddimah is the study of the rise and fall of dynasties, which he thought "has a natural term of life like the individual."[234] He traced the strength of the dynasty to the blood ties and family traditions which bound members to the state and created a sense of solidarity and mutual responsibility which he called, ʿasabiyah.[235] At the first stage, the formation of the dynasty, a primitive tribal ʿasabiyah --that of the first wave of uncivilized nomad tribes bent on domination-- is at its peak. These tribes eventually achieve their objective of seizing power over the cities and establishing their dynasty. In the second phase, the dynasty would become a sovereign political state, where the ruler would govern his people according to his will, and not according to the mutual consent of his followers. "The third phase is one of quiet ease and leisure to gather the fruits of the rule and dominion, since human nature tends

---

[233]Sadr, Muqaddamat, 104.

[234]Quoted in Erwin I. J. Rosenthal, Political Thought in Medieval Islam, An Intoductory Outline (Cambridge: Cambridge University Press, 1962), 88.

[235]Ibid., 87.

to acquire wealth and leave behind... fame."[236] At this time the sovereign would regulate taxes and impose new civil rules to govern people instead of relying upon the communal solidarity of ᶜasabiyah. He becomes careless about the welfare of his followers, and increasingly concerned with his own leisure, building palaces and stocking his treasury with the wealth of his people. "The fourth phase is one of extravagance and waste."[237] The corruption of the ruler becomes widespread and taxes on the people are increased to finance his lust for pleasure. The civil laws become the norms that govern the society, not the strong bond of ᶜasabiyah. The tradition of solidarity is weakened. People become divided into factions and have little interest in defending the dynasty. The ruler has a standing army to do the job. In the fifth phase, the whole system shows signs of decay. The rulers are more corrupt and may even spend part of his army's pay for his own pleasure. This weakens his troops' desire to defend the state. Subjects of the dynasty are busy with their own daily affairs and survival. There is nothing bonding them to the state. By then, "the ᶜasabiyah collapses completely, and they forget about the defense of their dynasty against attacks of the enemy."[238] The dynasty is open for invasion by a new nomadic group.

The cyclical process of historical development of Ibn Khaldun emphasizes the importance of the social relationship for the survival of political entities, thus considered by him as the prime mechanism that shapes history. He was a pioneer in showing the effect of economics on the strength of the social solidarity of the people.

Rousseau had reached the same conclusion that the social relation is negatively influenced by the economic relationship, but he looked at the problem from a different perspective. He viewed the 'state of nature' as a harmonious social affair, where man lived in nature and exploited its resources with other men in a cooperative way. Life, then, was not threatening, and man thus did not have an aggressive attitude toward other men and nature. He was governed by his inner feelings, instincts, and impressions, which made him a patient and compassionate creature with empathetic feelings toward other men. He does not calculate personal advantage in dealing with his fellow men, and his social relations are based on seeking approval from them. It is private property that made man think about his self-interests and his personal welfare instead of the welfare of his community. Once he built a fence around his property and was willing to defend it, then the social phenomenon of haves and have-nots started to take shape and became an acceptable norm in human relationships.

The basic characteristic of civil society is inequality of ownership. Private property came into existence as an historical accident and it has subsequently shaped the mentality

---

[236]Rosenthal, _Political Thought_, 89.

[237]Rosenthal, _Political Thought_, 89.

[238]Ibid., 88.

and relationships of mankind. On the psychological level, it has introduced greed, and made human beings calculating, and aggressive and rational creatures. On the social level, it has divided human society into various classes of haves and have-nots where the former exploits the latter. Therefore, Rousseau concludes that the consequences of private property are all negative. It made slaves of every one; even the owners are slaves to their greed and to their property. To elevate human beings above such unhealthy and destructive relations, man must abolish private property, i.e, transform the civil society into 'the state of nature.'

Marx, while making use of Rousseau's analysis of historical development, did not agree with his conclusion. Although private property has negative consequences for human relationships, it is the prime factor of historical development. History, according to dialectical materialism, is a progressive process that centers around the ownership of property, but leads eventually to the abolition of private ownership by social ownership. In this way, according to the Marxist view, negative effects of materialism are eliminated while producing the essential positive effects.

While Sadr confirms that there are effects of the social and economical relationship on the process of historical development, he thinks that they do not subsume the whole process. It is man's relationship to God that ultimately explains the development of history. Sadr considers man as the sole agent in the shaping of the course of history, because only man can strengthen or weaken the vicarage relationship. Man commits to or deviates from the divine purpose of his existence.[239] The social and economic structure in any society is the by-product of his deeds. Sadr, therefore, differs from the Marxist view, which considers the superstructure of the society (i.e., the state, economic relations, values, culture, laws and knowledge) as the manifestations of material conditions. Sadr, then, asks what is inside man that makes the outcome of historical development different from one society to another, and from one epoch to the next? His answer is al-mathal al-aᶜla (the ideal, or the ultimate goal), which defines the purpose that social action seeks to achieve during its life span.[240] It is derived from people's views about life and nature, that is, from a socially determinate view. Social policy would be only the reflection of this al-mathal al-aᶜla, and the community's life, values, and temporary goals would be a determinant of it. "To the degree that al-mathal al-aᶜla of the social group is righteous, superior, and comprehensive the social goals will be right, and comprehensive; and to the degree that al-mathal al-aᶜla is limited, and low the goals derived from it would be limited and subdued too... So when any group chooses a al-mathal al-aᶜla, it has in fact determined its goals, means and the drawbacks of achieving such goals through those means."[241]

---

[239]Sadr, Muqaddamat, 116.

[240]Sadr, Muqaddimat, 120.

[241]Ibid., 120-121.

Sadr specified three types of <u>al-mathal al-aᶜla</u>. The first is that which reflects the environment and the conditions people experienced in their life.[242] In other words, it is the present condition (with all its limitations and faults) that shapes the future of a people. This 'conservative' <u>mathal aᶜla</u> (as I call it) would halt the progress and development of history. It would make the future a repetition of the past, and form out of the relative and limited standards and values an ultimate goal. In fact, the commitment to a conservative <u>mathal aᶜla</u> can be considered an act of suicide for a social group. It would lead to a degeneration of society or nation because it would not give it the opportunity and moral energy to develop the socioeconomic resources, or to mobilize the talents of its members.

However, why would any society determine to go in this historical route and choose its own demise? Sadr states two reasons for such a suicidal social mission: First is a psychological reason where people are accustomed to their way of life, praise their condition and are protective of what they have.[243] A member of the society becomes the product of his environment, and is unwilling to change. His social environment has made of him an empiricist, not a rational being; thus he lives for the day and cannot foresee any progress in the future. The <u>Quran</u> describes such an attitude:

> .. We follow that wherein we found our fathers. What! Even though their fathers were wholly unintelligent and had no guidance?(2:170)[244]

> .. they say: Enough for us is what is that wherein we found our fathers. What! even though their fathers had no knowledge whatsoever, and no guidance?(5:104)[245]

Second is a social reason where an authoritarian and tyrannical rule would impose standards and goals on the people to shape and mold the society according to its will for the survival of the regime itself.[246] The survival of such a type of a social system throughout history is critical. Because of this sensitivity, the political ruler or elite tries to resist any changes within the existing social norms which might bring a challenge to his reign. The <u>Quran</u> mentions such social dilemmas:

> And Pharaoh said, 'Council, I know not that you have any god but me.(28:38)[247]

---

[242]Ibid., 122.

[243]Sadr, <u>Muqaddimat</u>, 123.

[244]<u>The Glorious Quran</u>, trans. Pickthall, 26.

[245]<u>The Glorious Quran</u>, 116.

[246]Sadr, <u>Muqaddimat</u>, 125-126.

> Said Pharaoh, 'I only let you see what I see; I only guide you in the
> way of rectitude.(40:29)[248]

In reality, the ruler himself or the political regime becomes <u>al-mathal al-a^cla</u> per se. The goal is to prevent the realization of an alternative <u>mathal a^cla</u> that would transform the present circumstance into a completely different future that would eventually culminate in the withering away (to use Engles' term) of the existing political system.

The historical consequence of the conservative <u>mathal a^cla</u> is the gradual decaying of the society and the waste of its resources. No solidarity emerges that unites people together, producing goals that articulate their resources and opening up a future that is worth struggling to achieve. Rather, the social system is doomed to collapse. Sadr lists three possibilities that would bring about the ultimate termination of such a society:

1) a military invasion by a foreign power that cannot be resisted by scattered social resources.[249] The will of the people had long dwindled, having been wasted upon the immediate concerns of daily-life. A good example of such a case is the Mongol occupation of Muslim territories and the subsequence collapse of the Muslim Empire. The ^cAbbasid state was not able to muster a strong resistance to the invasions.

2) the intellectual encroachment of a foreign ideal and the adaptation of foreign <u>mathal a^cla</u> to bring about the revival of society.[250] The people by then have lost their identity and do not believe in their capacity to survive, as they become the shadow of another society. Sadr cited the example of Muslim appropriation of western values and the Western <u>mathal a^cla</u> and their satisfaction at being the peripheries of Western civilization. Notable instances of this are the regimes of Reza Shah of Iran and Mustafa Kamal Ataturk of Turkey, which attempted to foist the ideals of European man on their countries.[251]

3) the emergence of a new <u>mathal a^cla</u> that would put an end to the old political and social structure and bring about a new system to satisfy the immediate needs of the society and delay its eventual death.[252] Example of this type are the leaders of the Islamic revival movement such as Jamal al-Din Afghani and Muhammad ^cAbduh who, at the beginning of the twentieth century, tried to introduce a new <u>mathal a^cla</u> that would re-created the new

---

[247]<u>The Koran</u>, trans. Arbarry, 90.

[248]Ibid., v. II, 178.

[249]Sadr, <u>Muqaddimat</u>, 134.

[250]Ibid., 134-135.

[251]Sadr, <u>Muqaddimat</u>, 135.

[252]Ibid., 135

Muslim <u>Ummah</u> out of the ashes of the Ottoman Empire.

The second type of <u>al-mathal al-aᶜla</u> is that derived from futuristic ambition of a people. This 'utopian' <u>mathal aᶜla</u> (as I call it) is not a carbon-copy of the present conditions as in the first case. Rather it drives the nation towards development and progress. The members of the society are striving for a better future, for change of their present conditions, and for accomplishing certain goals. Such a society is looking for an advanced and utopian state.

However, the short-sighted vision of the society would not produce a utopia in a meaningful sense of providing a solution to the human problem. The mental capacity of man is limited, and therefore, unable to visualize the ultimate goal. The conditions he thought of as paradise would soon be discovered to be imperfect. Though such a <u>mathal aᶜla</u> can mobilize the people into challenging their values and environment and utilizing their resources in the production of improved material conditions, and motivate their effort to a powerful historical movement, the social achievement would be for a limited time only. The capacity to grow is proportionately related to the capacity of <u>al-mathal al-aᶜla</u> to picture the reality of the future. Man soon would achieve his goal, and the <u>mathal al-aᶜla</u> would stagnate and eventually kill the achievement because the utopian conditions proposed by the <u>mathal al-aᶜla</u> have become living circumstances. It would eventually be a 'conservative' <u>mathal aᶜla</u> that halts progress, and the people committed to its stagnating principles face the same historical determinism.

Sadr identified two ways in which a utopian man-made <u>mathal aᶜla</u> fails to visualize the ultimate state of affairs and make valid generalizations about the future outcome:

1) Failure in 'horizontal generalization'(or prediction of conditions). Man visualizes his future from the circumstances he faces and will rebel against everything that is linked in one way or the other to his present environment. Rousseau's man, 'born free, but everywhere in chains,' would strive to break all of them. He is on the march to create a new world that is unrelated to his past and in opposition to its values and principles. The Enlightenment movement of eighteenth century Europe is an example of this phenomenon. The European man, suffering from religious persecution of the church, economic exploitation of feudalism, and political oppression of the monarchies, was determined to gain freedom from all those impairments. However, he later discovered that he had created a monster out of human nature by the new unbound and unlimited forms of freedom. When moral standards were abolished, values became relative, and every cruel action got some kind of justification. Hence capitalist democracies failed to produce a utopia for Western man. The result is a political system controlled by big capitalists. The society is wounded by moral ailments, as people adhere to amoral political ideologies, and workers all over the world are severely exploited by the new economic system.[253]

---

[253]Sadr, <u>Our Philosophy</u>, trans. Shams C. Inati, (London,

2) Failure of 'temporal generalization' (or prediction of a future epoch). Man, while rejecting the ills of the existing social conditions, may adhere to his vision of a splendid social situation in the future, i.e., the invention of a utopian social state. Marxists of nineteenth century Europe, for example, who had witnessed the failures of their social systems, proposed the utopia of communism. However the socialist movement in Russia and China may claim the success of their experiments on many levels, they are witnessing that the utopia that have promised is all an illusion. If Sadr had lived to witness the recent transformation in Eastern Europe, he would have seen his historical analysis of ill-fated man-made utopias come true. His prediction was that such man-made forecasts of the future would soon be exhausted and were doomed to failure. Man may predict discrete events in time but he cannot envision the whole historical process, only God can. Part of Marx's failure in making an accurate prediction, Sadr explained, is that his thought is limited to his experience of the social system in Europe. Hence, his analysis and prediction would be limited to his case study. A man's mentality cannot transcend beyond his environment when making futuristic predictions.

So the second type of man-made mathal aᶜla would also bring an end to the survival of society. Since the gains of the mathal al-aᶜla are transient, the society would find itself in the midst of a stagnate situation that consumes all previous social advancement. The Quran narrates the outcome of such a situation:

> And as for the unbelievers, their works are as a mirage in a spacious
> plain which the man athirst supposes to be water, till, when he comes to it,
> he finds it is nothing; there indeed he finds God.(24:39)[254]

> The likeness of those who have taken to them protectors, apart from
> God, is as the likeness of the spider that takes to itself a house; and surely the
> frailest of houses is the house of the spider, did they but know.(29:41)[255]

Sadr, furthermore, gives an account of the stages of stagnation of the society that went through the adaptation of a 'utopian' mathal aᶜla. At first the society would grow and develop rapidly since the mathal al-aᶜla is truly the outcome of people's aspiring to of a better future.[256] However the span of development is short-lived, and the gains are limited. Time would pass too quickly to achieve the goals prescribed by the al-mathal al-aᶜla. The Quran calls the period of prosperity al-ᶜajl (the immediate, or hasty world) because the gains are not long

---

Muhammadi Trust, 1987), 11-14.

[254]The Koran, trans. Arbarry, v. II, 50.

[255]Ibid., v. II, 101.

[256]Sadr, Muqaddimat, 143.

lasting:

> Whosoever desires this hasty world, We hasten for him therein what We will unto whomsoever We desire; then We appoint for him [hell] wherein he shall roast, condemned and rejected. And whosoever desires the world to come and strives after it as he should, being a believer--those, their striving shall be thanked. Each We secure, these and those, from thy Lord's gift; and thy Lord's gift is not confined.(17:18-20)[257]

The second stage starts when the dynamism of al-mathal al-aᶜla become static, and is not able to entice people to participate. They have found that the utopian situation is not real.[258] The mathal al-aᶜla cannot deliver new promises so as to make the society believe again in future paradise. The stagnation, thus, transforms the *ideal* into an *idol*, the leaders into masters and sovereigns, and the people into followers but not participants in progress and development. The third stage is only a continuation of the stagnation of the mathal al-aᶜla where the society is divided into two distinct groups: an elite governing class with one purpose in mind, which is to keep and protect its privileges, being careless about the future of the society; and at the bottom a divided mass that neither has hope in its future or in the social system.[259] The last stage is where the 'criminals' would take over the leadership positions to bring about the final destruction and immediate death of the society.[260] The Quran has a reference to those criminal-leaders with no moral quality and indifferent about the survival of the society:

> And thus have We made in every city great ones of its wicked ones,
> that they should plot therein. They do but plot against themselves, though
> they perceive not.(6:123)[261]

One nation Sadr refers to as an example of his cycle of the rise and fall of nations that adopt the second 'utopian' mathal aᶜla is Germany.[262] The German nationalism in few decades had delivered its promises of building a great nation-state. However the idealism of national solidarity of the German people, when achieved, made an idol of the Aryan people, which was considered the superior race. By then, the German people who felt lost in their historical

---

[257]The Koran, v. I, 302.

[258]Sadr, Muqaddimat, 144-145.

[259]Sadr, Muqaddimat, 145.

[260]Ibid., 145-146.

[261]The Glorious Quran, 136.

[262]Sadr, Muqaddimat, 146.

mission and could envision no future to their lives became indifferent about their social system and their leaders. It was easy then for criminals like the Nazis to seize power in Germany. While mobilizing people around the idol, the Nazis were able to deliver final destruction not to the German nation alone, but to modern European civilization that was built around the idol of nationalism.

The third type of <u>al-mathal al-aᶜla</u>, according to Sadr, is the 'real' one. The <u>mathal al-aᶜla</u> is actually Allah himself. The mission of mankind in earth is to work toward the ultimate, that is God.[263]

> O Man! Thou art laboring unto thy Lord laboriously, and thou shalt encounter Him.(84:6)[264]

Here, Sadr argues that religion, or the divine utopia, is only the means for the long historical process of man's ascendancy to God. It is religion and utopian social order that make it possible for man to progress spiritually and physically. Since God is the ultimate in existence, therefore, man's mission is a progressive one to achieve higher value. The mission is also a divine patterning of the historical process, which cannot be avoided by man. Thus, all mankind is part of a historical process regardless of their immediate goals and the temporal missions that have embraced in life. Nations may adopt a different <u>mathal aᶜla</u>, groups may resist change, men may have alternate goals in life or disbelieve in God, but the whole historical mission is directed towards God. God in this case represents the end of everything, as He was the beginning of everything. This ultimate end is not a geographical or historical end.[265] God is the ultimate and the absolute of existence, which means he is everywhere and anywhere. Man cannot achieve the ultimacy of God, but encounters Him at any moment or point at which man might decide to halt his mission. Encountering God is relative to where man (who is the limited) cannot achieve the ultimate and the absolute. Hence, the progress of his historical development is not limited at all.

Man may progress toward God in two ways: He may be fully aware of the mission and its goal, or he may be ignorant of the historical development and be proceeding towards Him without his determination. The former is called by Sadr *responsible progress*, and the latter *irresponsible progress*.[266] Irresponsible progress is when man adopts a <u>mathal al-ᶜala</u> in his life other than God. Responsible progress is known in <u>Fiqh</u> as the act of worship, or the submission of man to God and following his guidance. Such submission would make man compatible to progress of the historical process.

---

[263]Sadr, <u>Muqaddimat</u>, 148-149.

[264]<u>The Koran</u>, v.II, 331.

[265]Sadr, <u>Muqaddimat</u>, 150-151.

[266]Ibid., 150.

Responsible progress will have a positive impact on man. On the one hand, it will open the opportunity for continuous development and growth and achievement. There are no limits to that progress or to temporal goals that can be achieved at any point in history.[267] Man will, in discharging his mission and duty toward the ultimate, to be in a constant struggle to abolish all idols and other mathal a^clas that impede his progress. There are no boundaries or limits for man's development, and no historical stages of stagnation during the mission.

On the other hand, the responsible undertaking of the God-given mission would put an end to the contradictions facing man in his social life. The source of these contradictions is neither the economic relationship nor the social relationship, but rather, according to Sadr, man himself. Man will have the responsibility to account for his deeds before God. Such accountability to his All Powerful Lord will end all forms of oppression by man of man. Other mathal a^clas also create some forms of accountability, such as laws, norms or moral values that make man responsible before different social authorities; but their effectiveness is limited because man always finds a way to avoid his responsibilities. However, the case of accountability before God is not a contingent he can escape. In the latter case, the responsibility is not accidental, but rather an essential and continuous one aimed at eliminating the contradiction within man himself, which is the source of all forms of oppression in the social setting.

Man by creation is formed from part of earth and part of God, the soul.[268] The former part inclines him towards fulfilling his passions. In order to satisfy his sensual needs to the maximum, man is willing to oppress others. The latter part will make him ascend to the ultimate, beyond his earthly needs. He will search for the attributes of God, for His justices, His mercy, His beauty, and His knowledge, to the rest of the one hundred attributes of God. His role is to be the vicar of God, not to resemble animals. Thus, the purpose of the religion of God is to give man the ability to restrain his inner passions from getting out of control and harming others so as to establish a divine utopia on earth and not a jungle. Therefore, the only way to constrain his animalistic features is to make him accountable to the All-Seeing, All-Hearing.

In sum, Sadr concluded that monotheistic (tawhid) religion is the only mathal a^cla that could give man the potential to progress throughout history and end the contradiction of mankind.[269] The attribute of God's justice represents the ideal on which man should model his relations on earth. Moreover, the belief in the Day of Judgment would give the spiritual power to man to restrain his passions and make him fully responsible for his deeds before

---

[267]Sadr, Muqaddimat, 154.

[268]Sadr, Muqaddimat, 156.

[269]Ibid., 160-167.

God. Meanwhile, God would reveal his message to mankind through prophets. They guide man in his mission under God and safe-guard his historical development. Finally, the Imams would lead the struggle of mankind against all forms of idols and corrupt mathal aᶜlas that hinder the progress of man.

The Pattern of the Historical Process

Sadr interprets of the historical development as a complex process that takes different forms and involves multiple actors. However, the main factor that shapes history is man's adopted ideal, which he called al-mathal al-aᶜla. The rise and fall of civilization depend solely on the power of a mathal aᶜla to mobilize human energy and its ability to solve his contradiction. His conclusion is that the only mathal aᶜla that can guarantee the ever-lasting human progress is divine monotheistic religions revealed to divinely guided prophets. While other mathal aᶜlas might govern human progress, their impact in human history is short because their remedy to man's problems is not effective. In the meantime, human history is a process that functions according to God's blue-print. Man might curtail or speed up the process, but he cannot alter its direction. God not only made the dynamics of the process function in a certain fashion, but His will prevails.

History is a process in which the will of God or the power of his message do not endure. History is functioning according to man-made-mathal aᶜla that brought a constant reign of oppression to man, and there is no end in sight. Sadr asserts that God's final victory will prevail at the coming of the Mahdi (the messiah), who will rule the earth and establish a reign of justice and peace that will last to the Day of Judgment. The victory of righteousness over wickedness is a predetermined fact that will surely come about. The whole of human history is progressing toward the realization of God's will.

How is the mechanism of history thus functioning? One of God's laws that govern history is that oppression necessarily precedes the rise of just order. The Quran explicitly calls attention to such a fact: "So truly with hardship comes ease, truly with hardship comes ease."(94:5-6)[270] So the more severe the forms of oppression, the better the chance for justice to emerge victorious. Thus, the oppression would beget eventually its antithesis, to speak in Hegelian terms. The oppressive forms of relationships in human history will result in more demands and calls of justice and peace. Victory will come dialectically to the oppressed people. Since the oppressed people are always adopting a mathal aᶜla that is limited in its ability to solving human problems, while some forms of oppression are eliminated by human struggle and revolution, others will prevail. Throughout history many forms of oppression accumulate and are reinforced within the structure of human society. In the time that precedes the coming of Mahdi, the world will conform to the prophetic description of "full of oppression and tyranny." The dialectic outcome of this situation will

---

[270]The Koran, v.II, 331.

be the final victory of the forces of good and justice over all forces of oppression and tyranny. These forces led by the Mahdi will adhere to the message and the guidance of God and end once and for all the contradiction of man and set up the historical stage for the everlasting progress toward the eternity of the Absolute.

Sadr thinks that man would not only progress in his material condition then, but also would ascend beyond this physical world into the unseen world. The spiritual part of man will predominate over that part made of the 'dirt' of earth. Or put another way, the physical world will ascend in a progressive manner toward the spiritual world. Sadr seemed to believe in the al-harakah al-jawhariyah (substantial motion)[271] of Sadr al-Din Shirazi, a Muslim philosopher (d. 1640), in which the matter continues to develop to a higher state.[272] "Matter in its substantial movement pursues the completion of its existence and continues its completion, until it is free from its materiality [physical being] under specific conditions and becomes an immaterial [metaphysical] being - that is, a spiritual being."[273]

At the fourth historical stage (the Epoch of Justice of Mahdi's reign and beyond), man will progress, and his material being will develop to the state of an immaterial being. Such development will allow man to cross the dividing line between the material world and spiritual world. Sadr came up with this idea in his interpretation of the Shi^ca doctrine of raj^ca (The return of Holy Imams to rule the earth in the post-Mahdi era, prior to the Day of Judgment). Although this doctrine is not an essential part of Shi^ca belief, it is supported by many traditions (sayings) of the Prophets and Holy Imams.

Sadr interpreted the raj^ca, not as the return of the dead from the world of Barzakh (purgatory world after death and before Day-of-Judgment) to our world in a descending manner, but as an entirely different process: "...it is our world that will transcend and come close to the world beyond."[274] His idea is that once matter ascends to the spiritual world (the immaterial or Platonic world of 'forms') of the hereafter, it is not possible for it to return. It is during the Epoch of Justice that man will develop to the point where ascent to the metaphysical world is possible. At that point, Sadr explained, "we could say some of the

---

[271]On the substantial motion see Sadr's explanation on pages 175-6.

[272]On Shirazi, also known as Mula Sadra, see Encyclopedia of Philosophy, Sayyid Hussein Nasar, "Mula Sadra", v. 5., 413; also Abdullah Ne`ma, Falasifat al-Shi`ah, Hayatahum, Ara'ahum (The Shia's Philosophers, Their Lives, and Their Views) (Beirut: Maktabat al-Hyat, n.d), 346-368.

[273]Sadr, Our Philosophy, 280.

[274]al-Ha'iri quoting Sadr's view on Raj`a in "Tafsir," Al-Hiwar AL-Fikri Wa-al-Siyasi, v. 32 (Nov. 1985), 47.

dead return to life, and it is right to call this encounter <u>raj^ca</u>."[275] Therefore, the Holy Imams will lead the world in the post-Mahdi era because the physical and metaphysical worlds will intertwine.

Sadr discovers a different pattern of development in history, unlike the linear process of Christian thought which pictures history as moving between two events, from the creation to the Last Judgement. Though St. Augustine added other important events that influenced man's history, the basic linear process was kept in Christian thought. The coming of Christ, which is considered as God's act of redemption, had no effect on the development of man. The history of man is governed by his original sin, and his fall to the lower world on earth. The second coming of Christ will put an end to the city of man and establish the heavenly city of God which will enable man to transcend his original sin and return to God. However, this development is a progressive linear process of history, similar to that of the Enlightenment thinkers of eighteenth century Europe. While the Enlightenment philosophers thought the scientific revolution is the basic factor for man's development, St. Augustine thought that man overcoming his original sin of disobeying God's order is the reason for his development. In other words, the former thought that religion hinders the development of man, yet the latter thought otherwise, that religion is the salvation of man and the only cause for his development.

Sadr seemed to agree with St. Augustine's views about divinely revealed religion, but his interpretation of history takes into consideration a rise and fall connected with man's progressive trials. However these attempts are not in conflict with the grand design of God in the development of history. They function with the divine blue print, but do not constitute the whole mechanism of human history. Plato thought that there is a cycle of degeneration of the ideal state, the rule of the philosopher-king; first into temocracy, the rule of officers for the pursue of honor and prestige; then into oligarchy, the rule of aristocrats for the pursue of material interests; and into democracy, the rule of the masses for the pursue of their interests; and finally into tyranny, the rule of the corrupt one for his own interests. Ibn Khaldun's historical cycle, unlike Plato's, which is centered around the quality of the ruler, is centered around the solidarity of the social group that formed the political state. The degeneration of Plato's republic is caused by inferior educational background of the ruler, while Ibn Khaldun's monarchy is caused by growth of the economic life of the kingdom and the subsequent breakdown of <u>^casabiyah</u>. However, the cause of the degeneration of the progress of man, according to Sadr, is the limited efficacy of the <u>mathal al-a^cla</u> adopted by man.

Sadr's historical process is not cyclical; rather the dialectic of history looks like a spiral. At each point of ascension, a man-made <u>mathal a^cla</u> had brought an oppressive condition which caused man's progress to degenerate. However, out of these worsening

---

[275]Ibid., 47-48.

conditions, man would ascend to a new epoch of progress. Then a new cycle of rise and fall of human civilization will be repeated. In the meantime, the message of the Divine prophets gives the alternative <u>mathal a^cla</u> to mankind whereby man can end his misery and inner contradiction. While the prophets succeeded in revealing to man the solution to his social problems, the problems persisted because man did not commit himself to the implementation of the message. However, the messages of the Five Great Prophets (Nuh, Ibrahim, Musa, ^cIsa, and Muhammad) represent the five advancing periods in human history. Yet again, at each time man deviated from following the guidelines of the message, and went into a period of darkness, which is symbolized by oppression and conflicts. The hope for humanity will be in the coming of the Mahdi who will end the historical stage of diversification, and lead man into salvation and progress. Mahdi, therefore, is considered the fruit of human progress, and the conclusion of the historical process. Sadr eloquently expressed this metaphoric dream:

> The <u>Mahdi</u> is not an embodiment of the Islamic belief but he is also the symbol of an aspiration cherished by mankind irrespective of its divergent religious doctrines. He is also the crystallization of an instructive inspiration through which all people, regardless of their religious affiliations, have learnt to await a day when heavenly missions, with all their implications, will achieve their final goal and the tiring march of humanity across history will culminate satisfactory in peace and tranquility. This consciousness of the expected future has not been confined to those who believe in the supernatural phenomenon but has also been reflected in the ideologies and cult which totally deny the existence of what is imperceptible. For example, the dialectical materialism which interprets history on the basis of contradiction believes that a day will come when all contradictions will disappear and complete peace and tranquility will prevail.[276]

---

[276]Sadr, <u>The Awaited Savior</u> trans. of <u>Bahth Hawla al-Mahdi</u> by Mustajab A. Ansari (Karachi, Pakistan: Islamic Seminary Pub., 1979), 20.

The Nature of Man and Reality

> Surely We created man of the best stature
> Then We reduced him to the lowest of the low,
> Save those who believe and do good deeds.
>
> The <u>Quran</u>

In his interpretation of history, Sadr gives man a great role. While man has no influence in the final outcome of the historical development, he has an influence in delaying or speeding up the process. Man may adhere to the message of God and bring to existence a just state of the "city of God" (to borrow St. Augustine's term), or deviate from the grace of God and risk exposing himself to the misery of the unjust city of man. The question that might be asked is how man is capable of assuming such a great role in the historical process? Does he have the faculties to act as vicar of God on Earth? This question can be answered through the understanding of human nature, and the capacity of man to realize in the world around him the purpose of his great mission on earth.

The importance of epistemological questions is that they set the framework for the formation of the theory as a whole. When a theorist, for example, equates the whole of reality with the realm of the phenomenal world so that man can only discover this reality with the faculty of his senses, then he will conclude that moral values are relative, and that the goal of the political system is to satisfy the physical well-being of man. On the other hand, when reality is defined to include the metaphysical world, then the logical conclusion is that the theory will incorporate the view that there are universal moral values and that the goal of the political system is to achieve their implementation. This is why, in order for us to understand the political theory of Sadr, we must determine how he defines reality and human nature, for they are considered the substructure of the theory in general. This also will give us some indication as to whether Sadr's formulation of his theory is consistent with his epistemological assumptions. In the previous section of this chapter, Sadr has already set the agenda for his epistemological ideas. Man is a creature of God and is responsible before Him. The over-all historical process is divinely ordained, yet man has the free-will to change the course of its events. Therefore, reality according to Sadr includes metaphysical forms, and religious beliefs are part of human knowledge. This includes detailed analysis of these philosophical questions.

Human Knowledge

First of all, Sadr divides knowledge into two kinds: 1) conception (<u>tasawwar</u>), which represents the primary knowledge acquired by man and consist of the apprehension of particular forms and concepts; and 2) assertion (<u>tasdiq</u>), which represents any knowledge that involves making a judgement, thus relating concepts to each other.[277] There are two main philosophical schools regarding the sources of primary knowledge.

The empiricist school believes that "only sense perception supplies the human mind with concepts and ideas, and that mental power is that which reflects in the mind the various sense perceptions."[278] Human knowledge is nothing but a derivative of sense perception, while complex knowledge is either the combination or the division of these simple perceptions, or the ability of the mind to make abstractions or generalizations out of this perceptional knowledge. Senses are the only means for man to acquire knowledge from and about his surroundings. It is impossible to think of any source of knowledge other than sensory perceptions.

In general, what man sees, hears, touches and tests is recorded in the faculty of his brain. There he tries to make complex ideas out of these simple perceptions, such as imagining a mountain of gold out of his early witnessings of mountain and gold. He can also, through the faculty of his mind, deduce out of the enormous data recorded by the senses generalizations and universal ideas about his environment. It is the combination of these data that enables man to generate complex ideas and concepts, and build up theories. Human experience acts as the main source for human knowledge.

This is the philosophy developed by John Locke, the father of modern liberal democracy. Karl Marx, the founder of communism, developed Locke's ideas further.

Yet, if the mind is limited to the senses in acquiring knowledge, it would be impossible for man to form any advanced ideas that go beyond these simple perceptions. For example, empiricism has no explanation for the development of the notion of causality in the human mind. The empiricist school has no explanation as to how man can obtain the assertoric, synthetic knowledge from the simple knowledge acquired by the senses. To solve such a dilemma, David Hume had "rejected the principle of causality and attributed [the development of this complex idea] to the habit of the association of ideas."[279] What this means is that if events are repeated many times then human beings will have the idea of a relationship that links causes to effects, as, for example, in experiments where someone uses

---

[277]Sadr, <u>Our Philosophy</u>, trans. Shams C. Inati (London: Muhammadi Trust, 1987), 39.

[278]Sadr, <u>Our Philosophy</u>, 43.

[279]Sadr, <u>Our Philosophy</u>, 46.

trial and error to produce the same phenomenon until he concludes the cause-effect relationship. However, experimentation might tell us something about the sequence and succession of events or phenomena, Sadr argues, but it cannot reveal to us the understanding of the causes behind them. We might sense the increase of heat, followed by the boiling of water, but these perceived events say nothing about the relationship between the two. In that case, Hume's idea led empiricism to reject the comprehension of the objective reality surrounding us, since the principle of causality is the means available for the human mind to make 'sense' (so to speak) out of the factual perceptions.

The rational philosophical school, in contrast, believes that sense perceptions are not the only source of knowledge available for man, but that there is another source of knowledge within the innate nature of man. "[T]he human mind possesses ideas and conceptions that are not derived from the senses, but are fixed in the innermost being of the innate nature."[280] Hence, philosophers differ on the nature of these innate ideas and conceptions.

Descartes, on one hand, believes that they include the idea of God, of the self, and of matter and its natural characteristics such as extension and movements. On the other hand, Kant believes in the whole field of conceptual human knowledge and science, including the two forms of time and space, as well as his twelve categories of conceptual knowledge.

However, the integration of the human soul is different from the Platonic idea of the descent of the soul from the world of forms to the physical world we live in. According to Plato, mankind is in the process of remembering the ideas the soul was exposed to in the higher world.

The Islamic philosophical school of thought, according to Sadr, rejects the rationalist views and Plato's views that man is born with knowledge about reality in its idealist forms. It affirms, rather, that human beings at the moment of birth do not possess any ideas, no matter how clear or general.

> God brought you out of your mother's wombs when you did not
> know anything. He gave you hearing, vision and hearts, in the hope that you
> will be grateful.[281]

Muslim philosophers recognize two types of mental conceptions. First are the primary conceptions, which are the outcome of sensory perceptions of the physical world and form the simple ideas in the human mind. The more complicated ideas are innovatively constructed out of those simple ideas to form what is called the 'secondary conceptions,' such as imagining a man with two heads. "These new ideas fall outside the scope of the senses, even though they are derived and extracted from the ideas that are given to the mind and to thought by the senses."[282] This theory is called by Sadr the Dispossession Theory

---

[280]Sadr, _Our Philosophy_, 41.

[281]Sadr, _Our Philosophy_, 43.

(<u>Nazariyat al-Intiza^c</u>).[283]

In light of this theory, we can understand how the notion of cause and effect, substance and accident, existence and unity came about in the human mind. All of them are dispossessed notions that the mind invents in light of the sensible ideas.[284]

Man has the capacity to build up his data beyond the realm of sense perceptions. In modern terms, the human mind, unlike the computer, is capable of generating new data out of its original data bank obtained from the senses to further enhance his mental capacity.

Moreover, at the level of propositional (assertoric) knowledge, Islamic philosophers, according to Sadr, side with the rationalist school stating that man possesses innate forms of knowledge. For that matter, they divide human knowledge into two categories. First is the necessary knowledge, which needs no propositions to prove its validity. Rather, one finds it necessary to believe in them. Examples are the principle of causality, the principle of noncontradiction and the primary mathematical principles. These principles are undisputable truths that are shared by every human being. They act as the basis of the human mind from which new concepts and ideas are developed. It is hard to imagine that any idea can be derived without making reference to these principles. They are the building blocks of advancing human knowledge.

The second form of propositional knowledge is the 'discursive knowledge' such as the theoretical propositions validity and rests on previously established propositions. So the "making of a judgement in those propositions depends on the process of reasoning and derivation of the truth from prior truths that are clear as they are."[285] Based on this, Sadr argues that:

> the rational doctrine shows that the cornerstone of knowledge is the primary information [necessary knowledge]. On the basis of such information, the superstructures of human thought, referred to as 'secondary information' [discursive knowledge] are built.[286]

Thinking itself, according to Sadr, is nothing but a mental process to derive the superstructure from the substructure.[287] Without this innate knowledge, human beings

---

[282]Ibid., 47.

[283]Ibid., 46-47.

[284]Sadr, <u>Our Philosophy</u>, 47.

[285]Sadr, <u>Our Philosophy</u>, 48.

[286]Ibid., 49.

cannot come to an understanding of reality. Generally speaking, the senses are the source of the elementary and simple forms of knowledge. They function as the data for the human mind which, with the help of 'necessary knowledge,' can apprehend the objective reality, i.e., formulate the 'discursive knowledge.'

However, if empiricists were to reject the existence of 'necessary knowledge' and depend totally on the knowledge from senses only, they actually would not be able to make any judgment or gain theoretical understanding in any field of knowledge. Experiments cannot provide human beings with the laws, generalizations, or general beliefs without resorting to the support of the innate knowledge. An empiricist always employs rational knowledge to analyze the data of his experiments. Without collating these data with basic innate principles, he cannot claim to have made any true judgement. The most basic innate principles of the necessary knowledge are:

> 1. The principle of causality, in the sense of the impossibility of chance. That is, if chance were possible, then it would not be possible for the natural scientist to reach a common explanation of the numerous phenomena that appear in his experimentation.

> 2. The principle of harmony between cause and effect. This principle states that things which in reality are similar necessarily depend on a common cause.

> 3. The principle of non-contradiction that asserts that it is impossible for negation and affirmation to be true simultaneously.[288]

These principles are not the result of derivation of experiments, nor the product of sensual perceptions. They cannot be proven by any acquired knowledge, but are in fact tools for testing the validity of other knowledge and conceptions. Even when empiricists attribute the human knowledge to the laws of probability they in fact acknowledge unintentionally the existence of inner principles outside the realm of experiments. The laws of probability are based on the mathematical principles in the human mind.[289] Principles of mathematics are

---

[287]Ibid., 49.

[288]Sadr, <u>Our Philosophy</u>, 57.

[289]Sadr has devoted a whole book, <u>al-Usus al-Mantiqiyah lil- Istiqra'</u> (The Logical Principles of Induction), to formulate a philosophical theory base on the basic principles of mathematics and laws of probability. He proved that the principle of causality might be derived from the laws of probability, but all are functions of the innate knowledge of human mind. Accordingly, the laws of probability are the primary source of knowing the physical phenomenon and metaphysical one. Therefore, he refuted his argument in <u>Falsafatuna</u>, which suggests that either the principle of

not the outcome of experiments because our belief in these principles would not be reinforced or weakened by the number of experiments we conduct. One finds dissimilarity between the experiments of natural phenomenon and belief in the unquestionable validity of the principles of mathematics. Sadr writes:

> The issues of mathematics and logic are accepted with certainty. There is a big difference between 1+1=2, or that a triangle has three sides, or that two is half of four; and between issues of natural phenomena such as magnet attracts iron, water boils if its temperature gets... one hundred degrees, or every human will die. In the former issues we cannot imagine the possibility of doubt in any way, however, it is possible to doubt the latter issues.[290]

What is Reality

Given the mental and sensory faculties possessed by mankind, a question that lingers is whether man can discover the objective reality around him. Sadr, and Islamic philosophers in general, suggest that man is capable of knowing or grasping the objective causality or the principle of harmony between cause and effect is part of the innate principle of human knowledge. Human being through their experiences in observing a variety of phenomenal events and their successions develop the idea of cause and effects. Thus, man's ideas about reality are derived inductively, and not deductively as argued in Falsafatuna. The origin of the 'innate' knowledge is derived from man's experiences. However, Sadr in al-Usus al-Mantiqiyah was not reinforcing empiricist philosophy nor rejecting rationalist philosophy, but he was deriving his own, which he called al-Madhab al-Dhatiyy (Essential Doctrine). In his philosophical doctrine, he proved that human experience of the phenomenal world is the source of deriving what is called the innate knowledge, yet this knowledge is the means to discover the physical as well as the metaphysical world. Our inductive knowledge, which is the basis of the scientific research and empirical experiments, is also our basis to acknowledge the existence of the immaterial beings and forms. Therefore, Sadr argues, empiricism is the means to belief in God and religion.

[290]Sadr, "al-Yaqin al-Riyadi wa-al-Mantiq al-Wazᶜi," (The Mathematic Certainty and the Phenomenal Logic) in Ikhtrna Lak, (Bairut: Dar al-Zahra', 1982), 13.

reality.[291] What is the objective reality?

The physical world that is perceived by our senses provides us with only simple conceptual ideas. The mind then constructs from these perceptions new conceptions that have no real existence in reality. The mind has the capacity to imagine the unreal based on the physical perceptions of the real. However, the senses can directly perceive only the existence of the physical aspect of reality. Is that the whole reality there is?

According to Sadr, conceptions as such are not knowledge at all. What is called knowledge is the second form of mental activity, that is, assertion. The human mind, working on the perceived conceptions of the senses and the imaginative ones, scrutinizes this information in the light of innate (necessary) knowledge in order to make a judgment about it. Conceptions are, so to speak, only the data bank of the brain, while necessary knowledge is the logical framework that the mind uses to process and order the data. The outcome constitutes reality. Reality is not merely the sensual conceptions, but is rather the mind's judgement about them. In other words, the phenomenal world is not the total reality, but the substructure of that reality, the means by which reality becomes manifest.[292] What we see, hear, smell and touch represents only the physical aspect of reality. The mind, therefore, through the faculties of the innate knowledge, can discover what is beyond the materialistic features of reality.

Consequently, the human mind can discover the metaphysical reality through the aid of the abstract innate knowledge it possesses. This innate knowledge makes it possible for the mind to reach far beyond the materialistic world. A rejection of the role of innate knowledge as a conduit to metaphysical reality would strike a blow to our grasp of the physical world as well! This is because of the principle of noncontradiction, the principle of causality, and the primary mathematical principles are the only means available for the human mind to assess the physical reality of the world. It is through these principles that man can apprehend the true knowledge about the physical world, mathematics and metaphysics.[293] The information gathered through the natural science experiments, and social experience gives us no real knowledge.

Sadr goes even further to suggest that the knowledge gained by philosophical argument is reality to a greater extent than are the conclusions of experimentation. Scientists in the natural and social fields may not be aware of all the aspects of the issues under study, data may represent merely a part of the subject matter, or there may be defects in the collection procedures. The result of the experiments may be influenced by the bias of the scientist. The conclusions of experiments, in many cases, reflect these deficiencies.[294] On

[291]Sadr, _Our Philosophy_, 77.

[292]Sadr, _Our Philosophy_, 121-122.

[293]Ibid., 113.

the other hand, philosophical arguments can be judged with reference to innate principles of knowledge. Moreover, the philosopher may confine himself to the walls of his room, and his efforts may concentrate on discovering the objective reality through the operation of the basic principles of the mind. Because of this, we find philosophy has surpassed the development of social and natural sciences in the discovery of reality. Case in point: the philosophy which was developed by Democritus (460-370 B.C.) maintained that reality is composed of atoms was not realized for its truthfulness and importance by the natural sciences until the modern time of our history when Dalton in 1805 used nuclear weight to classify the materials in chemistry.[295]

Sadr therefore concludes that:

1. the necessary rational principles are the general ground of the scientific truth...

2. The value of scientific theories and the result in the experimental fields depend on the degree of the precision of those theories and the result in applying the necessary principles to the totality of the empirical data collected. That is why one cannot offer a scientific theory with full certainty, unless the experiment covers all the possible objectives relevant to the issue under consideration, and is broad and precise enough to make it possible to apply to these possible objects the necessary principles; and consequently, to establish a unified scientific result on the basis of that application.

3. In non-experimental fields, as in metaphysical issues, the philosophical theory rests on the application of the necessary principles to those fields. However, this kind of application may be made in those fields independently of experimentation. Thus concerning the issue of demonstrating [the existence of] the first cause of the world, for example, it is incumbent upon reason to apply its necessary principles to this issue in order to pose its affirmative or negative theory in accordance with these principles. As long as the issue is non-experimental, the application occurs by means of an operation of thinking and a pure rational inference independent of experimentation.[296]

Hence, the mental concepts we have formed about reality is reality itself, which includes the physical reality as well as the metaphysical reality. The only difference between the two is that ideas in the human mind about the physical reality attain materialistic manifestation in

---

[294]Sadr, al-Insan wa-al-Mushkilah al-Ijtima^cia, 99.

[295]Sadr, Iqtisaduna, (Bairut: Dar al-Ta^caruf, 1980), 126.

[296]Sadr, Our Philosophy, 115.

the external world, yet both of them are merely subjective forms in the mind.[297]

One simple conclusion that can be drawn from Sadr's views is that the human mind, with the aid of innate knowledge, can truly discover reality. This reality is the same for everybody regardless of circumstances because people share the same basic principles of knowledge. The differing views about truth are due to the fact that there is a misapplication of innate principles during the reasoning process. The truth that was discovered by the Greeks is the same for Muslims, Christians, and modern man. Imam Ali's belief in God, Sadr proclaimed in one of his lectures, "is shared by the Greek philosophers; Aristotle also used to believe in God, Plato also used to believe in God; and al-Farabi used to believe in God."[298] Plainly speaking, there are certain principles of truth and belief systems that are shared by every one. People are of one kind and resemble each other in their thinking and conclusions if they have the opportunity to use their mental faculty in the proper way. In this regard, Islamic philosophy advocates that there are 'natural laws' which are standard for mankind regardless of race, age, gender, color or time.

One of these shared truths is the assertion that the existence of the universe was caused by supernatural forces. This assertion is the natural conclusion of the principle of causality, the same principle that enables man to be aware of all phenomena and discover their causes and effects. Sadr maintain that if it

> ...were not for the principle and laws of causality, it would not be possible to demonstrate the objectivity of sense perception, nor any scientific theory or law. Further, it would not be possible to draw any inference in any field of human knowledge on the basis of any kind of evidence.[299]

Since every event in reality has a cause, and every cause necessarily produces its natural effect, the whole of existence must have a first cause, a cause that was not produced from a prior cause. The whole chain of causality requires a cause in order to be initiated because "the succession of causes cannot regress to infinity."[300] The endless chain of cause and effect is rejected by the innate principle of finitude which states that causes that proceed from other causes must have a beginning. Once the principle of finitude is rejected, then everything in existence is caused by everything. This statement means there is no cause-effect relationship at all. Once the principle of causality is put in question, then the coming about of all existence is in question too. If we accept the principle of causality as a necessary

[297]Ibid., 116.

[298]Sadr, <u>Muqaddimat fi al-Tafsyyr al-Mawdh^cy</u> (Kuwait: al-Dar al-Islamiyah, 1982), 213.

[299]Sadr, <u>Our Philosophy</u>, 217.

[300]Ibid., 234.

innate knowledge of the human mind, the obvious conclusion is that the world must "proceed from a being necessary in essence, self-sufficient and not requiring a cause."[301] The 'first cause,' which is God, requires no cause prior to it; it generates its own effect. Since a cause does not require a cause to proceed it, it requires an effect, and since the 'first cause' initiates its own effect, then we need not to think of a cause prior to God.[302]

Motion and development are also considered in Islamic philosophy to be among the natural phenomena. Motion is defined as "the gradual advance of existence and the development of a thing to the level permitted by its possibilities."[303] This philosophical fact remains persistent since Aristotle first proved the presence of motion and development in natural phenomena and their attributes. In metaphysical philosophy, motion is a gradual and continuous progressive movement to actualize the potentiality of a thing, in Aristotelian terminology, the <u>telos</u>. Moreover, motion has two distinct features; on one hand, it is actual and real; on the other hand, it is the potential that any object would ultimately achieve. "Thus, motion continues as long as an [object] combines both actuality and potentiality, existence and possibility. [And] if possibility is exhausted, and no capacity for a new stage remains in the thing, life of motion ends."[304]

Sadr goes further to present the philosophy of 'substantial motion' of Sadr al-Din al-Shirazi as the most advanced conceptualization of motion in existence. He summarizes the basic tenets of al-Shirazi philosophy in the following:

> First, the direct cause of the accidental and outermost motion of bodies - whether mechanical or natural -is a specific power in the body. This idea is true, even of the mechanical motion that at first appears as if proceeding from a separate power. For instance, if you force a body in a horizontal or a vertical line, the primitive notion of this motion is that it is an effect of the external force and the separate agent. But this is not true. The external agent is just one of the conditions for the motion. As for the real mover, it is the power that exists in the body. Because of this, the motion continues after the separation of the moving body from the external force and the separate agent; and the moving instrumental agent seizes. On this basis, modern mechanics pointed to the law of essential limitation (<u>qanun al-qusur al-dhatiyy</u>). This law states that if a body is moved, it continues

[301]Ibid., 235.

[302]Sadr is elaborating on idea of Muhammad `Abd al-Rahman Marhaba, <u>al-Mas'alah al-Falsafiyah</u>, (Manshurat ʿUwaydat), 80, in <u>Our Philosophy</u>, 236.

[303]Ibid., 167.

[304]Sadr, <u>Our Philosophy</u>, 168.

moving, unless something external stops it from continuing its moving activity. However, this law was misused, since it was considered as a proof that when motion begins, ..., it does not need a specific reason or a particular cause. It was taken as a means for rejecting the principle of causality and its laws. But the truth is that scientific experiments in modern mechanics show only that the separate external agent is not the real cause of motion; otherwise, the motion of a body would not continue after that body is separated from the independent external agent. Due to this, the direct cause of [continued] motion must be a power existing in the body [known as momentum], and the external agent must be a condition for, and influences that power.

Second, the effect must be appropriate to the cause in stability and renewability. If the cause is stable, the effect must be stable; and if the effect is renewable and progressive, the cause must be renewable and progressive. In light of this, it is necessary that the cause of motion be moveable and renewable, in accordance with the renewable and progression of the motion itself. For, if the cause of motion is stable and fixed, anything it produces will be stable and fixed. Thus, motion becomes rest and fixedness. But this contradicts the meaning of motion and development.

On the basis of the above two points, we conclude the following: First, the power that exists in a body and that moves it is a moveable and progressive power. Owing to its progression, this power is a cause of all the accidental and outermost motions. Further, it is a substantial power, since it inevitably leads to a substantial power; for an accident exists by virtue of a substance. This demonstrates the existence of substantial motion in nature.

Second, a body is always composed of a matter made evident by motion, and a progressive substantial power by virtue of which the outermost motion occurs in the phenomena and accidents of the body.[305]

According to the 'substantial movement theory,' a human being and the reality around him are in gradual progressive development toward the ultimate. Not only is the physical being of mankind in a developmental state; so also is his metaphysical being. It is one of the laws of nature that the whole "realm of matter is in a continuous state of renewal and development."[306] Without such motion and development, nature does not exist. The fact is that one of the fixed principles of reality in the realm of nature is that of change, renewal and motion. It is the realm of nature that is changing and developing, not our mental

[305]Sadr, Our Philosophy, footnote number 7, 210-211.

[306]Ibid., footnote no. 8, 211.

comprehension about this factual phenomenon. Human knowledge and understanding about reality would not develop and grow out of dialectical conflict or contradiction, as in Hegelian-Marxian thinking.[307] The fact is that the realm of nature is developing and growing in gradual progressive movement, not out of dialectal conflict contradiction within the reality itself.

An awareness of the progressive development of human beings and the realm of nature is essential to the understanding of existence. A political theory must take into account this principle because the concept of returning to the good old days is contrary to the basic principle of existence. The stability of a political system rests on its adaptability to the dynamic movement of nature, and to the potentiality of man to progress through time. The law of nature will overcome any obstacle that hinders man's development.

<u>Human Nature</u>

From the above brief introduction to Sadr's epistemological views, one may conclude that man has two sides of existence. One is his materialistic nature, and the other is his rational nature. Of the former, man depends on his senses for satisfying his physical needs. He strive through life, struggles with nature and with the environment to secure his survival. There are essential needs that man is driven to preserve from his natural surroundings, otherwise his existence will be in danger. With the aid of his mental capacity, he is able to discover new ways to enhance his capability to secure his materialistic needs. No creature, save mankind, is capable of rapidly developing new techniques to balance the changing environment. Man, out of his physical needs, confines himself to the passions of his senses. He develops the feeling of individuality and the protection of his personal interests and centers his life around such needs.

On the other hand, the rational side of his nature makes it possible for man to develop beyond his materialist needs to discover the essence of his existence. Through his rational reasoning he discovers the metaphysical nature of existence, and broadens his visions to know the ultimate. His mental capacity gives meaning to his mission in life through defined goals and a clear understanding of his role on earth. The broader scope of his rational reasoning allowed him to transcend beyond the limited boundaries of this materialistic world.

It is because of the materialistic instincts of the senses that man felt it necessary to live in communal settings to secure his survival. The individual struggle with the environment is a great task and the cooperation with others makes it more efficient to preserve his livelihood.[308] To communicate his ideas with fellow men in the community, man developed language. He started assigning names to things and symbols to ideas to

---

[307]Sadr, <u>Our Philosophy</u>, 172-174.

[308]Sadr, <u>Iqtisaduna</u>, 162.

make others aware of what he thinks and needs.[309] Hence, the construction of the language came as an expressive means of man's intellect. Animals, who live in sociostructural types of communal settings, have not developed a sophisticated system of communication between them as human beings have developed languages. They lack the advanced mental capacity of man.[310] Another point worth mentioning here is that while the vocabulary expands according to the needs of mankind, the grammatical structure takes shape at the early period of the communal life and survives social changes.

Furthermore, Sadr recognizes the existence of what he called the 'self-love' instinct within the nature of man. The instinct of 'self-love' is so powerful that it overshadows all other instincts and desires. Self-love is defined by Sadr as the love human beings have for pleasure and happiness and the hatred of pain and misery.[311] It is self-love that enables us to understand human behavior in general. The instinct of self-love may be expressed in a variety of ways. Sadr explains:

> In human beings, there are many propensities for taking pleasure in a variety of things, such as taking pleasure in material things exemplified in food, drinks, the various kinds of sexual pleasures... [others] are those of the soul, such as moral values and emotional pleasures in moral values, in a spiritual companion or in specific doctrine.[312]

Man may find enjoyment or witness pain in the satisfaction of his materialistic or nonmaterialistic needs. While he finds enjoyment in eating, for example, he sometimes deprives himself of food to help others.

Human behavior is a function of the instinct of self-love. Man may concern himself with the materialistic instincts, or choose the other way. Here is where self-love plays an important role in directing the intensity of satisfying one of these needs. If the satisfaction of materialistic instincts is highly valued, then moral values will become less important. On the other hand, if social values are more important, man would sacrifice his materialistic needs for the welfare of social interests. For example, the more private property man acquires the more he will feel the satisfaction of his inner instincts. The same can be said of high moral values when someone sacrifices his life for his country. He feels the satisfaction of his self-love. Fulfillment of the desires for self-love may take an opposite stimulation. However, the fulfillment has to entail satisfaction of the self-love. A human being may give his life for a

[309]Sadr, <u>Durus fi °Ilm al-Usul</u> (Beirut: Dar al-Kitab al-Lubnany, 1985), 87-89.

[310]Sadr, <u>Iqtisaduna</u>, 83-84.

[311]Sadr, <u>Our Philosophy</u>, 21.

[312]Ibid., 22.

social cause only when he personally benefits from that action. His sacrifice for country is because he cannot bear the pain of the defeat of his nation, or because he will get the satisfaction of his victory.

If Rousseau and Marx thought that private ownership is the cause of social problems centered on individualism, they were wrong in their analysis. They looked at the effect but not at the cause. "Marxism holds that self-love is neither a natural inclination nor an instinctive phenomenon in the human nature. Rather, it is a product of the social condition that rests on the ground of private ownership."[313] Private property is only the manifestation of the natural instinct of the human self-love. If this manifestation is abolished, man will find other means to satisfy his inner instincts of self-love, such as the abuse of power. The emphasis on material possession in capitalism is because the system is built on the idea of protecting and maximizing individual interests. The ideological foundation of the modern capitalist countries is formed according to Locke who envisioned a government for the purpose of protecting the material interests of the individual. In these types of political systems, individuals are driven to enhance their material possessions. The more affluent a person is in the capitalist system, the more satisfied he feels, and the more impact he has on the system that was created to protect private ownership.

For this reason, the solution to the social problem resulting from the abuses of private ownership in the political system cannot be achieved by prohibiting private ownership in the society because other materialistic tendencies will take its place. "In reality, the social manifestations of selfishness in the economic and political fields are nothing but a result of individualistic motivation which in turn is a result of self-love."[314] The proper solution is the one presented by the religious message through upgrading the materialistic tendencies into a higher cause.[315]

Monotheistic religions carry an answer to this social problem; the goal of every human being in life is to achieve the absolute, i.e., God. In this case, the materialist possession will function only as a means to achieve that goal. Man may find it necessary to give up some of his property to others for the sake of the ultimate goal, i.e., the grace of God. The material he gives in this world will be rewarded with abundance in the hereafter. Instead of thinking about eliminating self-love, which is impossible to do since it is a natural instinct, the Islamic solution is to foster an ascent to an upper set of standards.

The religious beliefs provide the necessary mechanism to curb the desire individuals have for materialistic benefits and provide them with alternative benefits which are greater. The goal would not focus on the interests of this life, but in man's total journey to eternity.

---

[313]Sadr, <u>Our Philosophy</u>, 25.

[314]Ibid., 25.

[315]Sadr, <u>Our Philosophy</u>, 24.

Life does not end in death, but transcends beyond the bounds of this physical world. The happiness of man will not be found in achieving greater possession of private property or other materialistic wealth, but rather in satisfying God.

Religion beleif sees satisfying God as always in the end serving social interests. Man may give some of what he owns, sacrifice other material wealth, allocate part of his resources (physical or mental) to God's cause. All these donations have a positive social impact. Here the individual interest is intertwined with social interests. On the one hand, the instinct of individualistic self-love is fulfilled, while on the other hand, that fulfillment is directed toward the good of the society. "Therefore, religion guides man to participate in establishing a happy society, and in preserving the issues in society that are concerned with justice and that help attain God's satisfaction, be He exalted."[316] Sadr makes reference to some verses of <u>Quran</u> that reinforce this moral value:

> He who does right it is for his soul, and he who does wrong it is against his soul.(41:46)

> He who does right, whether male or female, and is a believer will enter Paradise where he will be provided for, without restriction.(40:40)

> On that day, people will proceed in scattered groups to see their deeds. He who does good and atom's weight will see it then, and he who does evil an atom's weight will see it then.(99:6-8)

> That is because no thirst, hardship or hunger afflicts them on the path of God. They do not take any step that harms the disbelievers. And they do not gain anything from the enemy; but by virtue of that, a good deed is recorded for them. God does not lose the wages of the good. They do not spend anything, be that small or large, nor do they cross any valley; but it is recorded for them that God will repay them the best of what they had done.(9:120-121)[317]

Value of Labor

Islam also has a different perspective about the social value of human labor which stems from its general theory about reality. It values human labor from a moral standpoint. ~~The moral standard is divinely~~ ordained and rationally accepted. According to Sadr, human

---

[316]Sadr, <u>Our Philosophy</u>, 29.

[317]Ibid., 35.

rationality is always consistent with the tenets of Islam.[318] Providence has never sanctioned a law that is contrary to human logic; a process that is created by Him. Hence, divine moral laws are the same as those ethical values derived by rational reasoning. Based on this premise, Sadr went on to evaluate the social value of human labor.

The empiricist school of thought measures human labor according to its physical value. Since the reality is only sensory, the materialistic manifestation becomes the only measurement to evaluate human deeds. The metaphysical moral values carry no weight in the empiricist perspective, since they do not have physical existence anyway. In this way, the value of any human action is determined by the amount of labor contained in it. What this means in the social level is that labor that has greater impact on a greater number of people is valued more. Capitalism, for example, which bases its social settings on the ideal of individual freedom and cooperative endeavor, regards any individual labor that benefits the society as worthy of praise.[319] Although the individual may do social work for his personal interest, the impact of that work on the society is what matters. It is the social benefit that is important, and not the moral values behind that deed. When a capitalist helps the needy, builds an orphanage, donates to schools, or participates in public programs, these activities are worthy of praise by the society. In that case, capitalist moral values are a function of social net-return of the individual labor. It is a realistic view that looks at the result of the deeds rather than the inner stimuli of the individual.[320]   Marxism,   though empiricist in its philosophy, has different interpretations of the social value of human labor. Since Marxism believes in the historical conflict of the social classes, social values are determined by the class that has control over the means-of-production.[321] Any individual action that benefits the governing class of the society is praised. However, when the governing class becomes the agent of stagnation and thus an obstacle to the dialectic historical change, the moral values change too. In the revolutionary struggle, moral values are those that serve the oppressed class, because they are the agent of historical development. Social values, according to Marxism, are not determined by the benefit that they produce for a society (because the society here is not a coherent entity, but rather conflicting groups) but by how they serve the deprived class struggling to overcome the existing economic establishment. Individual action that benefits the establishment is

[318]Sadr, al-Fatawa al-Wadhiha (Beirut: Dar al-Taᶜruf, 1984), 706.

[319]Sadr, "al-ᶜAmal al-Salih fi al-Quran," (The Proper Behavior According to Quran), in Akhtarna Lak (Beirut: Dar al-Zahra', 1982), 33.

[320]Sadr, "al-ᶜAmal al-Salih," 40.

[321]Ibid., 34.

considered reactionary.[322]

Islam, contrary to the empiricist view, does not value human labor according to the amount of the material benefits, but rather according to the inner intention (<u>niya</u>).[323] Reality in the Islamic perspective is not simple the material manifestation but is instead the entire knowledge that is constructed through human reasoning. The essence of things is registered in reason, not by what is preserved by the senses. Based on this philosophical stand, Islam is concerned with the intentions and purpose behind human labor and not its impact on the external world. Sadr writes:

> Thus we find that: Islam measures the value of works by its purposes, its bases, and its general ideological frames that conceal the seed within its sphere; whereas others measure the value of works by their result, outcomes, and by the various social fields that works take parts in reparation.[324]

For this reason, Islam puts greater emphasis on teaching man starting from his inner thinking and beliefs in order to change the external environment in which he lives. The 'substructure' of the society (if we are to use the Marxian concept) is within the human being, rather than the tools he uses, or the senses he utilizes. On the basis of this, individual labor, which has minor social benefits, may be heavily valued because of its intention. This perspective will encourage the participation of all people, because everyone is able to give with his capacity for the welfare of all.[325]

Since the ultimate goal of man on earth is God, man's social work should be undertaken for God's sake. Thus, human deeds, even within the social level, are linked to human destiny. When man gives to others for the sake of God, it will have a positive effect on his salvation. Hence the material manifestation of human labor when it comes to serving others has no value. Islam went further to encourage people to do public service in secret since the purpose of the work is not public praise and admiration, but God's satisfaction. "In this way we acknowledge that linking [individual] work with its essence is a realistic means that preserves the continuation of useful public service, nourishes it and urges it upon others."[326]

---

[322]Sadr, "al-ᶜAmal," 35.

[323]Ibid., 36.

[324]Ibid., 37.

[325]Sadr, "al-ᶜAmal," 40.

[326]Ibid., 42.

Social Process

Government arise either out of the people or over the people.
Tom Paine

Human activities have three types of relationships that determine the nature of historical development: 1) man-God, 2) man-man, and 3) man-nature. Providence plays a central role in determining the mechanism and outcome of the historical process as well as in determining the role of man through providing him with the rational mental capacity to know the reality and to enable him to execute his own judgment. Man has reason and can make judgements about reality around him. He can determine his will in every step he takes. The nature of the three relationships is determined by his own will. Islam advises man to practice total submission (taslim) of his actions to the will of God.[327] Man may submit or rebel against God's rules, but in both cases he has knowledge of his own actions and is responsible for the consequences before God. If he rebels he will be at the mercy of his own rationality, which lacks a complete and perfect knowledge of the nature of historical process. If he submits to the advice and the guidance of God, then he will protect himself from any misjudgment he might make. The total submission should be understood as a means to help man in making the right decisions to secure happiness in life. Sooner or later he will discover the wisdom behind the guidance of God in determining what is best for his survival on earth. In fact, the first type of relationship can be considered the divine guide for the other relationships, and not an impediment to man's rationality.

Human Freedom

The assigned role of man on earth by God is to be His vicar. No other creature of God in the whole universe was honored and entrusted with such a great role.

We offered the trust to the heavens and the earth and the mountains,
but refused to bear it and were afraid of it; and man assumed it. Surely he is
tyrant, and foolish.(33:72)

The role of vicar meant that man is to be over everything on earth: animal, plants, and natural resources.[328] This vicarage made humanity as a whole accountable before God.

[327]The name Islam is the derivative of the Arabic verb aslama which means submission, i.e., to the will of God.

Every human being is equally responsible before God, which implies that there are no distinctions between one man and another. The role of vicar abolishes all types of estrangement and considers people equal in responsibility. This means that all forms of estrangement are man-made.

Man was honored with the capacity to make his own decisions, making him fully accountable before his Lord. He was provided with the mental capacity to know realty and analyze facts. His rational measures are superior to any other creature. Accordingly, mankind is capable through reasoning to distinguish truth from falsehood, good from evil, and reality from myth without the aid of divine scripture.

Once men grouped themselves into communal units to meet their survival needs, there were various limitations placed on man's individual freedom. Man no more had the full liberty to chose and do anything he pleased. The social environment restricted his liberty as well as created competition to gain the most out of earthly resources. In the social setting, this natural wealth must be shared by all the members of the community. In other words, the social groupings, although they resolved some of the problems facing man, have become an impediment to individual liberty. Therefore, the call for freedom has become the utmost cry of mankind to liberate himself from his social chains. Such feelings stem from the fact that man is naturally a creature of free-will, and these social obstacles are impediments to his human nature. The restriction of his free-will is portrayed by Sadr as similar to tampering with some of his natural organs, the organ in this case being man's rational capacity, the essence of his human nature. The call for freedom, therefore, Sadr argues, is a natural instinct of mankind.[329]

However, no one denies that such full scale freedom of man in the social setting is not feasible. The freedom of one individual, within the social unit, eventually conflicts with the rights of others. Man's absolute freedom can be imagined only in the "state of nature," and is not even possible in the utopian form of society. The very concept idea of society means that man has to give up some of his freedom for the benefits gained from social relationships. The question within the social setting would therefore not be a question of how to regain man's absolute freedom, but rather of "how much freedom should be preserved for man."[330]

The capitalist political system, according to Sadr,[331] is a civilization that promotes

---

[328]Sadr, <u>Khalafat al-Insan</u>, in <u>al-Islam Yaquud al-Hayat</u> (Tehran: Ministry of Islamic Guidance, 1984), 133-134.

[329]Sadr, "al-Huriyah fi al-Quran," (Freedom according to Quran) in <u>Ikhtarna Lak</u>, (Beirut: Dar al-Zahra', 1982), 44.

[330]Sadr, "al-Huriyah," 45.

[331]Sadr, normally on the analysis of any concept, puts

securing the maximum amount of freedom possible for the individual within social system.[332] The personal freedom of the individual is extended to the point that it is limited when it harms the freedom of other individuals in the society. Personally, the individual is free to behave in any way he pleases. The function of the capitalist political state is to guarantee the protection of this 'sacrad' individual freedom. Sadr uses alcohol consumption in the West as an example. The individual is allowed to consume as much alcohol as he wishes, to the point of loosing his ability to think. This is considered in capitalist thinking as part of the freedom protected by the system, as long as is does not bring harm to others.

Consequently, the absolute freedom that is guaranteed by capitalism has made man a prisoner of his passions. While securing the ultimate needs of his material instincts, he abandons his rationality. He is no more a free-man, but rather a slave of his desires. The freedom sought for centuries turned out to be the greatest chain of all. It demolishes man's rationality by reducing him to a mere animal driven by his appetites, lust, and greed. Definitely, this is not the freedom mankind has been striving for throughout history.

> And humanity got drunk on the melodies of this freedom, dozing in its shadows for a brief time, feeling that for the first time it has destroyed all the chains. And the giant-monster [of the inner passions] which was suppressed for thousands of years out burst for the first time, and was allowed to do anything in the [open] without being frightened or apprehensive.[333]

---

emphasis on presenting and making critique of the world's dominating political systems, namely capitalism and Marxist-socialism, and mostly refrains from identifying the ideas with its political or philosophical thinker. For him, the ideological basis of political system is what is important, and not the individual who shaped these ideas. Hence, such a dichotomy is evidenced in Sadr's writings. For example, when he presents the Islamic view of freedom, he first critiques its capitalist concepts and understandings, which advocate the expansion of personal freedom and protection of individual liberty. Then he merges with this negative attitude on the Marxist-socialism views of freedom which advocate the curbing of personal freedom and advocate the social interests and welfare of the whole people. Finally, what conforms to his ideological belief that Islam presents humanity with the best understanding to the problem: A dualistic answer that secures individual freedom and cares about the welfare of the society.

[332]Sadr, "al-Huriyah," 45.

Sadr argues that capitalism misguided humanity about the nature and scope of freedom. According to him, there are two types of freedom: natural freedom and social freedom. The former is what nature bestows on humankind as liberty in his actions. A stone, for example, by nature possesses a limited amount of freedom of movement that cannot be altered or changed by the outside environment. Vegetation has the least amount of freedom of movement (enough to secure and preserve their natural survival) in comparison with living things. Plants, for example, make slow move to receive sunlight. Animals, however, have much greater freedom of movement, and greater ability to maneuver to choose the best possible environmental conditions for their survival. However, such freedom is driven by the animal's instincts. On the other hand, man sits at the summit of the hierarchy of natural freedom, possessing more of this freedom than other creatures. His freedom is not limited by his natural instincts as are animals, but he possesses the mental faculties that broaden his choices and give him the extra power to determine what are the best conditions for securing his interests. Man has the power to control his inner instincts and limit their drives:

> And this natural freedom enjoyed by man must truly be considered as one of the essential components of humanity, because it has the expression of dynamic power in it. For humanity without this freedom is a concept without a meaning.[334]

Thus, the natural freedom is out of the realm of evaluation because no political system or ideology can claim the power to suppress or expand such freedom. Epictetus was right when he thought that a tyrant can control only the external environment of a human being, i.e., social freedom. His spirit is free and out of the reach of political suppression. According to Stoicism, man may live happily under severe social coercion because he has the ability to control his desires and instincts. His public life may be like hell, yet his private life may resemble heaven because he can escape from his social reality to the liberty of his natural freedom.

The other type of freedom, social freedom, is the liberty granted to the individual by the society. While the first type of freedom is the reflection of human nature, the second type is the reflection of the social reality. The latter must be evaluated as to whether it is compatible with the social environment, and how much it helps to maintain the social survival. In order to circumscribe the social freedom and study its impact, one must distinguish between its essence and its perceptible form. "The essence of social freedom is the ability of man to acquire from his society the liberty to perform specified tasks."[335] In

---

[333]Sadr, "al-Huriyah," 46.

[334]Sadr, <u>Iqtisaduna</u>, 14th ed. (Beirut: Dar al-Ta͑aruf, 1981), 282.

this case, the society should provide all the necessary means to enable its members to achieve their physical survival. When the society allows its citizens to buy commodities in the market, it should also provide the means to possess them, i.e., the financial capacity and the availability of goods. Otherwise, the freedom to acquire such things is purely fictive. Sadr calls it al-hurriyah al-shakliyah, formal (or "fictitious" since he means to imply a negative connotation to the term) freedom. It is, for example, when one has the freedom to buy goods without being provided with the money to possess them. "The freedom to buy does not mean, actually, the ability to buy."[336]

Sadr acknowledges a certain positive effect of the formal freedom on the social life. A businessman, since he has the freedom to own a large corporation, although he may not possess the financial capital to own it, would be encouraged to work hard to achieve his goal. Accordingly, formal freedom can be a means to motivate people to release their energies in order to achieve higher objectives, although this may not guarantee success. In other words, this freedom does not entail ability, but it is the essential ingredient in the acquisition of ability. The formal freedom is the tool used to gain the essential freedom.[337] Basically, the capitalist doctrine concerns itself only in providing the individual with the formal freedom while detaching itself from any commitment to provide the means for man to possess the essence of that freedom. Socialism, on the other hand, considers the freedom provided by capitalism to be a false one and wants it replaced by an "al-huriyah al-jawhariyah (substantive freedom) by providing to the people the opportunities of work and decent living."[338]

Islam, according to Sadr, is the only political doctrine that advocates providing people with both types of freedom, formal and substantive. On the one hand, it wants to create a society that assures a certain amount of means of livelihood for the people; and on the other hand, it wants to protect the formal form of freedom, which motivates the will and energies of people. It is not true, as claimed by the democratic-capitalist doctrine, that if man losses some opportunities to do something, or his behavior is restricted in one way or an other, that he will be denied his humanity.[339] Social freedom can restrict formal freedom, but not natural freedom. A sound political system must take into consideration the importance of providing for the essential needs so as to bring about the realization of formal freedom by every individual. Human beings must be assured of a decent standard of living as well as the

---

[335]Sadr, Iqtisaduna, 283.

[336]Sadr, Iqtisaduna, 284.

[337]Ibid., 285.

[338]Ibid., 288.

[339]Sadr, Iqtisaduna, 289-290.

opportunity to live in peace and tranquility because material and psychological discomfort reduce man's ability to attain his natural freedom. Freedom should not go unchecked to produce harm to social relationships or curtail man's rationality. In either case he can harm his interests and make himself similar to the animals.

The process Islam proposed to achieve the measure of freedom is via the enslavement (ᶜubudiyah) of man to God.[340] It is a total submission to God that guarantees the full realization of freedom while preserving the human essence. Enslavement to God will enable man to break all chains that hinder his freedom.

The Islamic liberation struggle is launched on two fronts: On the one side it suggests an end to the inner contradictions of man to assure his rational power and make him aware of his reality and historical mission. In order to do this, man must have the power to control his passions to end his enslavement to his sensual desires and make himself his own master.[341] Once he has control over his appetites and passions, then he can claim to be truly liberated. Otherwise, he is no different from animals who are driven by their senses. The difference between the two, in nature, is that mankind is equipped with the will to command his passions through his rational faculty while animals lack such power. It is this rational will that distinguishes man from animals. The moment he loses his rational will he finds himself ruled by the lust of inner passions that make him enslaved by his sensual desires.

In order to preserve man's human essence, he must transcend beyond his materialistic desires to achieve an ultimate cause.[342] It is only in this way that man can claim mastery of himself and possess the will to change his social environment. It is attachment to earthly desires that the message of religion came to break in order to elevate man to a higher stature.

> Decked out of fair to men is the love of lusts-- women, children, heap-up heap of gold and silver, horses of mark, cattle and tillage. That is the enjoyment of the present life; but God-- with Him is the fairest resort. Say: 'Shall I tell you of a better than that?' For those that are godfearing, with their Lord are gardens underneath which rivers flow, therein dwelling forever, and spouses purified, and God's good pleasure [contentment]. And God sees His servants.(3:14-15)[343]

This power of the rational will that Islam generates through the idea of monotheism (tawhid), i.e., the enslavement to God, made the ummah of Islam able to abandon, for

[340]Sadr, "al-Huriyah fi al-Quran," 46-47.

[341]Sadr, "al-Huriyah," 47-48.

[342]Ibid., 49.

[343]The Koran, v. I, 74-75.

example, the drinking of alcohol. It is impossible to think in our time of any "civilized" nation being able to take such a drastic action of socio-behavioral control. The modern individual has lost control over his lusts and is being driven by them. "Islam liberates mankind from the slavery of the earthly [means] and its dazzling lusts, and attaches him to heaven, its paradise, ideals and the contentment of God; accordingly we know that monotheism is the [moral] support of humanity for its liberation from all types of slavery."[344]

On the social level, on the other hand, the ideology of monotheism seeks to liberate mankind from all forms of social idols to put an end to the enslavement of man by another man.[345] This can be done only, once again, through the enslavement of man to God which gives the feeling that all men are equal before God, all responsible to Him entirely on equal terms. Such a notion of equality will overcome once and for all the types of social hierarchy that man created throughout history, and no one could have the legitimacy to be the idol of others.[346]

> Say: 'People of the Book! Come now to a word common between us and you, that we serve [worship] none but God, and that we associate not aught with Him, and do not some of us take others as lords, apart from God.'(3:64)[347]

As long as man worships God only, he will consider that all men are equal to him and no one is superior to him except God, the rest of creation being servants of God as is he. In fact, the phenomenon of idolism, according to Sadr, came about for two reasons: First is man's enslavement to his lusts, which made him vulnerable to other types of slavery, one of which is social. Man consequently relinquished his freedom to social idols, such as another man like him, that could guarantee the repletion of his sensual appetite and lusts. The second reason is man's ignorance about the limited capacity of these social idols. Man naturally is looking for the ultimate, striving for the absolute to emancipate his life.[348] Such progressive ambition enables man to advance and be emancipated far more than other creatures. However, his ignorance deceives him by giving the impression that things are absolute and the finite is ultimate. It is man's knowledge of the true nature of reality around him that makes him aware of the fallacies of his idols. This is why Islam over and over again in the Quran encourages man to use his mental faculties to realize the discrepancies of his beliefs.

---

[344]Sadr, "al-Huriyah," 50.

[345]Ibid., 51-52.

[346]Sadr, "al-Huriyah," 52.

[347]The Koran, v. I, 82.

[348]Sadr, "al-Huriyah," 52.

Islam is a revolution in knowledge and an enlightenment movement. It is a revolution that is determined to abolish all forms of idols and set the stage for man's social and psychological transformation toward the ultimate emancipation where he could become the vicar of God. This is the true meaning of freedom, and the only way to liberate man from all forms of slavery. Accordingly, Islam does not allow man to adopt another form of belief, save monotheism, because it dilutes his thinking and subjects him to slavery.[349] Human freedom and monotheism are synonymous. If man is to attain freedom from slavery and succeed in breaking all chains, he can do so only through a total submission to God.

Worship of God

Since man's freedom is dependent on his enslavement to God, Sadr further shows how the act of worship in Islam and man's total submission to Him will be the means and the expression of man's liberation. Sadr also shows that other means of emancipation are actually stagnant and unprogressive. Islam proposes a certain and defined act of worship that must be performed by man throughout his life, unchanging over time. Sadr attributes the particularity of the acts of worship as meeting man's spiritual needs. Worship is a form of relationship between man and his Lord. Unlike man's relationship to nature, which is changing and developing over time, man's relationship to God is constant. Man's materialistic needs are enhanced in accordance with the development of his experience; however, man's spiritual needs are fixed. As such, the act of worship is to satisfy that invariable need.[350] To understand the nature of the acts of worship, one must, according to Sadr, understand also the permanent need that man faces in his mission on earth: the need for attachment to God. It is this attachment that makes man's historical progress to endless frontiers possible, as well as his emancipation. Any historical progress that is not linked to the Absolute is a random movement "affected by the surrounding conditions, but having no effect on man."[351] Thus, man's endeavor to relate to the absolute is the real cause of human novelty and achievement. But how does this work?

The real problem behind the fall of human civilization throughout history, according to Sadr, is man's fidelity to an absolute of his own making, or what Sadr refers to as the al-mathal al-aᶜla of man. Man's denial of the true absolute is reflected in both negative and positive ways. Negatively, man may reject the absolute altogether and disbelieve in any

---

[349]Sadr, "al-Huriyah," 53.

[350]Sadr, "Nazarah ᶜAmah fi al-ᶜAbadat," (General Outlook on Worship), in al-Fatawa al-Wadhiha, (Beirut: Dar al-Taᶜaruf, 1981), 703-705.

[351]Sadr, "Nazrah ᶜAmah," 707.

ideal; or positively, he may create a false absolute, and try to transform temporal things into an ideal. Islam refers to the former act as atheism (ilhad), and the latter as polytheism (sherk). Both problems hinder the continuous historical progress of man. If man rejects the absolute, his emancipation would lose a sense of direction and the objective of the progressive mission would become vague. If man believes in false absolute then his historical emancipation will become obsolete over time. The man-made idols of the ancient civilizations were the cause of their fall. In the same way, modern Western civilization, according to Sadr, has its own man-made idol: the belief in science. Today's man considers the empirical procedures to be the solution to all the problems facing him, and considers the findings of experiments as the absolute truth. Thus, the modern Western man does not reject all moral values, but he rejects transcendental truth and the existence of a metaphysical realm.[352] Naturally, he is also blind to his world, and his civilization is doomed to vanish by its own created contradictions. "Set not up with God another god, or thou wilt sit condemned and forsaken."(17:22)[353]

Therefore, the belief in God as the absolute will eliminate the negative side of the problem, and will put an end to man's regression by providing him with a sense of direction in his historical emancipation.[354] It will raise him to the position of vicar of God, a well-defined role within endless objectives. The responsibility of the vicar of the absolute makes man's mission in life meaningful. Belief in God will also put an end to the problem of idolatry, the magnification of temporal things into an ideal. God is not a man-made idol to serve some human purpose or to function in certain tasks or to satisfy man's limited goals. Rather, He will "with His everlasting attributes (such as knowledge, will, power, justice, and prosperity) replace the supreme ideals of al-mathal al-ᶜAla of man, the vicar on earth, and set the stage for the continuous struggle of humanity against all kinds of ignorance, impotence, oppression, and poverty."[355] Thus, the belief in God, as the absolute of humanity and the rejection of all forms of idols (the Islamic call of "there is no god but Him") will guide man into perfection and everlasting emancipation.[356]

Whosoever struggles, struggle for his own gain; surly God is All-sufficient nor needs any being.(29:6)[357]

---

[352]Sadr, "Nazrah," 708.

[353]The Koran, v. I, 304.

[354]Sadr, "Nazrah ᶜAma," 709.

[355]Ibid., 710.

[356]Ibid., 711-712.

[357]The Koran v. II, 97.

> Whosoever is guided, is only guided to his own gain, and whosoever
> goes astery, it is to his own loss.(39:41)[358]

On the other hand, worship is to function as the perpetual process that trains man for devotion to the higher goal or ideal. Objectively, man may behave either to benefit himself, or to benefit his society. His rationality always drives him to calculate the benefit to himself even when he ought to perform some task for the benefit of society. He is egoistical and always looking for individual glory and striving for his own interests. Such a self-centered personality is essential for his survival in earth. However, livelihood within a social setting pertains to certain actions that mainly benefit society. The social environment implies certain sacrifices by individuals for the sake of the survival of the social unit. Worship can be understood as an individual exercise of sacrifice. It is the continual individual behavior devoted only for the sake of God and it is not acceptable in any way if performed for the attention of personal gain. This is why Islam insists the intention (niyah) of the acts of worship should be for God. However, the act of worship is designed to serve and satisfy man's persistence needs. Although the effort which he puts into it varies, its objective is to enable man, spiritually and physically, to work for nonpersonal gains. Thus, a worshiper is trained to perform deeds for the sake of others. Performing the acts of worship, although they satisfy man's spiritual needs, is designed to help the society as a whole, and reinforce its tranquility and solidarity. Worship in Islam is not only praying and suplication, but also participation in a military struggle (jihad), paying alms and religious taxes (zakat), fasting (sa'um), cleaning (ghusul), and enjoying good and forbidding evils in the society, all of which are essentially social deeds. In fact Islam rejects both the limitation of worship to only a minor part of human activity, and the limitation of human duties to specific acts of spiritual worship. The Western civilization, Sadr believes, confines religion to the individual, thus worship is only for a few hours Sunday morning in church. On the other extreme, the Far Eastern civilizations emphasize the rejection of worldly pleasure and preach total devotion of man's efforts to all-embracing acts of worship. Worship should not be limited to the walls of temples but should include the entire realm of life, comprising every act that man performs for the sake of God. Concerning this, Sadr wrote:

> The cannon laws of Islam reject such an attitude because it wants
> worship for the sake of life, and not to confiscate life for the sake of
> worship.. [So] the mosque is only the center for the pious man in his daily
> conduct of worship, and not an obstacle to the life; for the Prophet has said to
> Abu Dhar, [a close companion], 'if you are able [to make your inner
> intention of] of eating and drinking only for the sake of God, you should do
> so.'[359]

---

[358]Ibid., v. II, 170.

Moreover, the social environment requires that man respect the rights of others, otherwise chaos and conflict will prevail. For this reason, society enforces security measures, i.e., coercive means to regulate the right of obligation of its members. However, such measures can always be manipulated and deceived by man. Man has the cleverness to find loop holes in laws to maneuver the system of coercion. One function of the act of worship is to train man that he is responsible before a higher authority, all-knowing and all-powerful, that makes man accountable for all his deeds. Since God also possesses the knowledge of the inner feeling and thoughts of man, this makes man honest with others. Worship trains people to have a self-regulating mechanism in their social behavior.

Finally, the act of worship in Islam is designed to tighten the social bond of the community. Religious duties have a great impact on protecting the social relationship and strengthening the solidarity of the <u>ummah</u>. Some of these acts of worship are: the <u>jihad</u> is a safeguarding of the homeland from foreign threat, <u>zakat</u> is a social welfare means for the needy, Friday and congressional prayers are the means of social solidarity and political gathering, and the most important is the <u>qiblah</u> as the source of unity and social identity for various communities of believers.[360]

At the personal level, the acts of worship are in accordance with human nature. Man is not only a rational being, but also a sensory one. The belief in the absolute may satisfy his rational side, but his materialistic needs must be fulfilled as well. The acts of worship in Islam intertwine the two needs, that is, they bring about attachment to God while performing symbolic functions. Examples are praying in the direction of <u>qiblah</u> (direction to Mecca), pilgrimage to the holy palaces in Mecca while performing various symbolic rites such as throwing stones at the representation of Satan, and so on. "These symbolic acts are to fulfill the sensory side of human nature of a worshiper, and satisfy its needs and give it its share of worship."[361] Worship in Islam is not entirely a rational exercise of the mind, although one might be inclined to view it as such, nor is it entirely a set of symbolic acts which make meaningless objects holy; it is rather a combination of the two equated to man's needs.

The Prophetic Mission

Human nature consists of two components: the senses and reason. The sensual perceptions play an important role in defining the way man perceives the world around him. The senses supply the human mind with visions and information about the surrounding world. On the basis of these perceptional visions, the human reason functions to discover reality. Man is therefore attached to his senses and dependent on them to derive his

---

[359]Sadr, "Nazrah ᶜAmah," 726.

[360]Sadr, "Nazrah ᶜAmah," 729-730.

[361]Ibid., 726.

knowledge. What this means is that mankind is more of a sensory creature than a reasoning one, an empiricist more than a rationalist.[362]

Thus the perceptions have a great deal of influence on man's reasoning and are the basis of his motivations and actions that shape the course of his behavior in life. Sadr explains:

> What this means is that theories and general rational principles ..., even if man believes in them strongly and being adopted by his mind rationally, would not motivate him, energize him, erect him, nor make him react nor reconstruct his being except in limited degrees.[363]

The rational ideals and knowledge are vaguely formed in the human mind, and do not take the level of certainty or belief. For this reason, divine messages were accompanied by miracles that astonish man's perceptions and compel him to believe through what he has sensed. This was true of the messages of such prophets as Noah and the worldwide flood, Abraham who was saved from the burning fire, Moses and his magic rod, Jesus's ability to cure an irremediable diseases, and the eloquency of the <u>Quran</u>, the holy book delivered to Muhammad.

Thus, influencing human beings by providence must be done with a pedagogy that appeals to the senses. Educators and teachers are "prophets" who are role models for mankind.[364] The divine ideal forms must be practiced by the prophets in order to embed them deeply in the human mind. Even the ideal city of God, i.e. heaven, is made to attract the senses of mankind. It is via this prophet-model that divine values and heavenly principles made it possible to bring man to a higher rational level. In that case, prophets were not only deliverers of the divine message, but also were examples to others. It is through them that man can ascend to the world of reason and metaphysical forms and go beyond animal instincts. The prophets and the messengers of God were the perceptional agents that made it possible for man to realize the higher moral values, rational principles and the metaphysical reality in order to progress toward the Absolute. A human being, through his rational reasoning, may attain a knowledge of the ideals proclaimed by the divine messengers of God, but he will not reach the level of belief that motivates him to the point of influencing his behavior and becoming part of his life. The divine teachers of humanity let the higher ideals descend within the reach of man by making them part of life

[362]Sadr, "Muda^cafat Wafat Rasul Allah," (The Implication of the Death of the Messenger of God) in <u>Ahul al-Bayat: Tanaw^c Adwar wa Wihdat Hadaf</u> (Beirut: Dar al-Ta^caruf, 1985), 46.

[363]Ibid., 46.

[364]Sadr, "Muda^cafat," 47.

and behavior. Greek philosophers, for example, although they believed in the unity of God, continued to worship idols; and Rousseau, although he believed in the republican-democratic system, could not visualize a world without a monarchy; and Marx, although he developed a socialist theory, claimed that he was not a Marxist.[365] It is through pedagogy that higher ideals and values enable man's deeds to accord with his thoughts.

Hence, prophethood was intended to raise up mankind into rationalism, to elevate his consciousnes and to guide him into a progressive responsibility toward the Absolute, i.e, God. For this reason, prophethood messages were changed and renewed throughout history. This gradual delivery in stages, according to Sadr, was due to an objective and subjective conditions. There are two objective conditions: First, because each message was meant to achieve a purpose, that is to meet a human need. In other words, it is to cure human problems.[366] Once the need is satisfied and the remedy is no longer needed, the message will get lost amid new social contradictions and human problems. The religion will become a mere dogma in the hands of demagogues and an instrument of the political system and social elites. The real message of the prophets will be corrupted. The time then will be ripe for a new message to meet the rising needs of man and overcome the social contradictions.

Second, the divine message is also linked to the personal capacity of the messenger. Some prophets were sent to guide small communities, a village or a town. Others were sent for one nation or race, while a few were to deliver a universal message and guidance. The latter were chosen to fulfill great responsibilities and needed superior ability. One can explain the scope and durability of the divine message and its relation to the capacity of the different prophets. The complex and persistent human contradictions require long-term messages to cure their effects and overcome their tragic tendencies. Such long-term and universal messages require highly qualified personalities that make it possible for the message to be influential and effective in human life. Any prophet "may not have the ability to handle the human contradictions in *toto*, everywhere, all the time."[367] The limited capacity of the prophet corresponds to the limited scope of the message, and the limited role that he plays in the course of history.

The final reason for the change and the renewal of prophethood was related to human development in history. The message must be compatible with the stage of human development and mental progress. At every historical epoch, the divine message advances mankind into new frontiers in his journey toward the Absolute, and cures his contradictions.

---

[365]Sadr, "Risalatuna wa-al-Daʿwah," (Our Message and those Who Preaches) in <u>Risalatuna</u>, 29.

[366]Sadr, "al-Taghyyr wa-al-Tajdyyd fi al-Nubuwah" (The Change and Renewal in Prophethood) in <u>Ahl al-Bayt</u>, 34.

[367]Sadr, "al-Taghyyr," 37.

Human development in history itself consists of three dimensions that are related to man's relationship to God to man and to nature: 1) consciousness of monotheism (or oneness of God), 2) the moral responsibility to carry the burden of the message, and 3) the ability to control the physical environment.[368] Prophethood is a function of the first two dimensions of development, but not of the third. The divine message is not a blue-print program to show man the best possible way to exploit nature and its resources, but rather it is to solve the human contradiction.[369] The means of exploiting and controlling the environment are endless; however, the resultant contradiction of this process of development is remaining the same.

Although the idea of the oneness of God is common to all prophetic messages, the idea varies in degree with respect to its depth, originality, scope and thoroughness.[370] Man was introduced to this idea in gradual stages in history analogous to the development of his consciousness.

Since man is bound to his senses and to the [physical] world, because of his human and physical nature, he must be called to, must be pulled from, the perceptional and the physical world up to the ideal of monotheism, which is a metaphysical idea.[371]

For example, God in the Old Testament, according to Sadr, is presented as a national Lord to the people of Israel. Thus, the Israelites must lead the struggle to destroy other idols and gods foreign to their culture and identity, and believe in the oneness of their national God. God is presented as a national symbol to replace other idols and to function as a mean of solidarity for the people of Israel.[372] The Gospel (New Testament), on the other hand, raises the idea of God from the Lord of a nation to the father of man. The God of Christianity, as presented by the disciples of Jesus, is not for one nation or race, but for all of humanity. However, he is still within the boundaries of the perceptional world, and confined to the limits of the senses. "The Gospel did not consider God as the father of Jesus in particular, but gives the consciousness that God is but one father of all the human race."[373]

In the Quran, however, God is totally a transcendent reality and universal Lord, and

---

[368]Sadr, "al-Taghyyr," 38.

[369]Ibid., 42.

[370]Ibid., 39.

[371]Ibid., 39.

[372]Sadr, "al-Taghyyr," 39.

[373]Ibid., 40.

has no physical relationship to anybody, even to His messenger, the Prophet Muhammad. All people, including prophets and saints, are his creatures and worshipers. No special privilege are given to anyone but to be the worshiper of God. "Prophet Muhammad [himself], in the words of <u>Quran</u>, stands before God as a submitting and humble worshiper to receive His commands, and he has no choice but to obey."[374] It is only in Islam that the idea of oneness of God reaches its summit, distancing God from the down-grading physical forms and from similitude to His creatures, yet keeping the powerful and dynamic link between man and his Lord via the concept of man's <u>submission</u> to God.

The last stage of development is the stage of man's maturing to the point of taking the responsibility to lead humanity in its mission under God.[375] A responsibility of the believers requires sacrifice and forbearing for the sake of saving humanity as a whole from the burdens of attachment to the physical world and to sensual desires. To achieve such a stage of progression in human thinking and beliefs, man must go through gradual preparation and a slow process of training. At every stage of development, man carries new and burdensome tasks connected with the responsibility of guiding others toward their Lord. Sadr explains:

> In the comparison between the [responsibilities of the people] of Moses and Jesus, and that of the responsibilities of Islamic <u>ummah</u> ... we reveal great variation in degree of forebearing, which represent the amount of growth of the ability of the latter. Moses [for example] died and the people of Israel were lost. This means that throughout his life Moses directed his efforts and his sacrifices and struggle for delivering his message, but the final result at his death is that the people of Israel were led astray. The decision of God, exalted be He, was to leave them in astray for forty years because they were not responsive to the task of the message. They did not respond ever to what the message of Moses requires from them... Were those from <u>ummah</u> [of Prophet Muhammad] who carried the burdens of the message?[376]

Leadership of <u>Ummah</u> in Islam

The social group entrusted with the responsibility of guiding humanity into the Absolute itself needs a guide to lead it to the level of conscious maturity. This guide must take the role of a model who perfectly represents the message he calls for. As a messenger

---

[374]Ibid., 40.

[375]Sadr, "al-Taghyyr," 41.

[376]Ibid., 41.

of God, the Prophet thus was the educator who wanted to bring about a society of committed believers. Also the leadership of the first community of believers that follow the Prophet must be held by those who totally resemble the messenger of God. This early community must be built on a solid foundation, disjoint from its <u>jahiliyah</u> (ignorance) past to be formed from the principles of the divine message. This total purity requires totally purified leaders. In fact, the leaders must assume the role of teacher to the believers and the rest of the society.

These model-pedagogues (which are called in Shi^cism as <u>ma^csum</u> from <u>^cisma</u>, literally mean sinless or perfect) must be entrusted with the absolute leadership of the society to reshape it according to the values of the new message. The idea of <u>^cisma</u> is not peculiar to Shi^cism only, but is, according to Sadr, a standard practice of every social doctrine that determined to build a society that resembled its vision. Marxists, for instance, who are critical of the Soviet system of government, claim that the Russian leadership is not a pure representation of Marxist values and teaching.[377] The definition of <u>^cisma</u> hence is "the total involvement in the message, and the total representation of its values in the spiritual, ideological, and practical dimensions."[378]

The leadership of the first Islamic community was held by the Prophet Muhammad. The Prophet was in full control of all aspects of life of the society. Such a 'totalitarian' authority, to borrow from the terminology of modern political science, was essential to reshape the new Islamic society according to Islamic values. The message of Islam is the program of heaven to end man's psychological and social contradictions and to guide him in the progressive movement toward the <u>absolute</u>. For that case, it is a message that is not limited to one aspect of man's life, but a comprehensive one that seeks to purify all human deeds and relations. Generally speaking,

> ...the Prophet was leading a revolutionary movement, and conducting comprehensive operational change of the society, its beliefs, its practices and its values. The way confronting such operational change is not short indeed, but is a long one extending beyond the great semantical obstacles separating <u>jahiliyah</u> (ignorance, the pre-Islamic period) from Islam. Which means that the message preached by the Prophet should start with the <u>jahili</u> man to rebuild him into a new one, and to make out of him an Islamic personality who would hold the new light, and release him from all the <u>jahili</u> roots and

---

[377]Sadr, "Badayat al-Inhiraf wa-B^cath al-Mashakl allati Wajahat Amir al-Mu'minin," (The early corruption and some of the problem faced by the 'Prince of Believers,' i.e., Imam Ali) in <u>Ahl al-Bayt</u>, 73-74.

[378]Sadr, "Badayat," 74.

deposits.[379]

Such a thorough revolutionary change definitely requires a long period of time to take effect, beyond the few years of the Prophet had with his followers. However great the accomplishments of the Prophet in the nearly two decades of his preaching and in one decade of his sociopolitical leadership in Madina, it was not enough time to bring about a purified Islamic community disenchanted with its jahiliyah past. The community that the Prophet had achieved in a very short period of time was the model society for humanity as a whole; however, this status was the outcome of spiritual contact the community had with the Prophet. That community sets the highest standards for mankind in its commitment to the divine goal, in its sacrifices of all the material conditions for the sake of Islam, in its coherent unity of its members, and in its bearing of the difficulties of struggling for the cause of spreading the message of the Prophet.[380] Notwithstanding, the high standards of the community are a reflection of the great leadership of the Prophet and not the result of values of social consciousness of the Muslim community.

The duration of the commitment to the highest values of the social group varies from time to time, and from one event to another. This is evidenced when the social group faces tragic events. If the social values are the reflection of the social consciousness, then they will not be influenced by historical events or emotional moments. Sadr cites the example of the Prophet's victory in Mecca and his liberation of the Grand Mosque of Ka^cbah. At that joyful moment in history, the Prophet did not show any joyful feeling, pride, or vengeance against his enemy, but rather he felt more humble and thankful to his Lord on achieving what God had wanted him to do.[381] On the contrary, when values and ideals are the reflection of enthusiasm, it winds down through time and people are quickly disenchanted with them at the moment of great emotion. Sadr cites two examples to prove his point that the social values of the people of the Prophet, generally, were the outcome of enthusiasm and not of their rational consciousness. At the battle of Hunin when the Prophet distributed the booty between Quraish people (the tribe of the Prophet) only, the Ansar[382] showed their

---

[379]Sadr, Bahth Hawla al-Wilaiyah (Kuwait: Dar al-Tawhid, 1977), 6.

[380]Sadr, "Bidiyat al-Inhiraf," 76-77.

[381]Sadr, "Bidiyat," 87.

[382]al-Ansar are the people of Madina who believed in Islam and welcomed the Prophet and his followers from Mecca to establish the first Islamic state in their land. Madina then became the center of struggle to liberate Mecca and the rest of Arabian peninsula.

dissatisfaction with the decision of the Prophet and claimed that he has abandoned them in the favor of his tribe. The Prophet at that emotional period 'energizes' them with a dose of enthusiasm when he told them that "it is better for <u>Quraish</u> to be left with booty, and you, <u>Ansar</u>, gain the Prophet himself."[383] In short, it was for the sake of the booty, a minor materialistic gain, at that joyful moment that the <u>Ansar</u> doubted the sincerity of the Prophet and the wisdom of his decision.

The other example concerns the <u>Muhajiryyn</u>[384] at the death of the Prophet, another tragic and emotional moment. In their deliberation with the <u>Ansar</u> about the succession of the leadership of the Prophet, the <u>Muhajiryyn</u> claimed the right of the leadership belonged to them only because the Prophet Muhammad was from their tribe. Thus they have the legitimate claim to the authority. This claim was based on the fact that they were one of the few original believers in Islam who withstood the oppression of <u>Quraish</u> for decades, migrated to Madina leaving behind everything they owned, and fought all wars in the defence of Islam. However, at the moment of emotion, the values of their triable heritage of the <u>jahiliyah</u> dominated their action, and, in their deliberation with the <u>Ansar</u>, they made no reference to their values and principles of their new faith.[385]

Hence, Sadr concluded that the Islamic <u>ummah</u> did not consciously grasp the high social standards associated with their beliefs, but were motivated by the effect of the charisma and strong personality of the Prophet. To eradicate the social values of the past, they needed instruction over several generations in the ideals, values, and belief system of Islam. It was not feasible during the short period of the leadership of the Prophet to accomplish such a giant sociohistorical task. We must keep in mind that the majority of the Muslim community then comprised people converted to Islam after the liberation of Mecca, who had at most three years of experience with the Prophet.[386] In that respect, Islam did not come to change the society, but it is revolution against the corrupt environment aiming at the creation of a new social order that determined to reconstruct human being from the inside out. However, the one decade of the Prophet's leadership was full of struggle to protect the newly created social order and not fully dedicated to the process of social pedagogy and education. The Prophet's relationship to his people, thus, was not like that of Jesus to his disciples, but was rather the kind of relationship where the Prophet used to lead armies and manage the affairs of the state.[387]

---

[383]Sadr, "Badiyat al-Inhiraf," 90.

[384]al-Muhajiryyn are the few people of Mecca who migrated with the Prophet to Madina.

[385]Sadr, "Bidiyat," 91.

[386]Sadr, <u>Bahth Hawla al-Wilayah</u>, 30.

The message of Islam faced also an ideological challenge from other religions and belief systems. That challenge was directed to the Prophet's efforts toward safeguarding the Islamic community from infiltration of foreign elements and a set of beliefs that corrupts the ideals of Islam. Quran presents clear proof that such a struggle was faced by the early Muslim community. Many passages show that the real threat confronted Islam revelation responded to make clear to Muslims the basic tenants of the religion. This confrontation hindered the Prophet's efforts to teach the Muslims.[388]

In that case, the Prophet's immediate objective was to build up popular support for the divine religion and secure its continuity for the future (since it is the final message of God and the end of the prophethood mission on earth.) The plan was to leave a pedagogue in the leadership role that would continue the guidance of mankind in its mission under God. What was required for the accomplishment of the divinely mandated revolutionary movement was a leadership like that of the Prophet which would instruct the ummah and bring to the consciousness of the community the divine values. The role of the model-pedagogue (maᶜsum leadership) should continue until Islamic values were fully realized in the life of the people. The effort to achieve this is known as the jihad al-akbar (the great jihad), which is directed at fighting man's desires and attachment to jahiliyah's values of ignorance and corruption.

The Role of Immhood

The first sign of decline in the Islamic political system started in the position of the top leadership. According to Sadr, the system consists of: 1) the structure of the political state headed by the leader; 2) the ummah, which consists of people devoted to the message of Islam and the belief in the prophethood of Muhammad; and 3) mujtamaᶜ (society), which includes the totality of people who conduct their affairs and social relations according to the rules and regulations of the message.[389] Since the leaders that succeeded the Prophet were not maᶜsum, the system of laws that guide the relationship and affairs of the society would be reshaped according to the wills of the leaders and the demands of the political conditions of the time and not according to the guidance of God. This process of degeneration occurs gradually and unnoticed. As time goes by, the Islamic society would function not according to the prescribed laws of God, but according to the common laws of man. Contradictions at the personal and social level will build up, and the mission of religion to solve human

---

[387]Ibid., 30.

[388]Sadr, Bahth Hawla al-Wilayah, 30-31.

[389]Sadr, "Dawar al-A'imah Baᶜda Wafat al-Rasul," (The Role of Imams After the Death of the Prophet), in Ahl al-Bayt, 57.

problem gets lost in the absence of any commitment of people to shari^cah, God's laws. A tradition of one of the Imams says: " The first impediment to [the laws of] Islam will be with the authority which God, the Exalted and most High, had assigned, and the last impediment to Islam is the prayer."[390]

The ummah would remain the last element of the political system to degenerate over time. However, the Islamic ummah did not go through the whole process of pedagogy in order to protect itself from being affected by the influence of others values and belief systems.[391] The people who were entrusted with the leadership of the Islamic state were from among the ummah, which was motivated by enthusiasm and not inner consciousness. The ummah was left with no guides to correct its behavior and watch over its conduct and commitment to the laws of God.

More specifically, the result of setting aside the ma^csum from his role as the leader of the state and pedagogue of the ummah would spread to the other pillars of the political system. First the ummah will lose its capability of safeguarding the message of Islam from alteration by the leaders and influences of other sets of beliefs and doctrines. The society as a whole will witness the rise of all sorts of contradictions that destroy its solidarity and give rise to social stratification and distinctions.[392] The ummah itself will face the dwindling of the commitment to Islam. It is then that the entire political system is doomed to failure in the face of any foreign attack against the state because the ummah is not able to protect it and defend the faith. The ummah at last will be consumed by foreign ideologies and doctrines, and ready to adopt any non-Islamic way of life. This is an actual description of what happened after the invasion of the Ottoman Empire by Western nations. Then, not only the Islamic political system disintegrated, but also the ummah became too weak to secure its commitment to Islam and fell short in defending it. "The ummah would then degenerate as the atheist world invaded its land, and the ummah would decline as well as the message and the doctrine [of Islam]; and the ummah would become a by-gone after a period of being a reality in history. It is only then that the role of Islam would vanish."[393] In other words, the military victory of the West ended up in an ideological victory as well, and this is where Islam lost its ability to control and regulate the life of Muslims. Paradoxically, what started as setting aside the divine choice of God for leadership, i.e., the ma^csum Imams, had brought the collapse of other pillars of the Islamic political system consisting of shari^ca as the social

---

[390]Ibid., 58.

[391]Sadr, "Dawar al-A'imah," 58.

[392]Sadr, "Bidayat al-Inhiraf," (The Beginning of Decline), in Ahl al-Bayt, 127-128.

[393]Sadr, "Bidiyat," 129.

regulative mechanism, and <u>ummah</u> as the committed adherent to the Islamic principles.[394] On that subject, Sadr eloquently writes:

> And this invader who came to destroy the [Islamic system], to destroy the Islamic society, to destroy the Islamic state, would bring also with him the culture and values of his civilization. This will have an effect on the Islamic <u>ummah</u> which did not comprehend Islam completely and really well during all this period of distorted practices [of leadership]. The <u>ummah</u> will find itself at the end [of the reign] of the distorted practices, after the humiliation of its honor, after destroying its determination, after chaining its hands by the leadership who led the distorted practices, after it lost its true spirit it would not be able to immunize itself against what will happen after the failure of [system]; It is then the <u>ummah</u> would collapse, too, right after the collapse of the [system].[395]

The primary task of the divinely chosen twelve Imams was to gain control of the leadership in order to end the process of retrogression once and for all. The vigorous attempt to achieve control of the state by Imam Ali had led his enemies to claim he was 'power-hungry.'[396] As years passed, the popularity of the Imams within the Islamic masses started to decline. The different nations that converted to Islam were not aware of the role of the Imams and their importance for the safeguarding of the tenants of Islam. One of the major political roles of Imams was to bring about the historical conditions to assume the leadership.[397] This would be done through the rise of a popular grassroots movement that will be committed to the goal of <u>ma^csum</u> leadership. Such an intense organizational and educational process of the <u>ummah</u> definitely will take generations to achieve. Sadr sums up the Imams role in the following:

> The Imams did not think that raising the sword and having a military victory is enough to establish the foundations of a just rule headed by the Imam. Establishing such a rule with a stable foundations does not depend, according to their views, on the preparation of expeditionary force only, but requires before hand the preparation of an ideological military force that believe with an absolute faith in the Imam and his ^cisam, understands his ultimate goals, support his plan in the realm of government, and safeguard

---

[394]Sadr, "Thalathat A'imah," (Three Imams) in <u>Ahl al-Bayt</u>, 122.

[395]Sadr, "Badayat," 129.

[396]Sadr, "Dawr al-A'ima Ba^cda Wafat," 59.

[397]Sadr, <u>Bahth Hawla al-Wilayah</u>, 52.

the prevailing interests of the ummah.[398]

The second political role of the Imams was the fortification of the ummah against decay by infusing it with Islamic zeal and sentiment, and safeguarding its beliefs against perversion.[399] This would give an extended life to ummah, enabling it to stand against the infiltration of various values and foreign beliefs and attach itself emotionally to the beliefs of Islam.

However, that tactical goal was achieved at two levels. In some cases, the Imams themselves were directly involved in the affairs of Muslims, either giving them advise to correct their policy or deviation from Islam, or stopping their corruption in a public opposition or armed uprising.[400] While the first Imam, ᶜAli, used to give advise to the second caliph, Umar,[401] he publicly showed his dissatisfaction with some of policies of the third caliph, ᶜUthman.[402] On the other hand, the second Imam, Hussein, led a revolt that resulted in his violent death along with members of his family and companions, against the corrupt rule of Yazid, the second Umayyad ruler. The fourth Imam, ᶜAli-Sajad, sent his son, Muhammad-Baqir, to ᶜAbdl al-Malik, an Umayyad ruler, to set up a financial policy for the Islamic state that was threatened by a boycott from the Byzantine Empire.[403] The eighth Imam, ᶜAli al-Rida, frequently gave religious and political advise to al-Ma'mun, an ᶜAbbasid ruler.

To safeguard the ummah's beliefs, the Imams were the pioneers in fostering religious studies and educating people as to the proper Islamic behavior. Imams throughout history were looked at as the symbol of purity of Islamic conduct, and the source of Islamic knowledge. The vast and quick spread of Islam throughout the lands of Africa, Asia, and Spain had two negative affects on the Muslim ummah: First the wealth generated from such expansion had created a prosperous society more tuned to luxuries and a comfortable life-style than to religious duty. Muslims began to think more of their materialistic conditions and needs, and slackened in their attachment to God and to the heavenly principles of Islam.[404]

[398]Sadr, "Dawr al-A'ima fi al-Hayat al-Islamiyah," in Ikhtarna Lak, 68.

[399]Sadr, "Dawr al-A'ima Baᶜda Wafat," 59.

[400]Ibid., 65-68.

[401]Ibid., 66-67.

[402]Ibid., 64.

[403]Sadr, preface to al-Sahifah al-Sajadiyah [of Imam ᶜAli ibn Hussein al-Sajad] (Tehran: al-Maktabah al-Islamiyah al-Kubra, n.d.), 8.

Imam ᶜAli al-Sajad, for example, reminded people of their metaphysical being and needs through his suplications which contained an encyclopedic references to the Islamic principles and showed the way of devotion to God.[405]

It was because of these types of political involvement and these high standards of Islam manifested by the Imams as well as their indubitable commitment to the faith that the Imams, and especially ᶜAli, become the symbol of all Islamic revolutionaries. "Getting the gratification of Imams of Ahl al-Bayt" was the slogan of their revolutions. For example, the first revolutions in Islam against the third caliph, Uthman, made Ali their symbol of Islamic purity as well as their choice for leadership. The second Islamic revolution, the Abbasid revolution, in the second century of Hijrah, rose from the mobilization of the Muslim masses around imams of Ahl al-Bayt.

The other negative effect was exposing the ummah, which did not go through a long period of pedagogy to understand fully the basic tenets of Islam, to different creeds, religions and philosophies.[406] Such exposure had influenced numbers of Muslim intellectuals and started to affect the social beliefs of Muslims in general. The imams took the initiative to set the foundations for religious schools to introduce and educate the Muslim ummah about the laws and ideology of Islam. The pioneers in this intellectual activity were Muhammad-Baqir, Jaᶜfar al-Sadiq and Musa al-Kadim, the fifth, sixth and seventh Imams, respectively.[407]

The second tactical role of Imams in the affairs of Muslims consisted of an indirect involvement aimed at safeguarding the belief of the ummah against deviation. The strategy of the Imams was to raise the consciousness and determination of the ummah to the level of protecting its identity and defending its rights. Such a role was accomplished via "Alawi (followers of Imam ᶜAli) revolutionaries who through their struggle and courageous sacrifices wanted to preserve the Islamic consciousness and Islamic will, and the Imams, may peace be upon them, supported those who were sincere."[408]

---

[404]Sadr, preface to al-Sahifah, 11-13.

[405]A collection of Imam Ali-Sajad's sublication is collected in what is known as al-Sahifah al-Sajadiyah (Book of al-Sajad). The book, which contained sublications for specified for various human deeds, is highly revered book, particularly for shias, and regularly recited by believers along with acts of worship.

[406]Sadr, preface to Sahifah, 10.

[407]Sadr, "Thalathat," 115-116.

[408]Sadr, Bahth Hawla al-Wilayah, 53.

<u>Social Stratification</u>

Centuries of incompetent rulers heading the Islamic political system brought a social condition entirely different from the divinely prescribed one. The Islamic society in no way approximated the ideals of Islam: unity among tribes, solidarity of Muslims, brotherhood of believers, and universal equality of mankind. Since the turn of the century, and due to generations of corrupt rulers that weakened the social coherence of the Islamic state, and due to foreign invasions of Muslim lands, the <u>Dar al-Islam</u> (world of Islam) is not divided only into various nationalities and states, but each of these heterogenous social entities also breaks into even smaller and distinct social groups.

Sadr has developed a classification of social groups in what he called <u>al-mujtama^c al-Fir^cuni</u> (Pharaonic society) where the absolute ruler who resembles Pharaoh is its core. The division of the society is political in nature and is designed to serve the survival of Pharaoh's political system. The Quran portrays this disintegration in the following verse:

> Now Pharaoh had exalted himself in the land and had divided its inhabitants into sects.(28:4)[409]

In other words, Pharaoh society as such is disintegrated, torn apart into divisions with the socioeconomical resources lying in waste.[410] In that confrontational social environment, mankind loses his capacity to innovate and develop. Thus, the survival of the whole social unit is in question in the long run. This is the definite historical consequence of a society that considers Pharaoh as its <u>al-Mathal al-^cAla</u>. Pharaoh here is the symbol of the center of oppression, i.e, dictator, charismatic leader, institution, party or social organization. The objective of this <u>mathal ^cala</u> is continuation of political reign. It can be achieved in a hierarchical yet oppressive social structure that only functions to serve as the symbol of oppression. Human progress and development are unknown to this type of political system. The political goal of Pharaoh is 'divide and rule.' Following are Sadr's social classifications:

<u>Oppressed oppressors</u>. This group of people consists of those who execute Pharaoh's orders in society. In the modern political system, they represent those who function within the agencies of coercion of the state. Hence, they are the 'secondary oppressors' which the Imams referred to them as the 'aides of the oppressors.'[411] It is due to them that the type of Pharaonic political system survives and is nourished. However, some of them may fall victim to Pharaoh during the change of his policies. However, before the judgement of God,

---

[409]<u>The Koran</u>, v. II, 86.

[410]Sadr, <u>Muqaddimat</u>, (Kuwait: al-Dar al-Islamiyah, 1980), 190.

[411]Sadr, <u>Muqaddimat</u>, 192.

they will face a similar fate as their masters.

..When the evildoers (oppressors) are stationed [before] their Lord, banding argument the one against the other! Those that were abased will say to those that waxed proud, 'Had it not been for you, we would have been believers.' (34:31)[412]

Advisors and assistants. Those are not like the previous group who execute policies, but they are the one who make policies and plan options for Pharaoh. In this case, they are not his arms, but his eyes. Since they are aware of Pharaoh's demands and goals, they mostly instigate his actions and influence his behavior.[413]

Then said the Council of the people of Pharaoh, 'Wilt thou leave Moses and his people to work corruption in the land, and leave thee and thy gods? Said he, 'We shall slaughter their sons and spare (or rape) their women; surely we are triumphant over them!'(7:127)[414]

This group constitutes the flatterers and an inner circle that Pharaoh refers to for advice, or they may exist just for support of his policies. They are at his disposal for legitimizing his oppressive rule.

Rabble, hooligans. They constitute the masses of any authoritarian political state. They are often labeled by political scientists as 'mobs.' Sadr seemed to adopt this terminology from Imam ᶜAli's tri-class social order based on their acquisition of knowledge.[415] The group ranks the lowest of this hierarchical social stratification, i.e., they have no consciousness of their own, or a will of their own.[416] They are those who not only do not consciously feel they are oppressed by the regime, and do not realize there is terror in the state.[417] The Quran recount their state of affairs in the day of Judgment in the following

---

[412]The Koran, v. II, 135.

[413]Sadr, Muqaddimat, 193.

[414]The Koran, v. I, 135.

[415]Imam ᶜAli classifies the society into three groups: 1) divine scholar (or knowledgeable, wiseman); 2) those who seek to acquire knowledge; 3) al-hamaj al-ruᶜaᶜ (rabble hooligans) who follow every caller, and swing in every direction. See Imam `Ali, Nahj al-Balaghah (The Path of Eloquency) footnoted by Shaykh Muhammad Abduh, 2nd ed. (Beirut: Dar al-Andalus, 1963), v. IV, 594.

[416]Sadr, Muqaddimat, 195.

verse:

> They shall say [when they faced hell], 'Our Lord, we obeyed our chiefs and great [ones,] and they led us astray from the way.' (33:67)[418]

"In their conversation," cited in the above verse, Sadr argues, "nothing shows that they felt the oppression, or felt being oppressed, but only mere obedience, and mere dependency."[419] Their obedience to Pharaoh was beyond any questioning or reservation. For the most part, they act voluntarily and have abandoned their rational thinking. They are objects with mechanical movements that are directed as Pharaoh wants. For them, they have no ability to innovate and or to develop into full participants in mankind's historical mission of progress. Any manifestation of achievement attributed to this group belongs to those who control and direct these human-like machines.[420]

"Pharaonism," throughout history, tries, according to Sadr, for its own survival, vigorously to keep the bulk of the population within this group because it does not pose any challenge to the political system. Instead, they serve the goals and needs of Pharaoh. However, since the group lacks any ability to innovate and develop, they can be considered the source of decay of the Pharaonic social order because they lack the ability to defend the society in the face of internal or external crisis. The 'natural death,' as Sadr liked to call it, of the social order is the consequence of this group. The faster the growth of this group within the society, the more quickly death would come to the social order. Thus, Pharaonism contains the seed of its ruin.[421] On the other hand, the goal of al-mujtama^c al-salih (righteous society) is strive to vanquish the existence of this group. This should occur, not through a physical elimination, but through self-development and progression to the second level of Imam ^cAli's social hierarchy, i.e., those who seek knowledge for salvation to allow them to make use of their consciousness and rationality. In sum, the continuity and expansion of al-mujtama^c al-salih rests on its success in putting an end to the category of the rabble.

Self-oppressed. Contrary to the previous group, this group consciously opposes the unjust situation in the society, however they try "to appease it and keep silent."[422] They refrain from taking any political action against their oppressors and defending their rights.

---

[417]Ibid., 194.

[418]The Koran, v. II, 129.

[419]Ibid., 194-195.

[420]Ibid., 194.

[421]Sadr, Muqaddimat, 196.

[422]Ibid., 196.

> And those the angels take, while still they are wronging (oppressing)
> themselves--the angels will say, 'In what circumstances were you?' They will
> say, 'We were abased in the earth.' The angles will say, 'But was not God.s
> earth wide, so that you might have emigrated in it?' (4:97)[423]

Hence, their quietness and inactive attitude toward injustice, coupled with their awareness of it, make them live in a disturbed psychological state of mind that incapacitates them in innovating and developing in the realm of man's relationship towards nature. In that case, they will not help the society to progress.[424] Therefore, this group is not only useless to the Pharaoh and society; they also cause harm to their own psychological being. For this they are considered oppressors to themselves.

<u>Monks</u>. Although monks are conscious of the unjust social order of Pharaonism, their political reaction to injustice takes a negative expression. Instead of an active role to oppose oppression, they turn their backs and escape from reality. The phenomenon of monasticism is prevalent in every society that faces severe injustice throughout history.[425] It gives relief to those who calculate their historical role as insignificant in terms of accomplishing any meaningful result.

However, Sadr distinguished two types or trends of monasticism. The first group are the 'real monks' or those who would like to save themselves from the corruption of the society which was manifested forcefully in the unjust rule. Such running away from the facts-of-life is surrendering to injustice which Islam, therefore, condemns because it was considered a retreat from man's responsibility of his role as vicar of God.

> And We set in the hearts of those who followed him (Jesus)
> tenderness and mercy. And monasticism they invented--We did not prescribe
> it for them--only seeking the good pleasure of God.(57:27)[426]

The second trend of monasticism is represented by those 'artificial monks' who are not sincere in themselves, but have a mystic appearance for the purpose of deceiving others from gaining social status or benefits.[427]

> O believers, many of the rabbis and monks indeed consume the

---

[423]<u>The Koran</u>, v. I, 115.

[424]Sadr, <u>Muqaddmat</u>, 197.

[425]Ibid., 197.

[426]<u>The Koran</u>, v. II, 262.

[427]Sadr, <u>Muqaddmat</u>, 198.

goods of the people in vanity and bar from God's way.(9:34)[428]

Such a phenomenon is encouraged by Pharaoh to help divert the attention of people who otherwise oppose him and might threaten his rule by taking an active political role. This group acts as an agent of political passivism in the society, thus, prolonging the reign of Pharaoh.

The oppressed. At the bottom of Pharaoh's social hierarchy are the mustadᶜafin (oppressed) who are the focus of oppression and humiliation. This group only poses a political threat to Pharaoism by their willingness to take the risk of adopting political action to topple the reign of the unjust. Therefore, Pharaoh's social order will use whatever is at its disposal to crush this group and incapacitate their ability to move politically.

> And when We delivered you from the folk of Pharaoh who were
> visiting you with evil chastisement, slaughtering your sons, and sparing (or
> raping) your women; and that was a grievous trial from your Lord.(2:49)[429]

However, the oppressed, because of their consciousness of injustice and willingness to change their social environment for a better order, are the only social group under Pharaoism opposed to stagnation and actively participating in the human historical progress. They can be considered the source of dynamism and hope for the future. In this case, their status in the post-Pharaonic order is inversely proportionate to their status during Pharaoh's time. The revolution led by the oppressed will result, as the divine logic of history tells us, in making the slaves become masters, and in relegating the elite to the margins of the society. Their ultimate reward, as the Quran states it plainly in the following verse, is the grace of God.

> ..We desired to be gracious to those that were abased (oppressed) in
> the land, and to make them leaders, and to make them inheritors.(28:5)[430]

---

[428]The Koran, v. I, 211.

[429]The Koran, v. I, 35.

[430]The Koran, v. II, 86.

Political Movement

There is, however, a limit at which forbearance ceases to be a virtue.

Edmund Burke

Basing his thought on his social classification, Sadr mapped out a political movement that aimed to guide the 'oppressed' (mustad^cafin) group to their final victory. According to him, this is the only social group that would bring about real change within the Pharaoh's social order, a political system that is prominent in the Muslim world. They are the hope and the source of change and progress in this type of political system. Therefore, Sadr's political design is to utilize the capabilities and energies of this oppressed group to lead them to their final victory over their oppressors. The determinate law of history that promised their ultimate victory is contingent on their determination and commitment to achieve their goal. For that cause, the oppressed must strive in a long march to their victory, which might take years of struggle and bring intense and severe oppression by their social enemy.

Political Program

Since the main reason for the 'rise and fall of nations,' in Sadr's political theory, is al-mathal al-a^cla, the reason why the Muslim ummah is unable to rise and move forward is that its al-mathal al-a^cla is the absolute itself. Sadr identifies three elements of the mathal al-^cala: 1) the nature of the mathal itself; 2) understanding its fundamentals; and 3) the belief of the ummah in it.[431]

In addition to the absolute being at the center of the Islamic belief, the mathal al-^cala of Islam has all the characteristics that are needed to motivate believers to commit themselves to the historical-political struggle to achieve the emancipation of man. Islam, first of all, is a religious doctrine. Its principles and teachings are sacred in the consciousness of its people. This is different from the belief in a philosophical or ideological doctrine where the validity of their principles will not reach the level of certainty in the

---

[431]Sadr, "al-Shart al-Asasi lil Nahdhat al-Ummah" (The Principle Condition for the Emancipation of Ummah) in Risalatuna (Beirut: al-Dar al-Islamiyah, 1981), 21.

consciousness. People who believe in religions have no question in their minds about the validity of religious teachings and principles.[432] These constitute the divine truth revealed from God, the most knowledgeable and knowing. They are unlike those derived from ideological or philosophical premises, which represent only views and opinions of men. A Marxist, for example, may think that Marx himself was wrong in understanding certain historical conditions, as in the case of Lenin when he realized the naivety of Marx's view when the latter thought workers would organize themselves to lead a revolution of the proletariats. Thus, Lenin saw the need to organize a communist party led by the intelligentsia to guide the workers to their final goal. On the other hand, a believer in a divine religion would never think that God, or His prophet, had erred in their prescription for enduring man's contradictions. Divine teachings are the final truth and are everlasting.

Islam also gives the 'hope' to the believers that victory is always on their side. It is this 'hope' that gives the "glimpses of light" to those who struggle to change the social conditions. "And once the (political doctrine) loses hope in victory and success, it loses its existence and its real essence."[433] In Islam, it is God's promise that his servants who believe in Him will be victorious and prevail over their enemies, regardless of the historical conditions which overpower them. The hope of Islam, in the early days of the message, acted as a strong motivational force for Muslims to overcome the overwhelming oppressive conditions and rise beyond them to liberate the land of Persia and Byzantine.[434]

Still, up to now the Islamic message is, as it was, able to incarnate the hope in the soul of believers; to actually incarnated, through the lights of its Quranic and prophethood verses that promised victory, provided the attention (of believers) is devoted (to God) and plans (of action) are drawn according to Islam.[435]

The third unique characteristic of Islamic belief is that it integrates the personal-egotistic motivation with the ideal motivation of religion.[436] Any social doctrine must reshape the society according to its image and must commit its adherents to its ideals. The adherents must be motivated by the ideals and sacrifice for the promised goals; yet unless man finds some net return to his self-interests, his ideal motivations fade through time.

---

[432]Sadr, "Risalatuna wa al-Duᶜat," (Our Message and the Callers) in <u>Risalatuna</u>, 28.

[433]Sadr, "Resalatuna wa al-Daᶜwa," 30.

[434]Ibid., 31.

[435]Ibid., 31.

[436]Sadr, "Resalatuna wa al-Daᶜwa," 32.

Islam, however, motivates the believers to achieve ideals through personal net-return, felt by the believer. A sacrifice by a believer for the ideals of the message will be compensated by personal benefits, a heavenly gratitude from God to him. The ideal of Islam, which has a sociohistorical goal, is at the same time a personal gain to the believer himself regardless of the outcome of the struggle.

A lack in understanding the fundamentals of Islam causes the oppression of the ummah. Sadr questions why, if the ummah has a strong belief in the religion of Islam, the people still have a vague understanding of its teachings and principles! He answers that the colonization of the Islamic world by the West resulted in weakening the belief of Muslims in Islam.[437]

Sadr totally disregards the internal conditions that might have caused the problems faced by the Muslim community, such as weakness in understanding their beliefs, and places the cause of the problems in the realm of external conditions. In this situation, he does not seem consistent, or objective in accounting for all aspects of the problem of understanding the message by the ummah. Western colonization might have caused the great drift of the ummah from its belief, but definitely it is not the only cause. In his analysis of the previous section which is mainly quoted in his Ahl al-Bayt, Sadr refers to the problem of the cessation of education of the ummah by a maᶜsum leadership. The short period of indoctrination and education of the ummah has caused it to drift through time from understanding the basic fundamentals of Islam. Western colonization of Muslims can be considered as the last stroke in a long historical process of detachment of the Muslim ummah from Islam.

Based on his analysis, Sadr wanted to bring an understanding of Islam to the ummah , to let them rediscover their religion, and comprehend its truth. His political design aimed to "uncover its everlasting treasures so Islam may fulfill the longing of the ummah and its thoughts, and be its motivational force, and trusted means of its true and comprehensive emancipation."[438] This design explains the wish of Sadr to write well-argued, highly elaborate, and forcefully presented treaties that contained a comprehensive study and critique of the major Western philosophical and sociological schools of thought, at the same time, presenting Islam as the only truth and solution to man's problems. Two of his major works, Falsafatuna (Our Philosophy) and Iqtisaduna (Our Economics), are pioneer texts in the effort to achieve his goal. He wanted to show Muslims that the solution to their social problems, to their underdevelopment, is not Western ideas and experience, but, rather Islam.

He also wanted to develop committed believers, who not only have a strong belief in Islam, but also conduct themselves in harmony with the commands and teachings of the religion. Islam is a way of life and not only a system of beliefs. What is comprehended in

[437]Sadr, "al-Shart," 23.

[438]Sadr, "al-Sart," 24.

the mind must be manifested in deeds since the emotions, which are expressed in conduct, are the representations of the thoughts and ideas present in the mind; they must concur with the teachings of Islam. Islam, as a religion, wants ideas to form the emotions of a human being, which in return define human conduct and deed.[439] Man's social relationships, personal behavior, and individual attachment must be coordinated with Islamic beliefs. In this way, a believer in Islam finds harmony within his personality because his emotions are correlated with his thoughts. A Muslim, therefore, finds no conflict between his behavior and belief. He is a confident person, more so than those who find themselves in a continuous contradiction between their beliefs and their behavior.

<u>Political Goal</u>

Three elements define the personality of a human being, according to Sadr:

1) thoughts, which give rise to philosophical views about existence and life; 2) emotions, which include all the psychological components derived from thoughts that affect the behavior of human beings in life such as retreat, love, hate, support, opposition, forgiveness, honor, and disgrace; and 3) behavior, which includes all the personal deeds, positive and negative, that are the outcome of the thoughts and emotions.[440]

In sum, an individual who fully understands what he believes and behaves according to that belief is called by Sadr <u>al-shakhsiyah al-multazimah</u> (committed personality). In contrast, those whose behavior is not shaped by their beliefs are not committed.[441] Thus, an Islamic personality would not include those who only recite that "there is no god but God, and Muhammad is His prophet," while the teaching of Islam and its laws have no significant role in regulating their behavior and social relationship. It would definitely include those who place the interests of Islam above their personal interests, who are attached to God through their commitment and behavior, and who try to be a social model whereby others may learn about Islam.[442]

---

[439]Sadr, "al-Masha^cir wa al-Afkar," (The emotions and the Thoughts), in <u>Risalatuna</u>, 33-35.

[440]Sadr, "al-Shakhsiyah al-Islamiyah," (Muslim Personality) in <u>Min Fikr al-Da^cwah al-Islamiyah</u> (Of the Thoughts of Islamic Da^cwah), no. 13, (Islamic Da^cwah Party-- central propagation, place and date of publication unknown), 14.

[441]Ibid., 15.

[442]Ibid., 17.

According to Sadr, it is this type of believers that is the essential components for the emancipation of the <u>ummah</u> and the rise of Islam again to a leading position among Muslims after having been set aside by the colonized Western powers in the past two centuries. The more 'committed Muslim personalities' there are within the <u>ummah</u>, the greater the hope to achieve the goal. The process of struggle entails hardship and suffering, both of which require deep commitment to the goal and sincere devotion to God. Unless there is a reserve army of such individuals the struggle for the cause of God will eventually be interrupted by oppression and a long wait for victory. It is the indispensable army of committed personalities that secures the victory of Islamic movement in the long run. Regarding that, Sadr states:

> Our task at this [historical] stage, O Brothers, is to recruit the greatest number possible of those Muslim personalities that incorporate Islam as a living phenomenon in their lives, and who will change, God willing, the path of human history and reinstate to humanity its honor and emancipate it to the highest level of civilization man has ever witnessed.[443]

In addition to being committed to their beliefs, Muslim personalities must strive to achieve a sociohistorical goal. This striving makes them different from those committed Muslims who have no such goal in their lives. The latter might have deep beliefs and an understanding of the religion and coordinate all his behavior according to the commands of Islam, yet live on the edge of history with no social role to play. Therefore, they are insignificant as factors in the historical progress of humanity. It is the goal that gives a meaning to life, "for the value of man's life is equal to the ideas which he believes in and contends to achieve."[444]

Therefore, <u>al-Insan al-Hadif</u> (man-of-purpose) would strive to obtain for his belief the most suitable environment, which can be done in three ways: 1) by bringing to his belief a directive role in social life; 2) by reinforcing its foundations and survivability; or 3) by spreading its message among people and extending its influence in life.[445] Simultaneously, the Islamic movement should not only increase the number of committed Muslims, but also discover among them those who are 'objective,' because they represent "the real leaders the <u>ummah</u> is waiting for, and depends on, to achieve its hopes of regaining its sovereignty and recovering its national pride and international prestige."[446] To distinguish the 'objective

---

[443]Sadr, "al-Shakhsiyah," 17.

[444]Sadr, "al-ᶜAmal wa al-Ahdif," (The deeds and the goals) in <u>Min Fikr al-Daᶜwah</u>, 21.

[445]Sadr, "al-ᶜAmal al-Hadif," 24.

[446]Ibid., 24.

personalities' from those who are not is very vital to the current struggle of the movement.

<u>Political Means</u>

To achieve the goal of making Islam the social doctrine of society that dictates the rules of behavior for both the ruler and the ruled requires planned political activities that organize the efforts of the objective committed Muslims into one specific political program. Although the random activities of those dedicated Muslims activists may be the outcome of sincere efforts and total commitment of the participants, they will not produce tangible results in the political life of the Muslim society due to the lack of a comprehensive rational plan for achieving a definite goal.[447] The task that Sadr is vigorously stating is not to reform the existing social order of Muslims, but rather to embark on a radical course of action that ultimately aims to wipe out the existing political systems that are not based on Islam and replace them with Islamic ones. In this connection, he called his political plan a "revolutionary movement," which is different from the "reformation movement," where the goal of the latter being merely to reform the system in some aspects while disregarding, in the course of its activities, other aspects or the fundamentals on which the current situation is built."[448] However, the revolutionary movement is determined to change the enduring social situation, because it conflicts with the basic fundamentals of its beliefs, and creates a new situation based on the doctrine of the movement and restructure human life and social order according to its principles.[449]

The current political system, which is the heritage of the postcolonial period, is contradictory to the basis of Islam and the cultural values of Muslims. The effects of Western colonization cost the Muslims dearly. The <u>ummah</u> lost not only its political structure, which was replaced by a foreign one, but also its religious values and Islamic principles, which were supplanted by Western ones. The <u>ummah</u> forgot its religious message and surrendered to the colonizing masters not only politically, but ideologically as well.[450] He exuberantly exclaims:

> ...that the situation of Islam at the current condition is not a matter of reforms, but rather a revolutionary one. The reformation movements which played a part in building religious schools some times and published books and magazines at others; established committees to preach and sermon the

[447]Sadr, "al-ᶜAmal," 26.

[448]Sadr, "Daᶜwatana il al-Islam Yajeb an Takun Enqilabiyah" (Our Call for Islam Must be a Revolutionary), in <u>Fikr al-Daᶜwah</u>, 35.

[449]Ibid., 35.

[450]Sadr, "Daᶜwatana," 36-37.

next time; and all those sorts of services...would constitute marginal activities and are not part of the real crisis. The major conflict Islam is facing today with its enemies concerns the return of the leadership role and the restoration of the Islamic doctrine to its proper position in the life of ummah...

The situation--O Brothers--is not a situation of youths being corrupted by schools, and not of a group that needs sermons and guidance, and not of an environment that needs to be cleaned and purified from immorality and rottenness; but a situation of an ummah that must be emancipated according to the principles of Islam so as to be fortunate in this world and the hereafter.[451]

The solution for this situation, therefore, would not come from efforts to reform some aspects of the social order but from a comprehensive change in the whole structure. Reformation movements were conceivable when the social system was based on the fundamentals of Islam, although what contained some corrupt elements within its structures. However, in the case of a system, Sadr argues, which is in total conflict with Islam and is structured on anti-Islamic principles, reformation is incomprehensible. The only conceivable course of action is a revolutionary one to reinstate Islam as the ruling force of the society.

The goal of restructuring the social system according to Islam can be realized only through the organization of Islamic activities so as to intensify the scattered efforts of committed Muslims into a unified purpose. The various efforts and activities of Muslim activists must not deviate from the goal of the Islamic movement as a whole. Sadr could foresee different means to achieve the goal, but he defined the specificity of the goal itself with reference to the current political conditions, i.e., the establishment of an Islamic political system. Once the goal is embraced by all Muslims, then it is permissible to adjust the means when "it becomes difficult or impossible to bring the goal to realization."[452]

However, Sadr had engineered what he regarded as an effective means to achieve the revolutionary goal. He thought the best possible way to coordinate the random activities into one effective and unified force was through the mobilization of committed Muslims personalities through a political organization, that is a party. The organization of such political institutions is a progressive form of other types of existing movements. The party will not only organize the multitudes for one unified task to achieve one specific goal, but also will contribute to educating the members who will take the task of propagating Islam within the ummah. "[Historical] experience of various international movements ascertains that organization is a successful means in changing the society in the direction either of

---

[451]Ibid., 37.

[452]Sadr, "al-ᶜAmal wa al-Ahdif," 26.

righteousness or of wickedness."[453]

Of course there are differences between Islamic party activities and that of other parties of different ideology, and these differences stem from the fact that "activists in an Islamic party strive for the message of God,.. obey the laws of God,.. and take their rewards from God, not from people.[454]

Additionally, the hierarchy in the Islamic party, Sadr states, is not according to position or status within the party structure, but rather according to closeness to God. This implies that members obey God's laws only and not the laws of those in the upper echelon of the party. However, such a spiritual hierarchy will cause chaos and disorganization, where a political party is institutionalized on the basis of obedience of its members to commands of the leadership. To overcome this problem, Sadr explains that party orders either should be in agreement with God's law, or have a religious connotation that makes it obligatory for Muslims to follow and obey its dictates: either 1) through a religious oath that the member voluntarily submits to, solemnly swearing to follow the guidance of the party in his efforts to serve the interests of Islam; or 2) through consideration of the necessity of achieving Islamic goals only through combined organized efforts of Muslims, "particularly, when one takes into consideration the nature of atheist powers in our times who use the weapon of organization to confront the religion of God and its advocates;"[455] or 3) through a decree of a Muslim jurist (faqih) requiring obedience to the orders of the party.[456]

According to Sadr, the organization of an Islamic political party is consistent with the teaching of Islam, and the obedience of party commands can have religious connotations. Furthermore, "Islamic shari‎c‎ah," Sadr holds,

...does not dictate the means to be followed by the Muslims in campaigning for [social] change, therefore, it is religiously permissible for us to adopt any suitable way to spread the teachings of Islam and its commands, and to change the society as long as the way will not entail a violation which is religiously forbidden.[457]

---

[453]Sadr, "Hawla al-Ism wa-al-Shakl al-Tanzimi li-Hizb al-Da‎c‎wah al-Islamiyah" (On the Name and the Structural Organization of Islamic Da‎c‎wah Party), in Min Fikr al-Da‎c‎wah, 10.

[454]Sadr, "Hawla al-Ism," 10.

[455]Sadr, "Hawla al-Isma," 11.

[456]Ibid., 10-11.

[457]Ibid., 9.

Since a political party is an effective means to achieve the goal of Islam, and does not cause Muslim members to violate any religious laws, then it can be utilized for Islamic purposes. Not every Western or non-Islamic means should be rejected on the basis that it is wrong and contrary to Islam, Sadr contends. A means adopted by an ideological doctrine is not necessarily derived, directly or indirectly, from its basic fundamentals but rather its employment may not be in conflict with the fundamentals of the doctrine at all.[458] If party organization is the common means of political activities in the west, it does not mean that it is a means that should not be employed by Muslims. In fact such a type of political organization is not alien to Islamic heritage. According to Sadr,

> If the Prophet, may peace be upon him and his household, had lived in our age, he would have, as a result of his wisdom, used the suitable modern means of propagation and communication. The truth is that his means of propagation was not far different from the cellular organization.[459]

Moreover, the Prophet, before his call to prophethood, had joined a social group called <u>Hilf al-Fudul</u> whose aim was to protect the rights of oppressed foreigners in Mecca. He was quoted, while in Madina, when he was faced with a similar situation of foreigners being harassed by the local people, to have said: "I wish I had an alliance like that of <u>Hilf al-Fudul</u>."[460]

Sadr concludes that the organization of an Islamic political party is not only a legitimate political activity according to Islamic laws, but is an indispensable task in the current political conditions. It can mobilize committed Muslims, utilize their efforts, and organize their activities to accomplish the goal of establishing an Islamic political state. Simultaneously, Muslims who become members of the party must coordinate their activities with the planning of the party and should not deviate from its general program. In fact, a party member should always refer to the party for guidance to see if his political activities are in harmony with the general goal of the party "so all political streams would flow into one source."[461] Concurrently, members of the party must execute the plans and the responsibilities delegated to them by the party, and must make the members main political activities his priority. In this situation, Sadr concludes that the political party's activitie, can

---

[458]Sadr, "Risalatuna Yajib ᶜan Takun Qaᶜidah" (Our Message Must Be A Standard), in <u>Risalatuna</u>, 52-53.

[459]Sadr, "Hawla al-Ism," 10.

[460]Quoting Muhammad Baqir al-Nasiri, the current chairman of <u>Jamaᶜt al-ᶜUlama'</u>, in his speech at the eighth conference of Muslim Group, 1987.

[461]Sadr, "al-ᶜAmal," 27.

only be endured by "objective men," who dedicate their whole lives to achieve their objective in life.[462]

Sadr also outlines the stages a political party, confronting the historical conditions the Muslim World in general and in Iraq in particular must go through in undertaking to create an Islamic political system. The historical stages come from his political interpretation of the current conditions of the social order, which includes the recommendation of specific political programs and actions to realize the political objective. He mentions four stages: 1) the stage of party formation; 2) the stage of political opposition; 3) the stage of control of the state apparatus and the establishment of Islamic political order; and finally 4) the stage of serving and protecting the interests of Islam and the <u>ummah</u>.[463]

First of all, the Islamic movement needs to secure sufficient members who are committed personalities in order to insure its continued existence during unexpected political conditions. Thus, Sadr foresees in the first stage that the Islamic political movement must carry its effort to the stage of what he calls "<u>ideological change</u> (emphasis added), which is characterized by intense emphasis on spreading radical thought among the general public of the <u>ummah</u>, and to create and teach the revolutionary masses."[464] The "ideological stage" is not only a recruitment stage for the movement, but also has a social dimension as well. The movement, while recruiting Muslims to its rank and file, aims to have an influence within the social order that immunizes it from political oppression and to use its "reserve" of Muslim intellectuals to influence the social behavior, the collective mind of the <u>ummah</u>, and strengthen its attachment to the teachings of Islam.[465] It is through their behavior, deeds, and words that these intellectuals (or intelligentsia, as Lenin liked to call them) would affect the general behavior and thinking of the <u>ummah</u>.

However, Sadr thought the ideological stage of the party should continue indefinitely to await any change in the political environment that would favor direct political action with the existing regime. He saw the potential for change within the international political environment which could have a significant impact on the internal conditions of the regime. Rising world pressure on the regime for its human rights abuses, for example, might <u>relax some suppressive measures</u>, which in turn could facilitate a system for vocal

---

[462]Ibid., 26.

[463]Kazim al-Ha'iri explaining Sadr's political design for the historical stages of Islamic Da͑wah Party, in <u>Mabahith al-Usul</u>, 90.

[464]Sadr, "Hawla al-Marhala al-Ula min ͑Amal al-Da͑wah," (On the First Stage of Task of Da͑wah), in <u>Min Fikr al-Da͑wah</u>, 31.

[465]Sadr, "Hawla al-Marhala," 31.

opposition. On this subject he said:

> When we live in a democratic country which believes in respecting its people and their views, the authority would not confront them with massacre and deportation that have no accountability or legitimacy, in which case one can assume that any party can begin its activities underground to establish itself and then launch its stage of political opposition in its attempt to mobilize the <u>ummah</u> to its side and drive it to adopt its political positions. However, the condition in [a place like] Iraq is not as such. At any moment the oppressive authority feels the existence of an organized Islamic party functioning according to such [planned] stages to make Islam the rule, [that authority] starts killing, deporting, imprisoning, torturing the activists and suppressing the activities in the country before they fully achieve the goal of making the <u>ummah</u> sympathize with it [Islamic party], and motivate her to its side. Unless there is going to be another international change in the world arena that can overrun [domestic regime] stability it is not possible for the [Islamic] party to move from its initial stage to the next.[466]

There are no detailed characterizations of other political stages by Sadr, at least in his published works,[467] except for some comments about the structure of the Islamic state (political treaties published only after the success of the Islamic revolution in Iran and the formation of an Islamic republic.)[468] In this latter work, he recapitulates the role of the <u>marja^c</u> and the <u>ummah</u> in the structure of the state, which can be considered as his views of

---

[466]al-Ha'iri quoting Sadr (around 1392 A.H) in <u>Mabahith</u>, 91.

[467]It is possible to assume that Sadr might have written to the Da^cwah Party the detailed analysis of his thoughts about the other stages and kept exclusive to the party since it is currently engaged in political struggle with the Ba^cth regime in Iraq. In fact, his thoughts about the ideological stage were published only after his death in 1980, when the first stage, as declared by the party, was completed. Mahdi al-Hakim, for example, talked about some of Sadr's writings on the structure of the Islamic state which were written exclusively for the members of the Da`wah Party in the late 1950s which are still not available for general publication.

[468]Six political treaties compiled (by the Islamic government in Iran) in one publication under the title, <u>al-Islam Yaqud al-Hayat</u> (Islam Leads Life), see the annotated bibliography of the book in the first chapter.

the third and, partially, of the fourth stage. Suffice it to say that Sadr places great emphasis on the role of the marjaᶜ in leading both the political struggle and the Islamic political state. The marjaᶜ would take the role of pedagogue left by the occultation of the maᶜsum leader, i.e., Imam Mahdi (the twelfth Imam) while the party would assume the role of the ummah in Sadr's political program.

Marjaᶜiyah

The role of marjaᶜ in Sadr's theory stems from his general view that the vicar of God on Earth would always have a constant need for some sort of divine intervention to protect him from corruption and guide him toward the goals of vicarage. Without this intervention, man can always be influenced by his instincts and passions which fade and weaken his potential for progress.[469] Accordingly, God established the role of shahid (witness), the shahid being the one who would take the responsibility of conveying divine guidance to mankind. Prophets were the first to be assigned to the role of shahid. Since the role of shahid is of vital importance to the communal role of vicar, while prophethood is limited to transmission of the divine message to mankind, men other than the prophets are appointed by Providence to continue the guidance of man in order to safeguard him from corruption.

> Surely We sent down the Torah, wherein is guidance and light;
> thereby the Prophets who had surrendered themselves gave judgment for
> those of Jewry, as did the master and the rabbis, following such portion of
> God's Book as they were given to keep and were witness to.(5:44)

According to Sadr, the Quran has designated the Imams, and then the scholars of religious laws (faqih or what the Shiᶜas refer to as marjaᶜ), to succeed the prophets in the role of shahid. Since the Imams and religious jurists understand divine laws and revelations, they will take the responsibility of safeguarding the message of God to mankind, and take on the active role of guiding man in his historical mission under God.[470]

> The shahid, from an ideological perspective, is the authority on belief
> and legislation who oversees the social journey and its congruence,
> ideologically, with the divine message. He is also responsible for getting the
> [human] journey back on its right course in case of any deviation that might
> occur during the application [of the message].[471]

The only difference between the three types of people who take the role of shahid is that the

---

[469]Sadr, Kalafat al-Insan, 143.

[470]Sadr, "Khalafat," 144-145.

[471]Ibid., 145.

prophet is the messenger who receives, delivers, and applies the divine message while the Imam is the divine chosen guide that interprets the message and the marjaᶜ is the one, according to Sadr,

> ...who possesses, through his human efforts and long period of hard-work the comprehension...of Islam from its original sources, as well as deep piety that disciplines him to control himself and his conduct, and [also possesses] a suitable Islamic consciousness of his environment with all its overwhelming conditions and surrounding interactions.[472]

The marjaᶜ thus becomes the successor of the prophets and Imams for the Islamic ummah in respect of his being a source of guidance and center of leadership. The man who possesses the ordained qualifications (knowledge of divine laws, ᶜilm; and self-control of conducts, ᶜadalah) shall take the responsibility of shahid. However, the marjaᶜiyah is not assigned to any particular person as is the role of prophets or Imams. It is the qualification for the role that becomes an important criterion to be satisfied by suitable individuals. A wrong interpretation of the role of *witness* occurs when it is thought of as belonging to the person of the marjaᶜ rather than to the role of the marjaᶜiyah itself. The marjaᶜ is the legitimate successor of Imams by virtue of his ᶜilm and ᶜadalah, although there are certain responsibilities for achieving specific goals connected with the role of *witness*. The mariaᶜiyah in shiᶜism had entailed the selection of an individual marjaᶜ but has made the role of *witness* the consequence of his ability, or the function of the political conditions. However, inconsistency in the marjaᶜs activities coupled with failure to define goals to be achieved had resulted in a weakening of the role of *witness*. Unless the marjaᶜiyah would entail certain well-defined objectives the ummah would find it difficult to ascertain its social missions.

Recognizing such a chronic shortcoming, Sadr conceived the idea of marjaᶜiyah al-maduᶜiyah (objective authority) that would replace, in the long run, the existing marjaᶜiyah al-dhatiyah (individualistic authority). In order to achieve the general goal of the role of *witness* (i.e., safeguarding the divine message and guiding mankind in their divine historical mission,) Sadr specified five objectives for the marjaᶜiyah:

1. The promulgation of the teachings of Islam as broadly as possible among the Muslims; and trying to give each individual a religious education which would safeguard his commitment to these teachings in his personal conduct.

2. Founding a wide-spread ideological movement within the ummah which embraces the right Islamic principles such as the fundamental principles which emphasis that Islam is a complete system comprehending

---

[472]Sadr, "Khalafat," 145.

the various sides of life; and using efficient means to consolidate such principles.

3. Sufficiently meeting the ideological needs of Islamic enterprise, which can be via facilitating enough Islamic studies in various economic and social fields, which would make ideological comparisons between Islam and other social doctrines; and expanding the field of Islamic fiqh (jurisprudence) in a way to enable it to provide all aspects of life with legislation; as well as ameliorating the hawzah (religious schools) as a whole to the level of this great responsibility.

4. Taking the responsibility of guardianship of the Islamic movement; and supervising what the activists contribute to understanding the path of Islam in the various parts of the Muslim world; and supporting every such proper move to maintain it, and rectifying what is improper.

5. Making sure the hierarchy of authority of the ummah belongs to the ᶜulama', starting from marjaᶜ to the lowest ranking jurist, through safeguarding its interests, being involved in the affairs of the people, and protecting and embracing the activists in the path of Islam.[473]

Although these objectives, by themselves, would distinguish al-marjaᶜ al-salih from one who conducts his social activities in an arbitrary manner, they would not make the marjaᶜiyah itself an objective one. The current process of marjaᶜiyah is centered around the marjaᶜ himself, and has no continuity at all. Each and every marjaᶜ establishes his authority and starts his activities from scratch with no reference to the preceding accomplishment of other marjaᶜs. The marjaᶜiyah is linked to the marjaᶜ himself, and begins when he establishes his credentials within the hawzah and the ummah, and concludes with his death. Another chronic ailment of long-established traditional marjaᶜiyah is its random selection of the individual who ascends to the rank of marjaᶜiyah. There are no certain qualifications for the position except that of ᶜilm and ᶜadalah. Although these qualifications might be considered as a necessary requirement for achieving the first goal of the role of shahid (i.e., safeguarding the divine message from corruption,) qualifications for the second responsibility of guiding ummah in its historical mission under God are lacking. Such a social task needs, in addition to an optimal fulfillment of the first ideological task, other skills that go beyond mere religious knowledge and righteous behavior. It requires an understanding of the social conditions, and what necessitates changing them in order to safeguard religion and guide the ummah. For these reasons, Sadr contemplates an evolution in the way the marjaᶜiyah conducts its business or adresses the state of affairs. Thereby, he

---

[473]Sadr, "al-Marjaᶜiyah al-Salihah" (The suitable authority) in Kazim al-Ha'iri, Mabahith al-Usul, 92-93.

proposed what he calls, a 'social foundation' that would make the impact of marjaᶜ in social affairs more effective and longer lasting. It is this 'social foundation' that will help the marjaᶜiyah achieve its objectives.[474] Sadr's prescription to the problem is to establish an institution in which the marjaᶜ himself forms the center, and where its structure, role, and process are thoroughly defined. Specifically, he wants to transform the marjaᶜiyah from being a traditional, individualistic, and arbitrary process into a modern, institutional, and objective one. His political engineering focuses on what he calls: 1) the improvement of marjaᶜiyah's procedures; and 2) stages of marjaᶜiyah.

To bring stability and coherency to the procedures of marjaᶜiyah, the marjaᶜiyah itself must function with a framework of well-established institutions where tasks and activities are specified and accountability enforced. On this issue, Sadr envisions two types of organizational set-ups of the marjaᶜiyah: the 'office of marjaᶜiyah,' which acts as the central administration; and the 'representatives,' which act as the social arm of marjaᶜiyah.

The central administration consists at first of six socio-political offices that perform the planning and executive activities of the marjaᶜiyah and in which the marjaᶜiyah is administered by qualified and specialized people as the tasks of each office are differentiated in order better to meet the responsibilities of marjaᶜiyah and achieve its goals.[475] The marjaᶜiyah, later on, can further develop these offices as tasks and responsibilities expand, to include the whole spectrum of affairs of the ummah. These offices will "replace the court [of the marjaᶜ] which represents an arbitrary individualistic structure made up of individuals grouped by chance who fulfill some immediate needs but exhibit a superficial mentality without any defined and clear objective."[476]

Sadr specifies some of the tasks of these offices (or committees, as he like to call them):

1. Committee to administer the educational affairs of the hawzah,..., which regulates its curricula, assigns the texts; gradually develops the education process of hawzah to the level that allows it to participate in achieving the goals of the objective marjaᶜiyah; provides the necessary data about the enrollment of students according to their geographical locations; and searches to fill the vacancies and increase enrollment.

2. Committee on scientific research, which takes the responsibility of founding scientific centers to conduct research and follow up its completion; administrates good achievement of hawzah; and follows up the intellectual achievement in the world which concerns Islam; and is able to produce

---

[474]Sadr, "al-Marjaᶜiyah," 93-94.

[475]Sadr, "al-Marjaᶜiyah," 94.

[476]Ibid., 94.

publications such as journals or other; and to encourage qualified individuals to enroll in <u>hawzah</u> or associate with it if living abroad.

3. Committee(s) responsible for the affairs of <u>ulama</u> in areas linked [to <u>marja^ciyah</u>] which keep records of their names, places, representations; follow their activities, behavior and relationships; meet their needs and vacancies; and write general reports regularly or at <u>marja^c</u> requests.

4. Committee on [foreign] relations that will be responsible for opening new links in areas where <u>marja^ciyah</u> has no contacts. It is also responsible for making studies and surveys of the areas and the possibilities of making relationships, and sending envoys, from the <u>marja^c</u> himself, or at any other level; and assigning the areas which are willing to welcome such envoys; ..as well as responsible for communicating in the proper manner with the intellectuals and scientists in various parts of the Muslim World and providing them with books; and utilizing ceremonies such as the event of <u>Haj</u>.

5. Committee to sponsor the Islamic movement and be aware of its impacts on the Muslim World, and make a judgment on each one and give guidance and support when needed.

6. Committee on financial matters for keeping records of capital and sources; finding financial representatives; searching for investing the regular resources of <u>bayt al-mal</u> (central treasury); and paying for the necessary expenses of <u>marja^ciyah</u>.[477]

The quotation above of Sadr's detailed descriptions of the committees of the central administration of the <u>marja^ciyah</u> proves his organizational capabilities and shows his dedication to upgrade the <u>marja^ciyah</u> to the level of an institution able to carry on its social objectives.

Sadr also wanted to create a hierarchical setup in which the <u>marja^c</u> would represent the top of a pyramidal structure. In addition to having a central administration, the <u>marja^c</u> has been traditionally represented by ^c<u>ulama</u> in various parts of the world who serve the religious needs of Muslims and act as liaison officer for the <u>marja^c</u>, carrying on such task as transmitting his <u>fatwas</u> (religious opinion or decree) or collecting the religious taxes. However, such a relationship between the <u>marja^c</u> and his parochial representatives has been "in most cases, theoretical (not effective) and formal which does not facilitate centralization."[478] A more centralized structure becomes indispensable in situations when the <u>marja^c</u> seeks to commit himself to achieving a political goal or implementing radical

---

[477]Sadr, "al-Marja^ciyah," 94-95.

[478]Sadr, "al-Marja^ciyah," 96.

change in the society. Sadr's prescription is to make the local representatives more active participants in the process of marja°iyah. He proposes that the marja° form a council that proposes policies and suggests courses of action for marja°. The council will consist of, in addition to the individuals of the six committees of the central administration, representatives and high ranking °ulama. The whole religious establishment in this way becomes a full participant in the decision making process of the marja°, an arrangement which eventually would motivate commitment and insure dedication to the marja°iyah. Such a broad consultation process will protect the marja°iyah from adopting policies that might be influenced by personal excitements.[479] Although, individual traditional practices have some positive aspects, such as "quick action, ensuring higher levels of precaution and secrecy, and limiting the infiltration of unqualified individuals marja°iyah, yet the proposed arrangement will have greater and more important results."[480]

The formation of the central administration and 'council of marja°iyah' will insure the continuity of the role of the marja° beyond his life span. The structural organization will provide expertise and long-term planning for achieving the goals. The succeeding marja° would not have to start from nothing, but rather will use the institution to carry on the tasks of the former marja°. In addition, the institution of marja°iyah will serve as a training field and selection agency for the new marja°. Once the institution establishes its trust within the hawzah and the ummah, it could influence the choice of the next marja°.[481]

To establish such a type of an 'objective marja°iyah' which aims to replace the 'individual' one, it is necessary to go through the traditional stages in which a marja° build up his credentials and gains trust and influence within the hawza and ummah. At the first stage, the marja°, performing his duties as an individual marja°, must "start forming an institutional structure gradually, such as establishing a limited number of consultative committees and some of the specialized [offices] to perform some of the tasks of the marja°iyah."[482]

In the second stage, which regularly begins when the marja° publishes his al-risalah al-°amaliyah (book containing religious opinions), he should not, Sadr argues, make rash effort to complete the structural set-up of the institution which might cause resistance from the traditional sector of hawza and ummah who are not aware of its objectives.[483] The formation process of the institution should progress gradually so that its evolution will take place naturally. The marja° should emphasize bringing the consciousness of the ummah to

---

[479]Ibid., 96.

[480]Sadr, "al-Marja°iyah," 96.

[481]Ibid., 97.

[482]Ibid., 98.

[483]Sadr, "al-Marja°iyah," 98.

the point of realizing the goals and benefits of the 'objective marjaᶜiyah. This way the marjaᶜiyah will develop as a natural part of the culture of the ummah, and will reach its maturity. It is only then the 'objective marjaᶜiyah' will enter its final stage of being the sole marjaᶜiyah and dominate religious authority that will guide the ummah toward restoring the leading role of Islam in the society.

The Islamic State

The Islamic state, according to Sadr, consists of two main players, the ummah and the marjaᶜ, each with a different role. The ummah will act as God's vicar on earth; the latter, although part of the ummah, will possess the political authority. From this perspective, Sadr, in his last treatise (which included an essay on the constitution of the Islamic Republic of Iran), defined his views on the three elements of the Islamic polity the legitimacy of authority, the role of the people, and the structure of the state.

The Legitimacy of Authority

From Sadr's analysis of the marjaᶜiyah, one might conclude that the marjaᶜ will have a significant role to play in the Islamic political system. In fact, according to Sadr, the marjaᶜ as an individual is the legitimate heir to the political authority of the original Islamic state of the Prophet and Imams. He is the shahid who succeeds the prophets and Imams to guide the ummah and safeguard the shariᶜah. Politically speaking, he is the chief arbitrator, the grand advisor, the supreme jurist who will have the final word regarding issues that concern Islam.

After all, what is the Islamic political state? It is a polity of Muslims ruled according the laws and teachings of Islam. Who is more capable to define the tenets of Islam than the scholars of Islamic jurisprudence? In fact, the marjaᶜ, Sadr holds, is supposed to be the most knowledgeable of all Muslim jurists.[484] He is selected according to his intellectual capabilities by the hawza, the Islamic center of jurisprudence studies. It is his knowledge in religious studies of Islam that puts him ahead of everyone else within the ummah.

It is because of this fact that the marjaᶜ , in Sadr's Islamic political state, is the legitimate holder of authority. He is not specifically chosen by God as is a prophet or an Imam. What marks him out is his attributes. The shariᶜah has defined the qualifications that the marjaᶜ must meet in order to take the role of shahid (*witness*) during the occultation of Imam Mahdi. It is then left to the ummah to search for the one who meets those qualifications and entrust him with authority.[485] This is why once Sadr found some short-

---

[484]Although not all Shia's faqihs think that the marjaᶜ should be the most knowledgeable in shariᶜah, Sadr hold the idea that he should be. The supreme mujtahid is the one is considered the most knowledgeable of all; thus he is marjaᶜ which the ummah should refer to him for guidance. Sadr, al-Fatawa al-Wadhihah, 105.

comings in the marja^ciyah, he tried to overcome them by institutionalizing its activities while preserving the role of the marja^c as the sole authority of the ummah.[486] It is so because the marja^c is the only legitimate authority within the ummah, and thus, in the Islamic state. "The marja^c per se is the deputy (khalifah) and the vicegerent of the Imam (na'b al-Imam); and this vicegerent is the just mujtahid mutlaq (absolute jurist) who is aware of the process of succession."[487] However, there is a difference between the prophet or Imams and the marja^c. The former are infallible (sinless) individuals, or ma^csum. They represent the divine message perfectly in their teachings and deeds. On the other hand, the latter are not ma^csum and depend on their knowledge about Islam to derive their opinions and conduct their affairs. Thus, the role of shahid is entrusted by God to the marja^c, not to the person.[488] The marja^c as an individual must possess the attributes defined by the shari^ca in order to attain the role of shahid. Such spiritual training and continuous pedagogy of the marja^c will elevate him to the position of legitimate authority. As the eleventh Imam, Hassan al-^cAskari, narrated in one of the traditions:

> If one among the faqihs sustains [the virtue] of himself, safeguards
> his religion, defies his passions, and obeys his Lord, then the people should
> follow him.[489]

Sadr also goes on to specify other attributes that make the marja^c, with his lack of ^cisma, capable of leading the ummah and assuming the responsibilities of a shahid. He should possess the competence required for the position. Although attributes of 'knowledge' and 'justice' are lucid ones, competence, on the other hand, is a vague one. As described by Sadr, competence is a function of:

> ...wisdom, rationality, forebearance, and courage, which are the
> capabilities that God, Most Exalted and High, wanted the righteous of his
> servants to possess through the social difficulties, experiences, and hardship,
> which are faced in the way of God, and related them to status of shahid. [It
> is] said [in the Quran]
> 'If a wound touches you, a like wound already has touched the
> heathen; such days We deal out in turn among men, and that God may know

---

485Sadr, Kalafat al-Insan, 147.

486Ibid., 96.

487Ibid., 96

488Sadr, Kalafat al-Insan, 147.

489Ibid, Sadr is quoting al-Hur al-^cAmili, Wasa'il al-Shi^ca, v. 18, 94.

who are the believers, and that He may take witnesses (shuhada) from among you.'(3:140)[490]

<u>The Role of People</u>

Although man in general is the vicar of God, he may not have the capacity to discharge the responsibilities of his role if he is suppressed by unjust rule, or if he is being driven by his passions. In this case, only the <u>shahid</u> can be considered the vicar of God. However, the awakening of the <u>ummah</u>, which will eventually lead to the establishment of the Islamic rule, will restore its divine rights. Thus every individual within the <u>ummah</u> will carry the sociopolitical responsibility of implementing Islamic laws and teachings in his life, and participate in the historical mission of progress toward the <u>Absolute</u>. Sadr underpins this idea on the following verse from the Quran:

> And the believers, the men and the women, are friends one of the
> other; enjoining good, and forbidding evil.[491]

Islam, in this case, suggests a total equality between the believers, men and women, to carry on the political responsibility and participate in the social affairs of the <u>ummah</u>.

The believers are also being advised by God to manage their social affairs in consultation with others. In fact, the idea of consensus in Islam is derived from the following verse:

> Those who hearken To their Lord, and establish Regular prayer, *who*
> *(conduct) Their affairs by mutual consultation.*(42:38)[492]

In this regard, Sadr argues that Islam is suggesting that it is necessary to follow the opinions of the majority in matters where the <u>shari^cah</u> has not specified any rule or directions to be followed. Thus, the door was left open for people to conduct their affairs in a more careful way and follow the will of the majority. Politically speaking, the people, in Sadr's Islamic political system, are to be in charge of the executive and the legislative authority of the state. It is left to them to decide on any policy, and to take any course of action that does not violate the basic teachings of Islam. The <u>marja^c</u> role is to oversee their role of abiding by the rules of God, hence advising them, and showing them the right path in case of deviation from it. Needless to say, Sadr's argument seems to be based on linking the idea of <u>shura</u>

---

[490]Sadr, <u>Khalafat</u>, 148; the verse translation from <u>The Koran</u>, v. I, 90.

[491]<u>The Koran</u>, v. I, 215.

[492]<u>The Holy Qor'an</u>, text, traslation and commentary by A. Yusf Ali (London: The Islamic Foundation, 1975), 1316-1317.

(consultation among the believers) to his thesis about the role of vicar of God. Since man has rights and responsibilities that can be translated in political terms, then the whole <u>ummah</u> possesses these rights and responsibilities in the Islamic political system, although Sadr does not provide any logical basis from which to derive such a conclusion. The political process of his envisioned Islamic system is democratic since policies are grouded in majority rule. However, if every man is considered a vicar of God, the majority rule principle implies that some vicars of God lose their rights and are forced to uphold to the will of the majority. What theoretical or jurisprudential basis is there that justifies the tyranny of the majority? What religious claim does the majority have to impose its will on others who have similar rights to participate in the making of policies in the Islamic state? These questions are left unanswered by Sadr.

<u>The Structure of the State</u>

The Islamic state that Sadr envisioned would not, of course, be the ideal state, since the ideal state is led only by the <u>ma^csum</u>. It is the best possible polity during the absence of the <u>ma^csum</u>. In fact Sadr classifies three types of Islamic political states: First is the state where "the legislation is derived from the ideological basis of Islam, and the executive and legislative affairs are consistent with the laws of Islam."[493] This type of government is the *infallible state* which can be realized only with the leadership of the <u>ma^csum</u>. Here obedience is obligatory on everyone.

The second type of Islamic state is *apostate state* where the government in its executive and legislative affairs deliberately deviates from the line of Islam. The ruler(s), in this case, loses the attribute of 'justice,' implying there is no legitimacy for his reign. Therefore, the <u>ummah</u> should try to depose the corrupt authority. What if the <u>ummah</u> is not able to revolt against the authority? Sadr suggests that every Muslim should restrain the government from committing further sins, and people should not obey the government's laws except those which serve Islamic interests.[494]

The third type of Islamic state is *fallible state*, the one that accidentally deviates from the line of Islam, because of ignorance. It is this government that Sadr is planning to establish, where the ruler has some knowledge of Islam, but may accidentally adopt certain rules that are in conflict with Islam. The <u>ummah</u>, in this case, should obey the authority and uphold the law. Only those who are aware of the aberration of the government should give advice and consultation. If the government persists in its wrong-doings, then everyone should obey the authority in 'matters of unity' such as holy war or taxes. Otherwise, it is <u>permissible only for those who</u> are aware of the wrong-doings to defy the corrupt laws.[495]

[493]Sadr, "al-Dawlah al-Islamiyah" (The Islamic State) in <u>al-Jihad</u> (March, 14, 1983), 5.

[494]Sadr, "al-Dawlah," 5.

But when the ruler is a <u>marja^c</u>, i.e., possess the fundamental qualities of <u>ijtihad</u> (knowledge and justice), then the disagreement here is related to the differences in Islamic opinions. The rule of the <u>marja^c</u> is legitimate, and even other <u>mujtahids</u> should obey the rule of <u>marja^c</u>, placing him in command of the state.[496]

The <u>marja^c</u>, accordingly, is the "legitimate representation of Islam, as well as the general deputy of the Imam."[497] Hence, he should, according to Sadr:

1) be the head of the state and the commander-in-chief of the armed forces

2) designate the person(s) qualified for the presidential election, thus giving legitimacy to the election

3) specify the religious framework of the constitution

4) sanction the legality of the legislation

5) form a supreme court for constitutional jurisdictions

6) establish special courts all over the country to oversee the abuses of power by the government.[498]

However, such authoritarian supremacy of the <u>marja^c</u> is not in any way a dictatorial rule but rather a leadership constrained by Islamic rules and institutional oversights. The <u>marja^c</u> should in the process of decision making refer to the 'council of <u>marja^ciyah</u>' which consists, suggests Sadr, of one hundred intellectual and religious scholars as well as at least ten <u>mujtahids</u>.[499] It is through the aid of this council that the <u>marja^c</u> should derive his policies and make his political decisions.

On the other hand, since man is the vicar of God, he must be responsible for conducting his social affairs in accordance with God's will. The <u>ummah</u> should have the right to bear the divine trust and be eligible to form the executive and legislative branches of the government. Every member of the <u>ummah</u> has an equal opportunity under the law to realize the potential of the vicarage role, i.e., to have to express his views and thoughts, conduct his political activities through any means, not to mention the conduct of his religious or sectarian rites.[500] The <u>ummah</u>, according to Sadr, then should:

---

[495]Ibid., 5.

[496]Sadr, <u>Minhaj al-Salihin</u> (The Path of the Righteous) (Beirut: Dar al-Ta`aruf, 1980), 11.

[497]Sadr, <u>Lamhah Fiqhiyah ^cAn Mashru^c Dustur al-Jumhuriyah al-Islamiyah</u>, in <u>al-Islam Yaqud al-Hayat</u>, 12.

[498]Ibid., 12.

[499]Sadr, <u>Lamhah</u>, 13.

[500]Ibid., 16.

1) elect the head of the executive branch who then should reserve the right to select his cabinet

2) vote, through direct election, for the members of the legislative council who should have the power to:

First, approve the selection of the cabinet

Second, choose between the different alternative policies that are not contradictory to Islam

Third, make new legislation in areas where no definite regulations are defined by Islam

Fourth, have the power to overrule the executive branch's implementation of law.[501]

Thus, the political affairs of Sadr's Islamic state are shaped and nourished by the people. The marja‘, theoretically speaking, is limited to the role of the shahid, i.e., watching over the implementation of Islam by the ummah and safeguarding religion from the corruption of its enemies.[502] The ummah, by conducting its political activities, would be aware of its mission as vicar of God on earth, and take full responsibility for its behavior. "Because not even the ummah is the source of authority, but rather it is responsible before God, the most Exulted and High, to uphold the trust and carry on its duties."[503] The creation of an Islamic state is one of the means whereby man's role as vicar of God is realized. The state should be structured to facilitate the discharge of such responsibilities and give man the opportunity to accomplish his mission on earth.

---

[501]Sadr, Lamhah, 11-12.

[502]Sadr, Khalafat al-Insan, 170-171.

[503]Sadr, Lamhah, 11.

The Economic Structure

Poverty is the ultimate death.

Imam Ali

The economy of the Islamic state is divided between that of the individual as vicar of God (<u>khalifah</u>), and the ruler as the witness (<u>shahid</u>). The economic structure of the Islamic state, thus, consists of private property and public property. However, one should not think that the economic structure of the Islamic state is some sort of combination of capitalism and socialism. Sadr strongly rejects this misconception. He argues that the juxtaposition of private and public rights of ownership stems from the fundamental beliefs of Islam.[504] This is similar to the way that private ownership is advocated in the capitalist system or public ownership is advocated by socialists as the logical conclusion of their ideological and philosophical beliefs. To justify private ownership and public ownership in Islam, one must understand the rights and obligations of the individual and the state in Islam. Sadr's detailed description of the economic relationship in the Islamic state and the establishment of its economic structure represents the best available argument for the notion of Islamic economics.

Economic Relationships

Man's behavior, according to Sadr's theory, is categorized into three types of relationships: social, economical and religious. It is due to his inner instinct of self-love that "always derives him to bring good things to himself, to secure his interests, and satisfy his needs."[505] Accordingly, man, in his relationship with the environment, is predisposed to utilize all possible resources to satisfy his needs and increase his pleasure. In due time, he is willing to use animals and plants to help him in his struggle with the environment. Although his essential needs were simple in the early period of history, his mental capacity enabled

---

[504]Sadr, "al-Janib al-Iqtisadi Min al-Nizam al-Islami," (The Economic Perspective of Islamic System) in <u>Ikhtarna Lak</u>, 112-113.

[505]Sadr, "al-Nizam al-Islami Muqaranan bil-Nizam al-Ra'smali wa-al-Markisi" (The Islamic System Compared with The Capitalist and The Marxist Systems) in <u>Ikhtarna Lak</u>, 160.

him to develop new means to help him utilize the resources of the environment. Thus, his needs were always expanding due to the complexity of utilizing the resources of the environment.

Man's relationship with others of his kind was the natural outcome of his need to satisfy his desires. The complexity of life, i.e., his relationship with the environment, made it difficult for him to sufficiently cope with his needs. Cooperation with others makes the effort to satisfy his needs manageable. Cooperation with others results in a sharing of benefits with all participants of the community.[506] The inner instincts of self-love that drove man to create the first community are evident. These instincts gave rise to man's exploitation of his brother.

Because people were not equal in their physical and mental capacities, they obviously were different in their utilization of the resources of the environment. Such differentiation of capabilities is part of the divine plan for bringing cohesion, through the division of labor, to the human community. People of different capabilities function in different tasks within the social order.[507] However, man's desire to maximize his interests drove some men to exploit the situation for their benefit. Human needs were growing due to man's mental and economic development. His experience broadened his capacities to utilize the resources of his environment. His passion to acquire more of the environmental resources for himself became prevalent. Consequently, some men were willing to oppress others to satisfy their greed and egos (both instincts the outcome of self-love). It is then that the human community faced oppression in the form of economic exploitation.

This conflict between social peace and individual instincts of maximizing interests was persistent throughout history. This historical conflict, Sadr argues, is between two classes: those individuals who possess the environmental resources (economical and social) who are endeavor to protect their interests, and the rest of the society who strive to live in peace and cooperation. Marxists believe the problem originated with a few people controlling economic resources. The only way to bring about peace to the social order is through the revolution of the oppressed class of the society to destroy the special interests of the privileged class. Capitalists, on the other hand, believe such social conflict is the result of the limited natural resources of the environment which are not sufficient to satisfy the needs of all people.[508] Thus, social conflict will always be prevalent. Human society can only hope

---

[506]Ibid., 161.

[507]Sadr, _Iqtisaduna_ (Our Economics), (Beirut: Dar al-Taᵃruf, 1982), 311-313.

[508]Here Sadr seems to mention the view of Thomas Robert Malthus and disregards other capitalist economic thinkers who believe that the source of economic problem is the

to manage, through incremental and gradual reforms, the social conflict from overtaking human progress. Based on this, capitalists oppose any type of social revolution. However, Islam disagrees with both views and considers the environmental resources to be sufficient to satisfy people's needs.

> It is God who created the heavens and the earth, and sent down out of heaven water wherewith He brought forth fruits to be your sustenance. And He subjected to you the ships to run upon the sea at His commandment; and He subjected to you the sun and moon constant upon their courses, and He subjected to you the night and day, and gave you of all you asked Him. If you count God's blessing, you will never number it; surely man is sinful [oppressor], unthankful [kafur].(14:34)[509]

The problem rests with human nature: how can the instinct of self-love be directed in a proper manner? Unless a solution comes to control human desires and deflect the potential of human energies for exploitation of others, the social order rests on superficial foundations. The above verse clearly states that the social problem is the result of the misdeeds of man. It specifies two reasons for the socioeconomic problem: 1) the oppressive nature of man; and 2) man's inefficiency in the utilization of the economic resources.

According to Sadr's interpretation, man's oppressiveness comes in the form of inequitable distribution of economic resources; while his (kufran)[510] comes in the lack of utilization of these resources, evident in underdevelopment and waste of economic resources. A solution must overcome the two basic problems of the economy. Sadr specifies three components to the Islamic solution: 1) the cessation of forms of oppression which is manifested in the unjust distribution of economic resources; 2) purification of human nature to achieve control of the desires of self-love; and   3) utilization of economic resources to satisfy the needs of all humanity.

<u>The Islamic Theory of Distribution</u>

---

distribution of economic wealth.

[509]<u>The Koran</u>, V. I, 278.

[510]The arabic word <u>kafr</u> literally means to cover or hide. It is used in the Quran to means covering the truth about the belief in God, i.e., infidelity and atheism. However, Sadr in the above verse defines it in economics term. <u>Kufran</u>, thus, denote the unproductive means to utilize the full economic potential of natural resources; which is according to Sadr one of the two problems of political economy. The other problem is the uneven distribution of the economic wealth.

The first step to end the contradiction of the economic structure of society begins with the distribution of economic resources between people. A just social system is the one that allows all people to benefit from the economic wealth. The Islamic economic system is judged upon this criterion.

The first form of economic wealth is the natural resources of the environment. The unjust distribution of the economic wealth begins with the problem of ownership of these natural resources. One must know who has the right of ownership in Islam. Sadr, thus, must develop the theory of distribution of the natural resources at two stages: preproduction and postproduction stages, or what he calls primary wealth and secondary wealth, respectively.[511] For this reason, he is not concerned with the Islamic view on the distribution of economic wealth based on the parameters of the political economy, rather he is out to discover the ideological basis of Islamic teaching concerning economic ownership. For him, the study of economics as such is irrelevant to the issue of economic justice; it is ideological theory, rather, which must address this issue. The economic study comes later to evaluate whether the ideological theory has an adequate basis in reality.

Distribution of Natural Wealth

Sadr also disagrees with political economists on the subject of economic resources. He disregards "capital" and "labor" as part of the source of production. It is only nature that can be taken into account in the theory of distribution of natural resources. "For _capital_ is in fact a produced wealth and not a primary source of production, because it represents, economically [speaking], any wealth which is produced and generated through human labor that can be reinvested in the development of new wealth."[512]

On the other hand, nature itself is classified into four categories: 1) land; 2) raw material (minerals and others); 3) water; and 4) other natural resources such as living species in air,sea and on land.[513] Although the canon laws of Islam seemingly contain different regulations for each one of these categories, Sadr used his ingenuity to discover the common ground between them, and reveal the general economic theory of Islam.

The sole owner of the land and raw materials is the Islamic state/government. People may gain special rights of ownership if they invest their labor to develop these natural resources, such as cultivating land and mining minerals. Individuals may gain precedence

---

[511]Sadr, "al-Nazriyah al-Islamiyah li-Tawzi͏ᶜ al-Masadr al-Tabi͏ᶜiyah" (Islamic Theory of Distribution of Natural Resources) in _Ikhtarna Lak_ (Beirut: Dar al-Zahra', 1982), 136-137.

[512]Sadr, "al-Nazariyah," 138.

[513]Sadr, _Iqtisaduna_, 433.

over others for a piece of land or the minerals which they worked. The special right of ownership may be gained only through labor invested in developing that land or raw material, and such right expires as soon as that development ends.[514] People utilizing these resources must pay property taxes for their usage to the Islamic state.

Water, on the other hand, can be owned if it is possessed for economic development. Although the sole proprietor of the natural resource of water is the state, all people have access to it for their use. The only exception is underground water, where the individual who invests his labor to develop its utility has an exclusive right to its usage and benefits.[515]

Other natural resources, such as birds, animals, plants and marine life, are publicly owned. These sources of economic wealth may become private property through individual efforts.[516] As such, people, not the state, have the exclusive right to own resources via their labor. They may not loose this right indefinitely, or pay property taxes for their possession.

Based on this view, Sadr concludes that people themselves, or in a more concrete term, their representative government, are the sole proprietor of the natural resources. Individuals may gain special privileges to make use of these resources only through their labor to develop these resources. Other types of individual labor, such as the use of force to possess, are not considered legitimate means to ownership. Only work is of economic significance. In addition, Islam gives individuals the right to own private property only through their continuous effort to develop these resources to benefit society as a whole. Once private development of these natural resources is suspended, the right of private ownership would cease too.[517] From this Sadr derives the first principle:

> All natural wealth is part of the public sector and individuals gain
> the special rights to use them only on one ground, that is labor which
> characterized by development [of these resources] by the direct work [of the
> individual himself].[518]

According to the above principle, the individual may not use other individuals to develop the natural resource, otherwise they share the ownership and the benefits of that natural wealth on the basis of their labor. Islam totally rejects the capitalist principle of individual ownership of vast natural resources on the ground that they are developed by the labor of

---

[514]Ibid., 483.

[515]Sadr, _Iqtisaduna_, 519-520.

[516]Ibid., 52.

[517]Sadr, "al-Nazriyah al-Islamiyah li Tawzi^c," 148.

[518]Sadr, _Khatut Tafsiliyah ^cAn Iqtisad al-Mujtama^c al-Islami_ (General Basis of Economics of Islamic Society), in _al-Islam Yaqud al-Hayah_, 88.

others. As such, industries for the development of the natural resources, e.g., oil and minerals, can be owned and managed only by the state. Yet Sadr introduces the concept of the "priority right of use" of the natural economic resources by the individual. Those who possess the labor and the will to exploit the resources have the right to gain access to them such exploitation serve the public interest.

Distribution of Produced Wealth

Sadr develops an Islamic theory of distribution of the commodities. Produced wealth is classified into: 1) the primary commodities, such as agricultural produce and raw materials; and 2) the secondary commodities, which are the primary commodities manufactured into different products. In these stages of production, capital generated from previous economic endeavors as well as the means-of-productions (tools and machinery) take part in the production process of these advanced economic activities. Each of these components has no share of the product, as in the capitalist theory, but they gain special rights for their usage in the production process.

As in the previous theory, Islam gives the worker the sole right of ownership of the produced goods. However, human labor is one of the components of the production of the primary commodities. The other components are nature itself, and the tools used to help man in the process of production. The tools, or any means of production, according to Sadr, "contained potential works of previous stages of productions that will be exhausted and depleted during its usage in the process of production."[519] In this case, if the tools are not the property of the worker who participates in the production, then the owner of the tools must get paid for the amount of usage of his tools, i.e., the exhausted potential work of the tools.[520] Herein lies one of the major ideological differences between capitalism and Islam. The former regards the owner of the means of production as the sole owner of the produced commodities; where Islam considers the laborer to have the only legitimate claim to the produced commodities. In capitalism, tools get a share of the product because they, as human labor, expend a certain amount of work in the production process. In Islam, tools only assist and aid man to facilitate the process of production, thus, they must be gratified in rent, not in profit sharing.[521]

Accordingly, the worker owns the product of the natural resources. It is unthinkable in Islamic economics, for someone to employ others and provide them with rent and tools, where he alone owns the products of their labor.[522] The laborer only has the legitimate claim

---

[519]Sadr, _Iqtisaduna_, 619.

[520]Sadr, _Iqtisaduna_, 584.

[521]Sadr, _al-Khatut al-Tafsiliyah_, 97.

for the products of his effort. Thus, industries to develop natural resources, such as oil and minerals, cannot be owned privately.

Since the utilization of the economic wealth of the environment is the responsibility of the society as a whole, the sole proprietor and beneficiary of the natural resources, society gets a share of the product extracted from the primary commodities. The state, in this stage of production, has the right to collect what is known as tisq [property tax] from producers to finance the social welfare expenditure and meet the economics needs of the people.[523]

As for the production of the secondary commodities, Islam gives the owner of the primary commodities the right to establish his claim to the final products. The legitimacy of his ownership does not cease because someone aids him in transforming his product into different commodities. An individual who owns the raw materials has the right to the manufactured commodities produced out of that material. If a state owned company produced petroleum, for example, it also has the right of ownership of all the processed goods extracted from that petroleum. People who participate in the production should get paid for their labor.

Also, ownership is not affected by the usage of the means of production belonging someone else. The owners of the tools and machines get paid for the usage of these tools and machines in the production process. By the same token, the owner of the primary commodities may also hire someone else to manufacture his goods. The worker, in this case, gets the salary for his labor, which should be specified in the job contract. The worker has no claim for the final product he produces.[524]

Islam specified two means of payment for a hired worker: the first one is through wages, where he is paid for the amount of work he does in accomplishing a task; the second is the sharing in the profit of the final product. In this case, the worker gets only a percentage of the profit specified in the agreement between him and the owner of the primary commodities. The general principle, in Islam, for earning is:

> ...that earning is only based on contribution of labor during the
> process [of production], so the contributed labor is the only legitimate mean
> for someone to get paid from the owner of the process...and without such
> contribution, there is no legitimacy for his earning.[525]

Based on this economic principle, the owner of capital will not receive fixed

---

[522]Ibid., 99.

[523]Sadr, Khutut, 561.

[524]Sadr, Iqtisaduna, 605.

[525]Sadr, Iqtisaduna, 618.

payment from the owner of the primary goods, i.e., usury is prohibited. The monetary means will not contribute any amount of labor at all.[526] Fixed payment is allowed in Islam only in one case, when there is a consumption of work, either directly through a worker, or indirectly (reserved work) through the means of production. As for the monetary capital, no such work will be exhausted or depleted. In this matter, the owner of the capital is allowed to share the profit and the loss with the owner of the primary commodities. The legitimacy of earning, in this situation, is based on his help in facilitating the process of production, and he is deserving of gratitude and appreciation which is expressed in profit sharing.

<u>Purification of Human Nature</u>

The first task of the Islamic political system is to eliminate forms of oppression within the economic relationship and to lay the ground for the establishment of a just system of distribution of economic resources. However, the source of the injustice, according to Sadr, is neither the social settings nor the means of production, but rather human nature itself, the inner instincts of self-love that drive man to secure survival for himself only. Such an instinct is essential for the survival of human life on earth. Profit, which is the economic manifestation of self-love and is generated from private investment, is the great engine of human economic accomplishment. It gives the individual the personal incentive to work hard and to overcome difficulties and challenges. However, when left without moral control it will manifest itself in different forms of oppression. Man will be concerned only with securing his own interests to the point of abusing the interests of others. Unless a solution to the problem of human nature is found, man will find the escape routes to abuse even in the just system of distribution. In fact, the social contradiction stems from the individual prejudice of self-love. In the capitalist system, it manifests itself in the form of economic exploitation of others. In the communist system, where private property is eliminated, man's self-love manifests itself in political oppression, such as the struggle for power and the securing of special social privileges.[527]

Religion, according to Sadr, gives humanity the only solution to this basic and deep-rooted problems of human nature. Religion overcomes the problem of human nature by specifying many channels of self-control that properly regulate or direct man's instincts into the appropriate social behavior. In other words, it will end the contradiction between social and private interests.

The first of these mechanisms for self-control is a spiritual one, the psychological power that makes man control his behavior. Man is the vicar of God, which means he is the ~~representative of the Almighty~~ on earth. In the economic sense, he is the trustee of God for

[526]Ibid., 625-627.

[527]Sadr, "al-Nizam al-Islami Muqaranan," 170.

the wealth created for mankind. This sense of vicarage implies that man is responsible for his economic deeds before God. Vicarage also means controlling personal behavior, and limiting the usage of the natural resources according to God's will.[528] Improper behavior and the waste of the wealth of God will make man accountable for his deeds and bring severe punishment. In the same manner, abiding by God's will guarantees a good reward and overwhelming gratitude.

> It is He who has appointed you viceroys in the earth, and has raised
> some of you in rank above others, that He may try you in what He has given
> you. Surely thy Lord is swift in retribution; and surely He is All-forgiving,
> All-compassionate.(4:165)[529]

Accordingly, man is expected to receive guidance as to how the wealth of God should be distributed and treated. It is this link between the here and now and the hereafter that brings accommodation between social and private interests. Anyone who sacrifices for the sake of others is rewarded. The religious solution, then, is not materialistic, but spiritual and trains man in the service of others, and in the sacrifice of private interests for the sake of social benefits. In doing so, he is serving and benefiting himself as well. In Islam, it is the fear of God and the desire of His gratitude that replaces the competitive greed of human nature. Once religion succeeds in bringing up this man who has control over his inner instincts and passions, the social order can be saved from contradictions and individual abuses and manipulations.

Since this goal is utopian in its outlook, Islam has derived a social mechanism to secure peace and harmony in the human society. God has assigned the vicarage role not to the individual per se, but rather to mankind. It is the social group that is the trustee of God over economical wealth. They, as a group, hold the responsibilities of managing the natural resources and human wealth to benefit the welfare of the group. The following Quranic verse refer to such social responsibility.

> But do not give to fools their property that God has assigned to you
> to manage.(4:5)[530]

According to Sadr's interpretation of the above verse, God considers the financial wealth of the ignorants as the wealth of the general public. The whole society is then responsible for not allowing any misappropriation of the ignorants' wealth. Such social control over economic wealth makes the individual accountable not only before God, but before his own

---

[528]Sadr, _Iqtisaduna_, 536-537.

[529]_The Koran_, v. I, 170.

[530]_The Koran_, v. I, 100.

people.

Islam also disavows any values that a society attaches to the possession of economic wealth. Affluence and economic prosperity of the individual are not signs of social prestige.

> He frowned and turned away that the blind man came to him. And that what should teach thee? Perchance he would cleanse him or yet remember, and the Reminder profit him. But the self-sufficient [rich], to him thou attendest thought it is not thy concern, if he does not cleanse himself. And he who comes to thee eagerly and fearfully, to him thou payest no heed.(80:1-10)[531]

Islam wants the individual to consider wealth as burdensome and places a responsibility on the shoulders of the wealthy individual to serve both himself and others. It is a means to achieve the goal of humanity.[532] Affluence should not be the goal for the individual to achieve in his life, as in a capitalist society which makes man use all possible means to increase his possession of wealth, even if it brings harm and oppresses others' interests. However, if one thinks of wealth as the means to realize the appreciation of God, then helping others, not oppressing them, becomes the social norm of the rich and wealthy. In other words, Islam is determined to change the social values related to the possession of wealth and private property. There is no need to abolish ownership of private property as suggested by Marxism. The social policy of elimination of private property, according to Sadr, will not be successful because it goes against human nature. The only solution is to reform social values in such a way that wealth is changed from an individual goal to a social means to achieve a higher moral goal.

Economic Development

The third part of the Islamic solution to the economic problem deals with "fostering the production and the utilization of the natural resources of the environment to its fullest extent."[533] God has created an abundance of resources in nature to satisfy the human needs on earth. Man, accordingly, is encouraged to use the abundance of God's gift to his benefit. According to Sadr, "Islam, ideologically speaking, has set the development of economic wealth and the utilization of the natural resources to the greatest possible extent as a goal for the society."[534] Islam is similar to capitalism in affirming this economic objective; however,

[531]Ibid., v. II, 324.

[532]Sadr, _Iqtisaduna_, 568.

[533]Sadr, _Iqtisaduna_, 649.

[534]Sadr, _Iqtisaduna_, 650.

they differ in their approach to achieving it. While capitalism "rejects any means of development of production or increase of wealth that hinders the principle of economic freedom, Islam, on the other hand, rejects those means which are contrary to its theories of distribution [of the economic resources] and its principle of justice."[535]

Notwithstanding, Islam, as mentioned before, discourages individuals from pursuing strictly materialistic objectives, downgrading gains in this contemporary existence. Sadr regards economic prosperity as the goal of the virtuous society, not of the individual. God, after all, has created everything on earth and the heavens to serve the existence of man.[536] Islam only rejects materialistic gain as the ultimate ambition of man, which in such cases leads him to the oppression of others. Islam encourages zuhd [austerity] as a pedagogy which trains man not to consider materialistic wealth as his final goal in life.[537] Zuhd is man's mechanism for self-regulation which he utilizes to fight his desires and direct his objectives toward God. However, it is not the goal of social order of the faithful.

Suffice it to mention that affluence and a high standard of living help mankind in his journey to God. Suffering can hinder such efforts. In fact, there is direct effect between man's relationship to God and his relationship to nature. The more men strive for God, the more bountiful nature will be in providing for man's needs. Social affluence is the sign of God's gratification to man. On the other hand, man's thankless attitude to God, of which his social injustice is the outward expression or symbol, results in the ruin of the economic resources and productivity, and the degeneration of man's social existence.[538]

Islam also expedites the social drive toward production in its religious regulation. Under the Islamic economic system, earning is exclusively linked to working. All other means of earning and ownership are abolished. The possession of natural resources is not considered legitimate without continuous human efforts to develop it. Any type of earning

[535]Ibid., 649.

[536]Sadr, in support of his argument, cites a letter of Imam Ali to the governor of Egypt that exemplifies the social order of the believers as that witness the affluence of herenow and hereafter. See Iqtisaduna, 651.

[537]Here Sadr gives his interpretation of two set of contradictory prophetic traditions of which some of them encourage authority and reject materialistic gains, and others invite man to make use of the wealth for his benefit. He sees no contradiction between the two when the former looked at as discouraging man for making economic wealth as the final objective of his life. See, Iqtisaduna, 669-672.

[538]Sadr, Muqaddimat fi al-Tafsiyr (Kuwait: al-Dar al-Islamiyah, 1982), 104-107.

that does not require any human labor, in commerce as well as in production, is forbidden. For this reason, the usage of the financial capital to generate earning is abolished. The only legitimate way to make use of the capital is to invest it in the production process and share the risk of profit and loss. To insure the utilization of capital in the economic development, Islam strongly forbids the conservation of money and initiates a yearly tax to downgrade any wealth that is not enrolled in the production process. Additionally, any type of useless economic activities, such as gambling, magic and superstition, jugglery, are forbidden in Islam.[539]

Furthermore, Islam made it a requirement for Muslims to explore all fields of knowledge and seek any efficient means of production in order to utilize to maximum benefit the natural resources of the environment.[540] The economic strength of Muslims is analogous to their military strength. The power of the Islamic political state is judged on the merit of their economic progress and social prosperity. For this reason, Islam places a heavy emphasis on the role of political leadership to regulate social economic activities to enhance economic development and eliminate waste.

The Role of the State

As indicated in the theory of distribution, the Islamic state possesses the sole right of ownership of natural resources. Consequently, it has absolute control of all aspects of economic activities. The owner of the natural resources, or the primary commodities, according to Sadr, is the sole owner of the secondary commodities. Basically, the government of the Islamic state can determine the flow of wealth in the society and define the economic process. The major objective of the Islamic state is to set up policies to develop the natural resources to the fullest extent to benefit the entire bulk of the society.

To achieve such an economical objective, the state has the right to distribute the social economic resources to attain the maximum amount of production that brings prosperity to all people. The state has the responsibility to provide the minimum of the essential needs of the society and ensure the economy of the people. It is unlike the capitalist state, which leaves that function to the fluctuation of the market. Nor it is like the Marxist-Leninist theory that advocates the state control all aspects of the economic activities. The Islamic state sets the direction of the economic activities, while giving individuals the right of private ownership to achieve the social goal. The government has the role to oversee and regulate economic activities. Accordingly, Islam has left the government with a high degree of flexibility in developing new regulations to meet rising economic circumstances. Sadr called the absence of restrictions in the Shariᶜah as <u>manatiq al-furagh</u> (the discretionary sphere of the law), where the jurist has the authority to make judgments and rulings

[539]Sadr, <u>Iqtisaduna,</u> 670

[540]Ibid., 671

according to the principles of jurisprudence.[541] He considers this area of legislation on the part of the law-giver as a realistic approach to ensure the development of economic activities and the means of production. The leadership of the Islamic state then could initiate any new legislation and regulations that they see as appropriate to the new rising circumstance in order to meet the economic needs of the people and secure the maximum utilization of the economic resources. In other words, the Islamic government is free to adopt a wide range of economic policies from full control of the economy to free-enterprise in order to achieve its social goal. In this case, the government must depend on the economists and experts to watch for the best possible alternative policies to set the direction of the state economy (provided that it will not overrule the theory of distribution.)

Such an unlimited role of government in the economy of the Islamic state is justified because of its substantial social involvement. The state is responsible for the social welfare of the all people.[542] The economic resources in the Islamic state are distributed not only according to work and ability to produce, but also according to needs. Not all people in the society are able to work, or if some do, they are not able to satisfy their needs. Sadr identifies three economic classes in the society: 1) those who have the mental and/or the physical power to produce more than their needs; 2) those who are able to work, but only to the extent of meeting their essential needs; and 3) those who do not have the mental or the physical power to work productivity. The government's responsibility is to provide for the needs of the latter two classes, which are not limited to the essential human needs. The people in the Islamic state must live in dignity, i.e., their economic status must be raised to the acceptable general level. Therefore, the state must have the economic resources to be able to finance the social welfare program.

> Whatsoever spoils of war God has given to His Messenger from the people of the cities belongs to God, and His Messenger, and the near kinsman, orphans, the needy and the traveller, so that it be not a thing taken in turns among the rich of you.(59:7)[543]

The verse, according to Sadr, indicates two things: first, the allocation of economic

---

[541]The jurist, according to Sadr, shall not change any of the primary principles of Islam, i.e., the sphere of _halal_ and _haram_, "obligatory" and "prohibition," respectively; but rather he may act within the realm of "secondary" matters, i.e., the _mandub_ and _makruh_, "preferred" and "disliked," respectively. The jurist may forbid any preferred action, or encourage any disliked ones.

[542]Sadr, _Iqtisaduna_, 697.

[543]_The Koran_, v. II, 268.

resources between the government and the needy people; and second, the distribution of wealth in such a way as to prevent the rich from controlling the state of the economy. Based on the above interpretation, Sadr argues that the main principles of Islamic economics are: 1) public (i.e., state) ownership of the means of production and distribution; and 2) centralized economic planning. It is only through the control of all the resources in the community by the society that the common need of the ummah to be protected is guaranteed, and the essential economic rights of the individual are insured. Accordingly, the legitimate Islamic government has the responsibility to make a long-term plan for serving the common good and overcoming instability in the market.

Islam recognizes differences in income between people, but strives to create tawazin ijtimaⁱi (equitable standard of living). To realize such a socioeconomic condition, Islam, although it specifies fixed taxes to be collected from the prosperous people, establishes a social and moral mechanism. A lavish and extravagant style of living is totally discouraged in Islam. Islam also forbids waste in production and consumption in order to direct the resources of the economy to produce the commodities that satisfy the needs of all people and bring about social equity. The state also has the authority to regulate wages and prices so as to overcome the selfishness and greed of those who possess economic wealth and insure an equitable standard of living for all people. In sum, the major goal of the Islamic state is for the prosperity of all citizens.

CONCLUSION

The value of one's life is equal to what he gives out of his
time and thoughts [to others] and what is left of him to be the model
for the <u>mujahidin</u> to follow.

Sadr

Islam, Sadr argues, not only defines the final goal of human existence; it also precisely outlines the means to achieve this goal. However, unlike other deterministic philosophies or religious beliefs, which portray man as an atom in this ever-expanding cosmos and who must know his place and work according to the dictates of his role, Islamic scholars consider the whole universe to have been created to serve man's purpose in life. Man is not one small part of an immense universe in which he must find his proper place, but rather is the nucleus of the entire creation. Man is the *vicar* of God and was created to benefit from his service as God's vicar.

Man's superior nature stems from his free will, i.e., his rationality and the ability to determine his own course of action, or for that matter, the ability to embrace or withdraw from the guidance of God. In fact, the idea of submission to the command of God presupposes man's capacity for both obedience and rebellion. However, obedience to God is not incompatible with his free will. Obeying God's laws is for the benefit of man and the satisfaction of his needs in life.

The progressive nature of man, his ability to choose what is best for him, and to search for pleasure and good, gives him the ability to use his mental powers and take different approaches to satisfying his needs. However, mankind may not come up with the best solution to his needs and interests. Although he was provided with a capacity for rational deliberation, such rationality grows and develops according to his experience in life. His limited experience in life makes him unaware of factors that affect his survival. Such factors must be taken into consideration in order to determine the best possible way of life. Religion, the divine message to mankind, is intended to show man the essential factors to bring about his happiness. Religion is the extra step man needs to take; it is the divine knowledge that shows man how to attain happiness. It makes him aware of things of which he otherwise would be ignorant. In other words, it is the light that guides him away from darkness.

Social life causes extra mischief for mankind. Although the development of the social unit was intended to serve human needs, man strives to preserve his personal interests, which sometimes are in conflict with the interests of others. The result of such conflicts of interests is an inhospitable social environment where the strong and fortunate oppress the rights and interests of the others. Religion provides the only solution to the social problem. It not only puts constraints on the egotistical behavior of man by making him responsible before his Lord, but also teaches man to give up some of his individual interests and pleasures in return for the abundance of God in the hereafter.

According to Sadr, peace in the social context can be realized only through sacrifices of the individual's rights for the sake of social interests. Only religion can provide the spiritual guide for man to sacrifice his temporal pleasures for everlasting ones. Any other socialist philosophy and doctrine may promise man a utopian future as a reward for his sacrifices, but such promises will not limit man's egoistic nature. Man will eventually find other avenues to satisfy his individualistic needs and advance his social interests. Religion does not intend to suppress man's ego but rather to develop it, in order to make him feel that whatever sacrifices he makes for society will be rewarded in the hereafter. The teaching of monotheistic religions provide a solution to the social dilemma through the belief that social interests are part of the individual pleasures man is seeking. Religion is not meant to constrain man's behavior or to override his free will, but rather to be used as a guide and a source of nourishment for his thoughts and as a solution to his complex problems. It is the torch for his emancipation. When every social experiment fails to provide happiness and justice, man finds divine religions transmitted from God to his messengers, the light to resolve man's social conflicts.

Therefore religion, according to Sadr, provides the only solution to man's individual needs and social crises. It is a divine guide for humanity and the answer to man's problems. Man without the help of divine aid will live in estrangement. Man may have the capacity to progress and the power to emancipate, but his endeavors are short-sighted with undesirable side effects and downfalls. He may progress throughout history and realize development in certain aspects of life, but such human achievement, although visible, is not real. He will soon discover the poverty of his individual happiness and the rigidity of his social environment. Divine revelation emanates from the source-of-knowledge, i.e., God, and takes into consideration all variables which have been overlooked by man. It provides humanity with salvation and clears all obstacles that hinder man's historical progress. Without the aid of God, man can only build part of his happiness. With the aid of the divine message, man can actually achieve his dream and goal, that is total happiness in earth, and unlimited and continuous progress toward the <u>absolute</u>. It is sufficient to say that without guidance from God, all progress is a mere <u>mirage</u> and every solution to man's problems eventually gives rise to new problems.

The above introduction deals with the ideological aspect of Sadr's political theory. The unquestioned belief is that Islam is the only authentic monotheistic divinely reveled religion which not only guarantees the future salvation of man but also ends the social contradictions of man's communal setting. Such belief is the corner-stone of the theory in its general aspects. The answer is set forward, and Sadr's task was to find an objective supportive argument. What intrigued Sadr was the challenge posed by Western ideological and philosophical doctrines to the religion of Islam in Iraq, and the Muslim world in general. His theoretical formations are not considered scientific research per se, according to behavioralist approach (although he tries to present a scientific argument regarding the issues he studied) but an ideological exposition that advocates the rightness and the truthfulness of Islam. His major task is to falsify and critique the existing western political doctrines, and champion Islam as the only doctrine that can guarantee man's happiness on earth. However, this does not mean that Sadr's theory lacks the aspects of political theory.

The structure of political theory, as outlined in Chapter II, consists of three major facets: ideological, philosophical, and a program of political endeavor. Sadr provided a philosophical argument to support his theoretical framework. Accordingly, I will summarize the main concepts of his theory.

Concepts of Reality and Epistemology

Existence is a divinely created reality. It is God's will which brought the universe into existence. What we sense and comprehend, including our own existence, is the manifestation of God's will. The means through which we know reality is our rational power, which operates on data realized through our senses. The senses are thus the vehicle through which the mind discovers reality. However, the ability of the mind to comprehend reality extends beyond the phenomenal world to include the metaphysical world. The existence of the latter is as real as the former since both are known through the conceptualizing powers of the mind. The data supplied by the senses have no value as knowledge without the mind's conceptualization of this data. The mind's conceptualization view of the physical world and its conceptualization of the metaphysical world are the same. Either we accept both worlds, or we reject both. The mind's intellect is the final arbiter of reality. Consequently, man is rational as well as an empiricist because he uses the faculty of his senses and reasons to discover and understand his existence. The revealed words of God serve as an aid to the human mind. These scriptures are the guide to human rationality, enabling it to discover the reality of the world. They should captivate the mind with new dimensions of knowledge that have long been ignored by man because of the limits of his sensory perception and rationality. Notwithstanding, Sadr argues that the metaphysical world represents a higher stage of development than the physical world. In the final epoch of development, the latter will be absorbed into the former. It is metaphysical existence that is ideal, where physical existence is its manifestation.

Concepts of Human Nature

Since man uses his rational faculties as well as his senses, he is both a rational creature and an experiencing one. His knowledge depends a great deal on his perception of the world surrounding him. He is the product of his environment. Yet, his rational deliberations give him the capacity to go beyond sensory perceptions. He can reasonably react to the events that challenge his existence and find ways to overcome the difficulties he faces in his life. He, therefore, is an optimistic being who has the capacity to evolve and surge beyond the limits of his environment. Although striving for the satisfaction of physical existence, he seeks values of goodness that surmount the boundaries of his personal satisfaction. He might seek to satisfy his emotional needs, such as the need for family and property, while supporting the idea of justice and goodness. His instincts make him a pleasure-seeking person who is concerned about his self-interests, while his rationality makes him a sociopolitical creature who supports the interests of others and sacrifices his own individual interests for their sake. However, man is strongly driven to secure his own physical survival, so that his rational needs in most cases are set aside. It is only through religion that man seeks the values connected with the interests of society rather than allowing himself to be dominated by greed. The message of religion is to rise above individualistic needs to the level of universal values.

Concepts of Ethics

Ethical values, since they are the products of human rationality, are universalistic in nature and common to all people throughout history. In fact, God's gracious revealing of these ethical principles to man has the purpose of overcoming man's greedy nature. Man's instinct for self-love makes him manipulative and exploitative of the rights of others. God reveals values as religious laws, yet they are not contrary to the values deduced by human reasoning. Therefore, Sadr stands with those philosophers who argue for natural laws. Morality and ethics, although they have an Islamic character in his theory, are but basic principles for all humanity. There is no difference in these values from one belief system to another because they are consistent with the rationality of the human mind. Although the purpose of these values and principles of ethics is to serve the happiness of man, Islam adds a religious flavor to this purpose. Man may behave according to these standards in order to please God, while being aware of His punishment if he strays from ethical behavior. For someone to be righteous, he must refrain from committing sins. The most righteous person is the most pious and religious before God. Religion elevates the idea of being right from the level of one's relationship to the society to the level of one's relationship with God. Consequently, all men are equal before God and are judged according to their deeds, including God's prophets and messengers; for each individual understands the demands of the divine moral laws. Equality, as viewed in Sadr's theory, arises from one's relationship to God, and consists in the equal rights which each individual received from God. However, the social implications of the principle of justice as developed in Sadr's political theory do not entail equality so much as they entail <u>fairness</u>. Justice in the social order means, "from every one according to his capacity, to every one according to his needs." Islam seeks to satisfy one's essential needs, while insisting that one must strive to give to his full capacity. The responsibilities for each individual in the social order are according to his own capacity; however, essential rights are protected by Islam. Justice within the social context, Sadr argues, is a "distributive value," not an absolute one.

Concepts of Politics

Sadr maintains that the formation of the communal settings was intented to serve the basics needs of man. The complexity of human life is due to the expansion of his efforts to exploit (positive connotation) the natural environment surrounding him and to cooperate with others beneficially. However, man's instinct for self-love, which manifests itself in greed, causes some individuals to exploit (negative connotation) the social system for their own interests. Oppression becomes rampant and a normal trend in human society. God in His mercy revealed laws instructing prophets to lead the community and establish control mechanisms to end man's oppression of his fellow man. The formation of the political state, according to Sadr, was initiated with the prophethood of Noah, whose message was the first to contain social controls in the form of laws and guidelines for political leadership headed by the Prophet himself. However, the elite of the society have stood throughout history in opposition to the call of justice preached by prophets, while coercion has become rampant as a means of social control. The social laws of the man-made political states were enacted to serve the interests of the dominate group of the society. One of the successful experiments was the reign of the Prophet Muhammad, in which a divinely guided and highly qualified individual led a community of believers and established a just political order. However, such an experiment did not last long. The Muslim community was soon led by corrupt leaders who started another cycle of human oppression.

The cry for freedom and liberty from oppression continues to be the call of the mustad\u1ebfafin. Sadr planned a political program to lead this group to victory and to end social oppression and establish a political state based on the just laws of Islam. The program calls for an organized political movement of the believers to mobilize their efforts and the resources of the society to lead a struggle against the "Pharaohs" of the time. A political party of believers should work in secrecy, underground, in order to mature and revive society's awareness of their inhumane conditions. They must await the right historical circumstance to lead an active struggle against tyrants. Their party must be headed by jurists (faqih) who are knowledgable concerning Islamic laws, just in their behavior, and competent in their leadership. The sought for Islamic state is to be ruled by an elite (jurists belonging to no special social class or group) and the masses of the ummah. Such a state is a combination of oligarchy and democracy, rule by neither the few or the many. This arrangement is considered the best possible situation without the presence of a divinely-guided leader, the twelfth Imam, or Mahdi, who will appear at the end of time to "fill the

Earth with justice and moderation, after its suffocation with injustice and oppression." Sadr also realized that a jurist is not an infallible individual. He cannot be left without supervision. Therefore, constraints must be placed on his behavior and power. The old conventional institution of <u>marja^ciyah</u> was insufficient in this regard. It was based on moral limits, as the jurist selected to the position of <u>marja^ciyah</u> was scrutinized and vigorously judged and watched over by his peers, who focused on his dedication and knowledge of Islam. However, Sadr wanted to put a constitutional limit on his behavior and help him in his administration of the state. He wanted to organize a political institution, <u>al-marja^ciyah al-salihah</u>, consisting of offices and specialists in all matters of religion and politics, to be the jurist's agent and political arm of the state.

Summary

Sadr's political theory is not entirely without antecedents. Every theorist depends on the thoughts of the others who preceded him. Marx, for example, utilized the thoughts of Fourierback, Hegel, and the socialist ideas in France, which he molded into a grand design unique to human intellectual tradition. Hence, the philosophical aspects as well as the Islamic aspect of Sadr's theory derive from other intellectual figures. His ingenuity lies in the political context. He stood as an exceptional giant among the Muslim jurists one who thought in global terms as he pondered the particular issues of Islamic law. His formulation of a political theory is unprecedented with its unique development of the concept of "governorship of jurist" (<u>wilayat al-faqih</u>), the general participation of the public in the determination of what constitutes the "suitable condition" of their affairs, "absolute ownership" by government of the natural resources, and its direct interference in the social affairs in order to guard social justice and the "social equilibrium" of the economic order. While other Islamic jurists resort to deriving laws concerned with individual believers, Sadr was perhaps the only one known to widen the scope of Islamic jurisprudence to include social issues. His aim was to include all aspects of Islamic knowledge in order to derive one coherent theory that gives an understanding of major political issues. Here is the summary of Sadr's theoretical framework.

Aims

Sadr argues that Islam is a political doctrine as well as an belief system for individuals. He thus aims to develop a political theory that would be the basis for the establishment of a political system and would shape the social and economic structures according to Islamic principles. Consequently, he was struggling to change the scope of religious studies to include discussions of social and economic issues which concern the political state. His major works in economics, philosophy, jurisprudence, epistemology, banking, and politics were steps in the direction of changing the paradigm of religious studies.

Assumptions

1. Acording to Sadr, human nature is duality consisting of sensory and rational sides. Man has emotional as well as intellectual needs. Man's knowledge about reality arises from the rational side of his nature. The metaphysical world as conceived by the human mind is as real as the physical world. However, man is in actuality more attached to his physical world and to his physical survival.

2. God is the ground of existence and creator of the reality we know. He has created man with duties to fulfill and a mission to accomplish, while providing him with all rational and physical faculties and resources for his life on Earth as well as with the guidance found in scriptures.

3. The historical process is divinely programmed to bring about the emancipation of man and his elevation into the metaphysical, utopian world of the spirit. Human relationships are of three types, all of which are interrelated: 1) social (man-man); 2) economic (man-nature); 3) spiritual (man-God). The third is the dominate one. Man, using his free will to abstain from following the guidance of God to achieve his goal, can delay the process of development, but cannot stop it. The historical development is the struggle of man to ascend to the <u>absolute</u>, God.

4. Prophets are the agents of God who deliver his guidance to man and make man aware of his deviation from the planned historical progression toward Him. They were divinely appointed to lead humanity and put an end to the contradictions that exist in social settings.

5. Human change is gradual, yet deterministic, progressive, and beneficial to man. Accordingly, a prophet's message comes in stages in order to teach man and develop his capacities and rational faculty and satisfy his spiritual and temporal needs. There are no real contradictions between divine-monotheistic religions because the revealer is one and the same, God. However, the message of religion is to overcome the problems of social relations and satisfy man's spiritual needs through his submission to God. However, religion was designed to be man's guide in the realm of economic relationships. The contradiction of the economic relationship is the result of the inner conflict of human nature, i.e., self-love.

6. Islam, the final revelation of God, has the solution to the socioeconomic contradictions of the communal setting which are generated by man's self-love. Islam satisfies man's spiritual needs, justly distributes economic wealth, establishes a social structure free of oppression, and guides man toward God.

Methodology

As mentioned above, Sadr defined the conflict facing man within his social setting as originating from the inner conflict of human nature. Man, although rational, has an emotional side that is linked to the temporal world and his physical needs. The idealism he adheres to is a reflection of his sensual needs. Sadr's studies can be summarized as an attempt to find the cause of social problems. Once a human being finds the solution to these problems, he can achieve happiness in his life. Sadr's first approach to the problem was to develop philosophical arguments aimed at discovering the cause of human suffering in the social environment. Once Sadr pinpointed the main cause, he was able to find a solution: monotheistic religion, and specifically its final revelation, Islam. His second approach was to formulate the theory of a conflict-free political system, which was a religious one. He used shi^cah sources to draw the blue-print for both the social and the economic structures of his political state. He used arguments drawn from jurisprudence (usul), Islamic positive law (fiqh) and Quranic studies to support his political design.

Typology

One major typology inherent in Sadr's theory comprises the stages of development in the historical process governing man's emancipation starting with the creation of Adam and "continuing" with his life after the "judgment day" (yawm al-qiyamah). Three of the five stages concern man's life on earth, the other two are after his death. The third stage is signified by a unified world-wide Islamic political system, divinely guided by the twelfth Imam, which transforms the temporal being of man into a metaphysical one. However, the development of the historical process is not linear, but rather spiral. At every regression of man to the animalistic status, which occurs when he links himself to his emotional needs, God reveals new messages to help him ascend to the "right path." The five universal prophetic missions are the beginning of a new historical epoch of human emancipation.

Other minor typologies are related to 1) the structure of the economic classes and, 2) the social groups within the Pharoanic (tyrannic) society. The former is essential for the distribution of the economic wealth and the latter is essential to determining the revolutionary group that will lead the political struggle.

<u>Final Remarks</u>

Although the historical process in Sadr's theory is deterministic, human beings still possess the ability, not to alter the grand divine design of history, but to delay its progress. However, this capacity and the free will entailed in it honors man among all of God's creations by giving him the power to become God's vicar on Earth. Yet this divine grace to man entails responsibility and ever-lasting emancipation under God. In order to achieve such an exalted privilege, man needs to submit himself to God through total devotion to the guidance of His message. However, social conflicts may divert the attention of man from God to other man-made lords. Societies that are devoted to lords other than God may vanquish and destroy man's emancipation. Man ought to establish a social order based on the guidance of God, which guarantees a conflict-free social environment.

Such an analysis amounts to religious idealism, based on the Islamic principle of belief. Sadr's analysis of the historical process is similar in its approach to the psychological approach of Hegel, where history is the development of ideas that instigate new social and economic structures. Sadr links the development of history to divinely revealed messages. Sadr also borrows the idea of elevation from temporal existence to a spiritual one from the philosophy of Sadr al-Din al-Shirazi.

ASSESSMENT

According to Islam, in order to construct free thought, man should develop his deductive reasoning or argumentation for the purpose of not accepting any idea without analyzing it.

Sadr

The central theme of Sadr's theory is that the so-called <u>substructure</u> of a society is the inner emotion, understanding and ideological beliefs of the individual member of that society. The <u>superstructure</u> of the society, i.e., the socioeconomic structure and relationships, is a reflection of the substructure. Once man changes his inner contents, an envitable change will occur in the external social environment. Sadr's political program of changing man within himself (through the establishment of a political party and creation of a righteous core of the society) prior to bringing about social change is a faithful outworking of his theoretical framework. He argues that social change is independent of the objective conditions of a society, i.e., its political, social and economic structure and relative only to the subjective conditions of man, i.e., his inner emotions and rational understandings. If man purifies his soul, and behaves according to his rationality, his actions will give rise to justice and happiness in the whole soceity. The social reality is nothing but the by-product of human nature. Consequently, Sadr, in designing the course of revolutionary political movements, gives more attention to the reformation of man than to the reformation of a society. It is when man purifies his relationship with God that he will witness great benefits in his relationship both with nature and with other human beings.

In fact, the whole theory (or for that matter Islamic religious beliefs in general) is centered around the salvation of the individual soul. The sole purpose of religion is nothing but to bring happiness to man. To explain further, the journey of man toward the <u>absolute</u> (as protrayed in his theory) is an emancipation of man as an individual in an endless progression. In objective terms, the unit of analysis of the theory is individual man. Sadr's entire theoretical formation aims to disclose the final or ultimate cause of the contradictions in the social phenomenon. His analysis centers around the main factors that hinder man's emancipation. Although Sadr has rejected the Marxian notion of linking the whole misery of man to one factor (the economic relationship), he falls into the same theoretical trap by relating all human problems and social contradiction to the psychology of man. The inner feelings of man are the determining factor for the socioeconomic structure. To end social conflict and oppression in a society it is necessary to end the inner conflict of human nature, the conflicts between emotional lusts and rational aspirations. Only God is capable of giving guidance to man in overcoming this inner human crisis, for man cannot transcend the limits of his own nature. It is the monotheistic religions that pinpoint the means of ending the tragedy of his psycological being. Sadr's theory is a mono-causal explanation. Sadrists may claim that Sadr simply underscores the central factor while at the same time considering many others, including social and economical factors. Although this might be true to some extent, the real cause of the conflicts facing man in his theoretical framework stems from one major cause, that is his inner human crisis. This single cause is much in evidence in Sadr's solution to the social crisis.

Although Sadr claims that social conflict originated from the inner contradiction of human nature, his solution, albeit provided by religion, uses social forces to enforce man's good behavior. It is sufficent to mention that he proposes the creation of a righteous elite that function as the nucleus of the society, but this social force has as its historical mission the shaping of the social environment for others to follow message of God. Sadr's political program, thus, is only partially psychological, aiming at reviving Islamic teachings with the few, while proving to be mainly social, aiming at creating an Islamic social order that enforces Islamic conduct of behavior on the rest of the population. The Islamic state has the responsibility to create a sin-free social environment and eliminate all corruption from the society, not merely through education and pedagogy, but through coercion if necessary. The economic structure and relationship in the Islamic political system must be shaped in such a way as to reflect the fundamental principles of Islamic law; it should not be a mere reflection of the actual level of the people's spiritual commitment to Islam. The leader of the Islamic state would oversee the implementation of Islamic laws in his jurisdictions and reshape the society according to Islamic principles. Thus, social change comes from above as well as from below, i.e., a change of attitude in man. As can be seen, there is an inconsistancy in the political component of the theory. If social oppression emanates from man's inner instincts as the theory suggests, then the only logical solution to the social problem would be through the consistent education and pedagogy of man's mind and soul, i.e., the purification of human nature. What Sadr has provided as a solution is inconsistent with his earlier theoretical analysis of the causes of the social problem. Consequently, one might question the validity of Sadr's assertions, that is his very biased assumption that man's psychological condition is the factor which determines his social enviroment and the basic element of his historical emancipation. Quite apart from problems relating to his theoretical interpretations of religious beliefs, which are the building blocks of his dogmatic theory some assertions that are not related to the religious belief have no scientific proof, but only a philosophical justification(for the theory is essentially a religious one in which fundamental Islamic principles such as that of divine determination of the historical process, supported by unquestioned affirmations of Islamic jurisprudence, obviously are essential factors in his Islamic theory). Although Sadr has argued that philosophical arguments are as valid as the findings of empirical experiments, such a claim, especially when it concerns factual phenomenon itself, needs proof. The connection between man's psychological being and social environment, which is considered in the theory as the key to understanding the crisis facing man in his life, needs uncontestable evidence.

On the other hand, Sadr also seems to exhibit a degree of ambivalence in his outlook on the human problem. The individual's inner instincts determine the social outcome, while at the same time the social environment has a direct impact on the individual personality and behavior. Both man and society are important, and each plays a significant role in affecting the characteristics of the other. Both have real existence. Although man's free will determines the conditions of his social environment, his fate is linked to the fate of the society at large. Sadr's theoretical approach is thus circular and is highly dualistic in nature. The central bias of his theory is religious (the spiritual purification of human nature), but his solution is materialistic, i.e., the creation of a political environment that constrains man's behavior to make him follow the right path, if not voluntarily then by social coersion.

The dualistic nature of the theory goes on and on. Man was created as a viceroy of God, endowed with free will, and rationality. He deserves to have the angel bow before him; yet he is driven by his animalistic insticts, and his rationality plays no important role in his decisions. His values are the results of his enviornment, and his belief system is based on myths. Man is rational, yet empiricist. He derives his knowledge from his senses; but, at the same time, he possesses an inner knowledge that makes value judgements and evolves gradually. His susceptibility to the influence of nature makes him the product of his environment, yet his rational capacity makes him an agent able to shape his environment. In all respects, the theory takes into consideration the two extremes but considers only one as the ideal. The values man believes in, for example, are either relativist or absolutist. He is a relativist if he resorts to his senses, and an absolutist if he is guided by the revelations of God, or the rationality of his inner knowledge. Generally, man is always a relativist because his rationality is influenced mostly by the environment. The only way for man to transcend beyond the limits of his surroundings is to be guided by the divine message. It is the objective of the Islamic state to elevate man above his emotional attachment to the ideal of rationality. The ideal situation in the temporal world can be realized only during the reign of the coming messiah, the Imam Mahdi. The political program is designed for the salvation of man. This mission can be achieved only via the establishment of a political system that guides man until the coming of the Mahdi. Such a political regime seems to have one mission: the elimination of all corruption which dulls the rationality of man and diverts him from his ultimate goal. It is only the Islamic state that ensures the survival of the believers and immunizes them from the currupt influence of the environment. When it comes to underpinning the source of order in the Islamic state, Sadr suggests people, due to their rational faculty, have the capacity and the inclination to live according to laws of God because it is for their own self- interest. This applies to some people, while others are driven by their emotions to yield to power only. However, the Islamic state must bring about the "corruption-free" cultural environment in order to bring man's habits into conformity with the guidance of God, what Sadr calls the long process of pedagogy.

Of course, the dualistic nature of his theory is justified on the basis that Islam, to use the words of Muhammad Hussein Fadalallah, "is a realist religion" that takes into consideration all factors that are important to human life. It is not a utopian theory one that disregards some essential component of life. A realist theory, according to this type of thinking, must contemplate the different extremes of life in order to fully understand their impact on human life and in order to pinpoint the right solution to the problems that confront humanity. Without such a comprehensive consideration of all aspects of reality, any theory will fall short of giving the right and proper solution. Islam stands alone as the only divine message that is saved from alteration and corruption and considers all factors affecting humanity and provides a suitable answer. It requires knowledge of God to be fully aware of the entire reality underlying social phenomena and the historical progress of man. However, if that is the case (i.e., that Islam takes into consideration all factors influencing human life), then there is no need for a theory. For the function of a theory is to organize our thoughts and show us which are the important factors. To consider everything as important means that nothing is important in the final analysis, and Muslim intellectuals should give up their efforts to formulate a comprehensive sociopolitical theory. Sadr was on the right track when he stressed the psychological factor as the driving force behind social contradictions, but he lapses into confusion by including other factors in his theoretical framework.

Another theoretical inconsistency found in Sadr's political design has to do with the distribution of power in the Islamic state. He envisioned two players who have major roles to play within the political system, the _imam_ and the _ummah_ (the witness and the vicar, or the ruler and ruled, respectively). The ruler of the Islamic state obtains his legitimacy from God, the ultimate holder of power. On the other hand, the ruled have the divine right to express their opinion on issues that affect them. In this regard, their responsibility is to make sure that Islamic laws and fundamental principles are being implemented within the society, implying that the ruled have the right to oppose the ruler when they see him unfit or not following Islamic teachings. In other words, the Muslim masses have the right to rebel against their ruler. However, such rights of defiance are terminated when the ruler of the Islamic state is a grand jurist (_marja`_). Sadr, like other jurists who advocate the authority of the _faqih_, concludes that the most qualified individual, the one who best knows Islamic laws and doctrine, is the jurist. The masses know little of the details of religion. Theoretically speaking, the divine right of _khilafah_ (vicarage of God) meant that the individual holds the responsibility to create an Islamic social system; however, when this goal is achieved, this responsibility is then reduced to obeying the legitimate ruler. The jurist is entrusted with the governership because of his talents. Sadr goes further to say that not even other jurists have the right to defy the order of a ruling-jurist, even if they see wrongdoing. Since jurists possess almost the same level of knowledge and understanding about Islamic jurisprudence, disagreement between them is only a matter of different interpretations of the sources of Islamic law. Therefore, they should keep their opposition within the closed ranks of the ulamas, otherwise it will be an invitation to anarchy. Accordingly, their duty is similar to that of others in the state, namely to obey the authority of the ruling jurist. Sadr's structuring of the Islamic state seems to give the legitimate ruler, as an individual, or as the state, an "absolute" power, the right to run the affairs of the society. It is the obligation of the people to obey the legitimate Islamic ruler because he represents the ultimate interests of the believers, i.e., conforming to the divine laws and principles. The Islamic government has the great responsibility of leading the masses to their final destiny, God. Consequently, the individual Muslim must obey (for his own good) the rules of the government because it is working for his own salvation. In other words, under an Islamic political system, either one should be like Rousseau's man who voluntarily acts according to the "general will" (which in Islam is the conformity to divine laws and regulations), or the sovereign should take the role of Hobbes's "Leviathan" in order to enforce the social interest to bring about the salvation of man. In the Islamic political state, there are no means of social influence on the leadership. The masses, in the entire social setting, i.e., the social institutions and political organizations, play no major role in influencing the leadership. The marja`, after all, is the divine successor to the original leader of the state. Muslims, in their defiance of his leadership, are committing a sin before God. The unity of the Islamic state and its social coherency are valued more than the individual's rights of expression.

With this type of "absolutism" of the governership of the jurist, one may wonder what happens to the individual Muslim's Khalafah (vicarage). According to Sadr's theory, the Khilafah is supposed to have a continuing role in the elevation of man to the Absolute. In fact, according to Kazim al-Ha'iri, Sadr argues that in the final stage of the historical process man will emancipate himself to the point he will not need the role of shahid (witness), i.e., guidence of imam. In another words, the ummah will take the role of shahid, i.e, the state will wither away, to borrow form Engle.

The inconsistency in Sadr's views stems probably from the different interpretations that emerge from his theoretical framework on the one hand and his juristic opinions (fatwa) on the other. In the formation of his theory, Sadr is trying to "discover" (as he likes to call his intellectual task) the general concepts that are the common basis of Islamic doctrine. However, when he issues a fatwa, it is to express his own interpretation of Islamic law with regard to specific problems. In the former case, he is formulating from a general understanding about Islam and the grand design of the Islamic social system. In the latter case, he is giving his own opinion as deduced through the standard legal methodology of Islamic jurisprudence. In the former, he is taking the role of philosopher, and in the latter he is a jurist. Consequently, one should keep these two roles in mind in trying to make sense of his different political views; otherwise, one may see only inconsistencies in his views. al-

Hairi, for example, finds Sadr shuffling from one stand to anothers. At first, Sadr leaned toward the view that leadership in the Islamic state is a collective one (shura) where a decision is a result of the consensus of a group of jurists. Then Sadr changed his view and adopted the idea of wilayat al-faqih where one jurist is the final arbiter of the state. In his later life, he seemed, according to al-Ha'iri, to combine these two earlier views by giving a role to the masses, through their representation, and to the jurist as caretaker of the governership. However, I believe that Sadr gave different roles to the masses and the jurist in the political life of the Islamic state. The latter has the final word in all affairs. The inconsistency in his theoretical formulations rests on his vacillation between two different fields of Islamic studies, philosophy and juristprudence, in the formulation of his theory. A logical conclusion in philosophy may not find supportive arguments in jurisprudenc.

However, there are shortcomings in the practicalities of Sadr's political engineering of Islamic state. He emphasize the need to build a institutional structure for the marja`iyah because it is symbol of legitimacy and constitutes the head of the state. Sadr maintains that legitimacy of the state belongs to the individual, the marja` as a person. He proposes the selection of the marja` be based on additional qualifications beyond knowledge of Islamic jurisprudence and just behavior, such as administrative skills and political insights. However, Sadr's political theory still employs the traditional concept of assigning legitimacy to the individual marja`. Such a conceptual framework can be understood in the case of a divinely constituted people who will be the recipients of God's guidance, but the application of this framework to others has no justification. Sadr does not even assign legitimacy to the process or the structure of the state, nor to the rule of law.

Furthermore, if one takes into consideration the amount of power entrusted to the marja`, one will realize the grave danger this presents. Although the jurist is constrained by the dictates of Islamic law and is responsible to the Muslim ummah, he is still considered, politically speaking, the bearer of the law and above the ummah. He possesses a great deal of political power. He is the final authority in the interpretation of the law, and this law is totalitarian in nature in the sense that it encompasses the whole realm of social and individual life. The jurist is, therefore, in realistic terms, an absolute ruler. He is in fact the final legislator, the chief executive, and highest jurist of the state. Moreover, there is no limitation on the duration of the position of marja`. Once he is selected, he may serve for the rest of his life. If one takes into consideration that the state is the sole owner of all the natural resources and the means of production of the society, then one soon realizes that the Islamic political system is a "totalitarian" one, a conclusion probably not taken into account by Sadr, given his aim of creating a political process based on a sharing of power in the Islamic state between the kalifahs (masses) and the shahid (jurist). Not even his political blue-print for the marja`iyah al-salihah provided for any meaningful constitutional form of separation of power.

Moreover, the question might be asked: why are property and the means of economic life commonly owned and totally controlled by the state, the chief agent of the society, given that property is considered the prime source of corruption? Are there historial limits to the control by the state over natural resources? Would there be a time when individuals reached the stage of salvation and of "being on the right path" such that they would have the right to own property? At the early stage of the formation of an Islamic political system, such total control over economic means might be justified as preventing some corrupt individuals from using these means to oppress others. However, no justification is acceptable when Muslims are elevated to a higher level of spirituality. It is important to mention that Sadr criticized Marxist theory for eliminating private property on the ground that this artificial abolishment of man's nature instinct would cause stagnation in economic development. However, when Sadr talks about the distribution of economic power in the Islamic state, the government and not the people becomes responsible for economic development. His views are derived from the fact that the laws of economics that govern the markets in a capitalist system are inhumane and tend to corrupt people and make them greedy and profit-motivated creatures. However, Sadr does not mention the shortcommings of proposals of centralized economic development, such as the corruption of the Islamic leadership, or of its bureaucratic institutions.

This would bring us to another critical point relating to Sadr's theory. He seems to assume that the process of historical development comes to a halt after the establishment of the Islamic state. He has not specified at all the nature of the development of the Islamic political state, except that it will lead to Imam Mahdi's worldwide political system. He definitely sets aside any mention of the type of social contradiction that exists in the Islamic political system in the pre-Mahdi governership. The Islamic state under the leadership of a jurist is an imperfect situation, otherwise the need for the governership of the infallible Imams is not necessary, and the coming of Mahdi is redundant to human historical development. Therefore, the Islamic state must contain some form of social injustice that Sadr ignores. When it comes to the Islamic political system, Sadr seems to be a conservative and an idealist, even when discussing the nonutopian Islamic state.

One might also be confused as to where to place Sadr in the political spectrum. On the one hand,he seems to be conservative because of his conviction that social change and the political process must be introduced gradually --breeding new social values in the people's existing beliefs. The political phase of change seems to take a gradual yet revolutionary step. It is only then that the realization of _real_ changes in the society takes place. It is a political program characterized by waiting for the social revolution to happen. The Islamic political party may aid the revolutionary process, but it cannot create it. The historical process must take its course, and a revolution cannot happen before its time.

On the other hand, Sadr seems to be a radical revolutionary. Although he is waiting for the historical conditions to be fulfilled, he is willing to use all possible means to influence the outcome to the advantage of his ideological commitments. The Islamic revolutionaries must take any opportunity to influence the direction of the revolution and reshape its course. They must find the right slogans to appeal to different groups, utilize the means to inspire the masses, put aside differences to unify the Islamic forces, infiltrate the existing political structure, be prepared to use arms to achieve the revolutionary goal, and collaborate with others to add strength to the movement. In general, however, Sadr is ultraconservative when it comes to preserving the Islamic system. He definitly does not allow any disagreement with the jurist in power, and believes all efforts should be channeled to support him every step of the way. Disagreements should be handled in private, even in matters on which other jurists believe his decisions to be based on false assumptions. His decision should be respected even when it is wrong. The preservation of the Islamic state is supposed to continue until the comming of the Mahdi.

Moreover, there are some omissions in Sadr's conceptual analysis. For example, he fails to discuss the political process in the Islamic state and the role of the political forces that existed before the formation of the Islamic political system. He also fails to mention what means the Islamic government uses to subordinate these hostile or neutral forces to its will. Another question concerns the level of disagreement with which one might pose or challenge the wisdom of the leader's positions. Sadr has not specified the role of the Islamic political party, which supposedly paves the way for the formation of the Islamic state. Would the Islamic political parties and organizations, who supposedly carry the revolutionary struggle against the corrupt regimes, continue their role of mobilizing the masses or be dissolved? The revolutionary struggle may continue indefinitly to achieve victory and the establishment of an Islamic state, during which the Islamic organizations put down their social roots and create their grass-roots structure. There is no possible way to imagine their withering away as soon as they achieve their political victroy. Realistically, they will continue to determine the process of government and become a major social force in influencing the decisions of the state hierarchy and leadership. However, Sadr's structuring of the state seems to emphasize the creation of state institutions, i.e., the office of marja`yah, the presidency, the parliament, cabinets and the courts, but has not specified the impact which social forces will make on the governmental processes. Would these social forces carry only the Islamic conventional wisdom, the orders and wishes of the leadership? Would they not have their own dynamics and behave according to their own organizational logic?

The other idealistic aspect of the theory is in its political solution. Sadr provided no pragmatic steps to reform the currupt political regimes. His only solution is the total social revolution that changes the whole fabric of the society, its structure, values, and leadership. He is proposing the creation of a new society that is based totally on Islamic teachings and dismantles all non-Islamic social aspects, structures and values. The existing social orders are based on non-Islamic foundations. In order to make Muslims live in accordance with God's teachings, they must reorganize their lives according to God's will, including their personal as well as social lives. The old conventional wisdom of trying to save the individual from social ills by guiding his personal behavior according to Islam is fallacious. The social ills sooner or later will corrupt the individual, and the faithful will be in danger of losing their commitment to their ideals. The only proper means of action is to implement Islam in all aspects of society. It will control the leadership, organize the social forces, restructure the economy and redistribute the wealth, as well as guide the individual. What this radical social change means in real terms is the destruction of the entire foundation of existing societies, and the reestablishing of an Islamic one. Sadr gave no consideration to any reform movements or activity within his revolutionary state.

Given this dogmatic prespective, one senses that all the answers are already given and that Sadr's entire endeavor was a search for questions that matched these answers. His theoretical framework, in other words, entails a going backwards, as in all doctrinaire systems. The given answers are never about the religious principles, such as belief in God, prophets, or the hearafter, but are rather about the political solution called for by the theory. They are, in other words, about such things as the legitimaty of the marja`iyah to the governorship of the state, the amount of political power it possesses, the process of political struggle by the Islamic movement, the role of man in the state, etc. Although Sadrists may argue that there are perennial problems faced by man throughout his history to which Islam provides the solutions, thus offering salvation in both the social and personal spheres of life, such an argument makes sense only at the level of highly generalized matters such as religious beliefs which will fulfill man's spiritual needs, or the right of the individual to life, progeny and property. But there is no concrete blue-print for an actual social structure or political process. I wonder whether Sadr, if he were writing immediately after the major occultation of Imam Mahdi, or two hunderd years from now, would arrive at political solutions which were any different. There seems to be no logical correlation between circumstantial conditions and theoretical conclusions. No matter how variable the former, the latter remain constant.

BIBLIOGRAPHY

Muhammad Baqir al-Sadr

"al-ᶜAmal wa al-Ahdaf" (The Deeds and the Goals): <u>Min Fikr al-Daᶜwah</u>. no. 13. Islamic Daᶜwah Party, central propagation, place and date of publication unknown.

"al-ᶜAmal al-Salih fi al-Quran" (The Proper Behavior According to Qur'an): <u>Ikhtrna Lak</u>. Beirut: Dar al-Zahra', 1982.

<u>Ahl al-Bayt: Tanawuᶜ Adwar wa-Wihdat Hadaf</u> (The House Hold of the Prophet: Diversity of roles but unified goal). Beirut: Dar al-Taᶜruf, 1985.

<u>al-Bank al-la-Rubawi fi al-Islam</u> (Non-usury Bank in Islam). Beirut: Dar al-Taᶜruf, 1981.

<u>Bahth Hawla al-Mahdi</u> (Thesis on Messiah). Beirut: Dar al-Taᶜruf, 1983.

<u>Bahth Hawla al-Wilayah</u> (Thesis on Rulership). Kuwait: Dar al-Tawhid, 1977.

"Daᶜwatana il al-Islam Yajeb an Takun Enqilabiyah," (Our Call for Islam Must be a Revolutionary): <u>Fikr al-Daᶜwah</u>, no. 13. Islamic Daᶜwah Party, central propagation, place and date of publication unknown.

"Dawr al-A'imah fi al-Hayat al-Islamiyah" (The Role of Imams in Muslims' Life): <u>Ikhtarna Lak</u>. Beirut: Dar al-Zahra', 1982.

"al-Dawlah al-Islamiyah" (The Islamic State), <u>al-Jihad</u> (14 March 1983): 5.

<u>Durus fi ᶜIlm al-Usul</u> (Lessons on the Principle of Jurisprudence). Cairo: Dar al-Kitab al-Masri, 1978.

<u>Falsafatuna</u> (Our Philosophy). 10 ed. Beirut: Dar al-Taᶜruf, 1980.

al-Fatawi al-Wadihah (Clear Islamic Rules). Beirut: Dar al-   Ta^cruf li-al-Matbu^cat, 1981

"Hawla al-Marhala al-Ula min ^cAmal al-Da^cwah" (On the First   Stage   of   Da^cwah Political Program): Min Fikr al-Da^cwah.   no. 13. Islamic   Da^cwah   Party,   central propagation, place   and date of publishing unknown.

"Hawla al-Ism wa-al-Shakl al-Tanzimi li-Hizb al-Da^cwah al- Islamiyah" (On the Name and the Structural Organization   of Islamic Da^cwah Party): Min Fikr al-Da^cwah. no. 13.   Islamic Da^cwah Party, central propagation, place and date   of   publication unknown.

"al-Huriyah fi al-Quran" (Freedom according to Quran):   Ikhtarna Lak. Beirut: Dar al-Zahra', 1982.

"al-Itijahat al-Mustaqbaliyah li-Harakat al-Ijtihad" (The   Future Trends of the Process of Ijtihad): Ikhtarna Lak.   Beirut: Dar al-Zahra', 1980.

al-Insan al-Mu^casir wa-al-Mushkilah al-Ijtima^cyah (The   contemporary man and the Social Problem). al-Madrasah al-   Islamiyah, 3rd ed. Beirut: Dar al-Zahra', 1980.

Iqtisaduna (Our Economics). Beirut: Dar al-Ta^caruf, 1981.

"al-Janib al-Iqtisadi Min al-Nizam al-Islami" (The Economic Perspective   of   Islamic System): Ikhtarna Lak. Beirut: Dar   al-Zahra', 1982.

Khalafat al-Insan wa-Shahadat al-Anbia' (Vicory role of man,   and Witness role of Prophets): al-Islam Yaqwod al-Hayat.   Iran: Islamic Ministry of Guidance, n.d.

Khatut Tafsiliyah ^cAn Iqtisad al-Mujtama^c al-Islami (General   Basis of Economics of Islamic Society): al-Islam Yaqud   al-Hayah. Iran: Islamic Ministry of Guidance, n.d.

Lamha fiqhiyah Hawla Dustur al-Jumhuriyah al-Islamiyah (A   preliminary jurisprudence basis of the Constitution of   the Islamic Republic): al-Islam Yaqwod al-Hayat Iran: Islamic Ministry of Guidance, n.d.

al-Ma^calim al-Jadidah lil Usul (New Directions on the   Principles of Jurisprudence). Tehran: Maktabat al-Najah,   1975.

Madha Ta^cruf ^can al-Iqtisad al-Islami (What do you know about   Islamic   Economics).

al-Islam Yaqwod al-Hayat Iran: Islamic Ministry of Guidance, n.d.

Manabi^c al-Qudra fi al-Dawlah al-Islamiyah (The Sources of Power in an Islamic State). al-Islam Yaqwod al-Hayat Iran: Islamic Ministry of Guidance, n.d.

"al-Mihna" (The Ordeal). Sawt al-Wihdah, no. 5, 6, 7. (n.d).

Minhaj al-Salihin (The Path of the Righteous). Beirut: Dar al-Ta^caruf, 1980.

Muqaddimat fi al-Tafsir al-Mawdu^ci Lil-Quran (Introductions in Thematic Interpretation of the Quran). Kuwait: Dar al- Tawjyyh al-Islami, 1980.

"Nazarah ^cAmah fi al-^cIbadat" (General Outlook on Worship): al-Fatawa al-Wadhiha. Beirut: Dar al-Ta^caruf, 1981.

"al-Nazriyah al-Islamiyah li-Tawzi^c al-Masadr al-Tabi^ciyah" (Islamic Theory of Distribution of Natural Resources): Ikhtarna Lak. Beirut: Dar al-Zahra', 1982.

"al-Nizam al-Islami Muqaranan bil-Nizam al-Ra'smali wa-al-Markisi" (The Islamic System Compared with The Capitalist and The Marxist Systems). Ikhtarna Lak. Beirut: Dar-al Zahra', 1982.

"Risalatuna wa-al-Da^cwah" (Our Message and Our Sermon). Risalatuna. Beirut: al-Dar al-Islamiyah, 1981.

"al-Shakhsiyah al-Islamiyah" (Muslim Personality): Min Fikr al-Da^cwah al-Islamiyah (Of the Thoughts of Islamic Da^cwah). no. 13. Islamic Da^cwah Party, central propagation, place and date of publication unknown.

Surah ^cAn Iqtisad al-Mujtama^c al-Islami (A Perspective on the Economy of Muslim Society). al-Islam Yaqwod al-Hayat Iran: Islamic Ministry of Guidance, n.d.

"al-Usus al-^cAmah li-al-Bank fi al-Mujtam^c al-Islami" (The General Basis of Banks in Islamic Society). in al-Islam Yaqwod al-Hayat Iran: Islamic Ministry of Guidance, n.d.

al-Usus al-Mantaqiyah lil Istiqra' (The Logical Basis of Induction) Beirut: Dar al-Ta^cruf, 1981.

"Utruhat al-Marja^ciyah al-Salihah" (Thesis on Suitable Marja^ciyah). In Kazim al-

Ha'iri,Mabahith fi ᶜIlm al-   Usul.Qum, Iran: n.p., 1988.

"al-Yaqin al-Riyadi wa-al-Mantiq al-Wazᶜi" (The Mathematic   Certainty   and   the Phenomenal Logic): Ikhtrna Lak. Beirut: Dar al-Zahra', 1982.

"Preface to al-Sahifah al-Sajadiyah" (of Imam ᶜAli ibn Hussein   al-Sajad). Tehran: al-Maktabah al-Islamiyah al-Kubra,   n.d.

Sadr's Works in English Translation

The Awaited Savior. Translated by Mustajab A. Ansari. Karachi,   Pakistan: Islamic Seminary Publication, 1979.

Islam and School of Economics. Translator name unknown.   Albany, CA: Muslim Students Association, n.d.

Our Phiolosophy. Translated by Shams C. Inati. London: Muhammadi Trust, 1987.

Critical Studies

Ha'iri, Kazim al-. "Sunan al-Tarikh, part one." (The Laws of History) al-Hiwar al-Fikri wa al-Siyasi (Summer, 1985):   51-90.

Ha'iri, Kazim al-. "Sunan al-Tarikh, part two." al-Hiwar al-   Fikri wa la-Siasi. (Fall 1985): 40-65.

Ha'iri, Kazim al-. "Sunan al-Tarikh, Adwar al-Tarikh fi al-   Hayat al-Ukhra." al-Hiwar al-Fikri. (Winter, 1986): 47-   75.

Biographies

Abu Ali, "Lamhah Khatifah ᶜan al-Shahid al-Rabiᶜ al-Imam Muhammad Baqir al-Sadr" (Brief Study of the Fourth   Martyr, Imam Muhammad Baqir Sadr), Tariq al-Haq. 7 May   1980.

Hairi., Kazim al-. Tarjamat Hayat al-Marja^c al-Shahid al-Sadr. (Biography of the Martyr Marja^c al-Sadr). Qum, Iran: 1988.

Najaf, A. al-Shahid wa al-Shahyyd. (Martyrdom and the Martyr). Qum, Iran: Jam^cat al-^cUlama' al-Mujahedin fi al-^cIraq. n.d.

Qubanchi, Sadr al-Din al-. al-Jihad al-Siyasi lil Sayyid al- Shahid al-Sadr. (The Political Struggle of Martyr al- Sadr). Tehran, Iran: Suprem Council of Islamic Revolution of Iraq. 1404 AH.

Personal Interviews

A.H.F. (remain anonymous) Kansas City, Missouri. Interview. 1 January 1990.

Kubba, Ahmad. Los Angeles, California. Interview. 4 November 1989.

Rifa^ci, Talib al-. Salt Lake City, Utah. Interview. 12 July 1989.

Interviews in Published Sources

Askari, Murtda al-. Interview Liwa al-Sadr. (7 Gambit al-Thai 1409 A.H): 6.

Fadlullah, Muhammad Hussein. Interview. al-Jihad (14 Dec 1987): 9.

Hakim, Mahdi al-. Interview. Liwa al-Sadr (7 Jamadi al-Thai 1409 A.H): 12.

Hakim, Muhammad Baqir al-. Interview. al-Jihad. 14 (Gambit al- Thai 1401 AH).

General Sources

^cAskari, Murtada al-. "Juthor wa-Khalfiyat al-Taharuk al- Islami fi Muwajahat al-Ba^cth al-^cAflaqi" (The Roots and Backgrounds of Islamic Activities in Opposition to the ^cAfliq's Ba^cth). Liwa al-Sadr (22 Muharam 1409): 10.

Adib, Salih al-. "Rijal al-Harakah al-Islamiyah fi al-^cIraq yatathkarwun: Sanauat al-

Muawajaha maᶜa al-Mad al-'Ahmar" (Men of the Islamic Movement in Iraq Remember: The Years of Conflict with the Red Expansion), al-Jihad. 326 (1 Feb 1988)

-----. "Mawakb al-Talabah" (Students Procession). al-Jihad, (29 Feb 1988): 12.

-----. al-ᶜAmal al-Hizbi fi al-ᶜIraq (Activities of Parties in Iraq). Beirut: Dar al-Turath al-ᶜArabi, 1989.

Ajami, Fouad. The Arab Predicament. Cambridge: Cambridge University Press, 1981.

-----, The Vanished Imam, Musa al Sadr and the Shia of Lebanon. Ithaca, N.Y.: Cornell University Press, 1986.

Alawi, Hassan al-. Shiᶜism and the National State in Iraq (Paris: CEDI, 1989), pp. 226-227

Andrew, Haker. Political Theory: Philosophy, Ideology, and Science. New York City: MacMillan Co., 1961.

al-Asadi, "Hizb al-Daᶜwah al-Islamiyah" (Islamic Daᶜwah Party). Tariq al-Haq (August, 1980): 50-55.

Bakshi, Om. The Crisis of Political Theory: An Inquiry into Contemporary Thought. Delhi: Oxford University Press, 1987.

Catlin, George E. G. "Political Theory: What is it?" Political Science Quarterly (March, 1957): 1-6

Dann, Uriel. Iraq under Qassem. New York: Praeger, 1969.

Easton, David. "The Decline of Modern Political Theory." Journal of Politics (February, 1951): 36-58.

Encyclopedia of Philosophy, v. 2. "Empiricism" by D. W. Hamlyn. 1967.

Encyclopedia of Philosophy, v. 5. "Mula Sadra" by Sayyid Hussein Nasar. 1967.

Encyclopedia of Philosophy, v. 7. "Rationalism" by Bernard Williams. 1967.

Encyclopedia of Philosophy, v. 8. "Voluntarism" by Richard Taylor. 1967.

Fadlullah, Muhammad Hussein "Taq'dim", a preface to Sadr, Resalatuna. Beirut: al-Dar al-Islamiyah, 1981.

-----. "Mn Yaqud ᶜAmaliyat al-Taghir fi al-Ummah, Hizb al- Ummah aw Ummat al-Hizb" (Who Leads the Process of Change in the Nation, the Party of the Masses or the Masses of the Party). al-Muntalaq, 27, 28, 29 (10, 11, 12, 1985).

-----. "al-Marjaᶜiyah wa-al-Tahazub" (Marjaᶜiyah and Political Association) speech delivered in Fourth Conference of Muslim Group, 1982.

-----. "ᶜAlamat Istifham ᶜAla Tariq Harakat al Quwah fi al- Dawlah al-Islamiyah" (Question Marks on the Route of Movement of Power in the Islamic State). al-Tawhid (Tehran) 21 (March 12, 1986): 90-105.

Germino, Dante. Beyond Ideology: The Revival of Political Theory. New York: Harper & Row, 1967.

-----, "The Revival of Political Theory," in the Richard H. Cox, ed. Ideology, Politics and Political Theory. Belmont, CA: Wadsworth Publishing Co., 1969. 105-118.

Islamic Daᶜwah Party, Lamahat min Masirat Hizb al-Daᶜwah al- Islamiyah (Study of the Journey of the Islamic Daᶜwah Party). n.p., n.d.

-----. Min Fikr al-Daᶜwah al-Islamiyah: al-Shahid al Rabiᶜ, al-Imam al-Sadr.(Of the Thought of Islamic Daᶜwa Party: The Fourth Martyr, Imam Sadr). n.d, n.p.

-----. Shuhada' Baghdad (Martyrs of Baghdad). Tehran: Islamic Daᶜwah Party, 1403 AH.

Khalil, Samir al-. The Republic of Fear: The Politics of Modern Iraq. Berkeley, CA: University of Berkeley Press, 1989.

Khdouri, Majeed. Socialist Iraq: A Study in Iraqi Politics since 1968. Washington D.C.: Middle East Institute, 1978.

Kinloch, Graham C. Sociological Theory: Its Development and Major Paradigms.

New York City: McGraw-Hill Book Co.,   1977.

Marx, Karl. On Society and Social Change, edited by Neil J. Smalser   Chicago: The University of Chicago Press, 1973.

Mallat, Chibli. "Religious Militancy in Contemporary Iraq: Muhammas Baqer as-Sadr and the Sunni-Shia paradigm. Third   World Quarterly (April, 1988):

Ne^cma, Abdullah. Falasifat al-Shi`ah, Hayatahum, Ara'ahum (The   Shia's   Philosophers, Their Lives, and Their Views).   Beirut: Maktabat al-Hyat, n.d. pp. 346-368.

Minogue, Kenneth. "Neithzsche and the Ideological Project,"   The   Structure   of Modern Ideology. Edited by O'Sullivan.   London: Edward Elgar, 1989.

Mussawi, Ra^cad al-. Intifadat Sufr al-Islamiyah fi Iraq (Sufr   Islamic Uprising in Iraq). 2nd ed. Qum, Iran: Amair al-   Mua'minin, 1404 AH.

Nuri, Fadil al-. al-Shahid al-Sadr Fada'iluhu wa-Shama'iluhu (Martyr Sadr, His Virtues and Characters). Qum: Mahmuwd al-Hashimi office, 1984.

Nuri, Hassan. "Ma^ca al-Shahid al-Sadr Muhaqiqan" (With Shahid   Sadr as an Inquirer) al-Hiwar al-Seyasi. 28-29, (April-   May 1985): 70-71.

Partridge, P. H. "Politics, Philosophy, Ideology." In Ideology,   Politics   and   Political Theory, Edited by   Richard Cox. Ballmont, CA: Wadsworth Publication, Co.,   1969.

Qubanchi, Sadr al-Din. Buhuth fi Khat al Marja^ciyah (Studies   in   the   Path   of Marja^ciyah). n.p., 1984.

Rosenthal, Erwin I. J. Political Thought in Medieval Islam, An   Introductory   Outline. Cambridge: Cambridge University   Press, 1962.

Sabine, George. "What is Political Theory?" Journal of   Politics (Feb 1939): 1-16

Sabine, George H., and Thorson, Thomas L. A History of   Political   Theory. 4th   ed. Hinsdale, IL: Dryden Press,   1973.

Shaykh, Tawfiq al-. ^cAn al-^cIraq wa-al-Harakah al-Islamiyah,   Hiwarat   ma^ca   al-^cAlamah Muhammad Taqi al-Mudarisi (On   Iraq and the Islamic Movement, Interviews with Muhammad   Taqi al-Mudarisi). London: al-Safa, 1988.

Shubar, Hassan. "Dawr Hizb al-Daᶜwah al-Islamiyah fi al-Taghir   wa-Halat   al-'Istirkha' al-Sabiqa" (The Role of the   Islamic Daᶜwah Party in the Previous Period of Change and   Relaxation), al-Jihad, 363, (Oct 24, 1988)

Strauss, Leo. "What is Political Philosophy?" Journal of   Politics (August, 1957): 343-368.

Thompson, Kenneth W. "Toward a Theory of International   Relations." American Political Science Review (Sept. 1955): 733-746.

Tinder, Glen. "What Should be Political Theory Now?" In What   Should   Political Theory Be Now? Edited by John Nelson.   Albany, NY: State University of New York Press, 1983.   150-165.

Varma, S. P. Modern Political Theory. New Delhi, India: Vani   Educational   Books, 1985.

Waltz, Kenneth N. Theory of International Politics. New York: Random House, 1979.

www.ingramcontent.com/pod-product-compliance
Lightning Source LLC
Chambersburg PA
CBHW031103250726

48655CB00004B/1561